Chekhov: *The Cherry Orchard*

Chekhov's masterpiece, about a Russian family losing its ancestral home, combines a lament for a vanishing past with a hopeful dream of the future. In the century since its first performance, *The Cherry Orchard* has undergone a wide range of conflicting interpretations: tragic and comic, naturalistic and symbolic, reactionary and radical. Beginning with the 1904 premiere at Stanislavsky's Moscow Art Theatre, this study traces the performance history of one of the landmark plays of the modern theatre. Considering the work of such directors as Anatoly Efros, Giorgio Strehler, Peter Brook, and Peter Stein, *Chekhov: The Cherry Orchard* explores the way different artists, periods, and cultures have reinvented Chekhov's poignant comedy of failure and hope.

PLAYS IN PRODUCTION

Series editor: Michael Robinson

PUBLISHED VOLUMES

Ibsen: *A Doll's House* by Egil Törnqvist
Miller: *Death of a Salesman* by Brenda Murphy
Molière: *Don Juan* by David Whitton
Wilde: *Salome* by William Tydeman and Steven Price
Brecht: *Mother Courage and Her Children* by Peter Thomson
Williams: *A Streetcar Named Desire* by Philip C. Kolin
O'Neill: *Long Day's Journey into Night* by Brenda Murphy
Albee: *Who's Afraid of Virginia Woolf?* by Stephen J. Bottoms
Beckett: *Waiting for Godot* by David Bradby
Pirandello: *Six Characters in Search of an Author* by Jennifer Lorch
Chekhov: *The Cherry Orchard* by James N. Loehlin

CHEKHOV
The Cherry Orchard

*

JAMES N. LOEHLIN
University of Texas at Austin

CAMBRIDGE
UNIVERSITY PRESS

CAMBRIDGE UNIVERSITY PRESS
Cambridge, New York, Melbourne, Madrid, Cape Town, Singapore, São Paulo

Cambridge University Press
The Edinburgh Building, Cambridge CB2 2RU, UK

Published in the United States of America by Cambridge University Press, New York

www.cambridge.org
Information on this title: www.cambridge.org/9780521533300

© James N. Loehlin 2006

First published 2006

Printed in the United Kingdom at the University Press, Cambridge

A catalogue record for this publication is available from the British Library

ISBN-13 978-0-521-82593-1 hardback
ISBN-10 0-521-82593-8 hardback

ISBN-13 978-0-521-53330-0 paperback
ISBN-10 0-521-53330-9 paperback

CONTENTS

List of illustrations   *page* viii
Acknowledgments   x

   Introduction   1
1 *The Cherry Orchard*: text and performance   9
2 The Moscow Art Theatre production, 1904   40
3 Russian and Soviet performances, 1904–1953   72
4 *The Cherry Orchard* in English: early
   productions   89
5 *The Cherry Orchard* at mid-century: Barrault,
   Saint-Denis, Strehler   121
6 Radical revisions, 1975–1977   147
7 Brook and Stein, 1981–1997   171
8 *The Cherry Orchard* after one hundred years   190

Notes   215
Works cited   239
Index   245

ILLUSTRATIONS

1 Victor Simov's design for the nursery in Act I, in
Stanislavsky's original Moscow Art Theatre
Production, 1904. (New York Public Library.)   *page* 12
2 The final moments of the play, in Stanislavsky's
original Moscow Art Theatre Production, 1904.
(New York Public Library.)   38
3 Victor Simov's design for the exterior setting of Act II,
in Stanislavsky's original Moscow Art Theatre
Production, 1904. (New York Public Library.)   44
4 Olga Knipper as Ranevskaya, in a Moscow Art Theatre
publicity postcard. (New York Public Library.)   50
5 The servants from the Moscow Art Theatre production,
from a publicity postcard: Charlotta (Muratova),
Dunyasha (Khaputina), Yasha (Alexandrov), and
Yepikhodov (Moskvin). (New York Public Library.)   85
6 John Gielgud as Trofimov, in the first West End
performance of *The Cherry Orchard*, Lyric,
Hammersmith, 1924. (New York Public Library.)   98
7 Alla Nazimova as Ranevskaya, with Harold Moulton as
Trofimov, in Eva Le Gallienne's 1928 production at the
Civic Repertory Theatre, New York. (New York Public
Library.)   114
8 Eva Le Gallienne as Ranevskaya and Joseph Schildkraut
as Gayev in Le Gallienne's Broadway *Cherry Orchard*
from 1944. (Photofest.)   118

9 John Gielgud as Gayev, with Dorothy Tutin as Varya and
Judi Dench as Anya, in Michel Saint-Denis's 1961 Royal
Shakespeare Company production. (Photofest.)   131
10 Giorgio Strehler's production of *Il Giardino dei Ciliegi*
(Piccolo Theatre, Milan, 1974). Act II, with the train
passing in the foreground and the veil billowing above.
(Piccolo Theatre, photo by Luigi Ciminaghi.)   138
11 Santo Loquasto's design for Andrei Serban's 1977
Lincoln Center production, New York City, with Irene
Worth as Ranevskaya and Michael Cristofer as Trofimov.
(New York Public Library.)   158
12 *The Wisteria Trees*, Joshua Logan's Broadway adaptation
of *The Cherry Orchard*, reset on a Louisiana plantation,
with Helen Hayes in the Ranevskaya role. (Photofest.)   196
13 Suzuki Tadashi's Japanese adaptation *The Chekhov*, with
Ranevskaya (Shiraishi Kayoko) making a grand entrance
watched by Lopakhin (Tsutamori Kôsuke), Gayev
(Sakato Toshihiro), and Anya (Takemori Yôichi). (Toga
Sanbô, 1986.)   204

ACKNOWLEDGMENTS

I would like to thank my editors at Cambridge University Press, Vicki Cooper and Rebecca Jones, along with series editor Michael Robinson, for their support, patience, and detailed attention to this project. I also want to thank the staffs of the Theatre Museum, Covent Garden, the New York Public Library, and the Moscow Art Theatre. I am very grateful to John Freedman for welcoming me to Moscow and offering many helpful suggestions. Thanks to Kevin Haynes and Graham Schmidt for their thoughtful comments on the manuscript.

I have depended heavily on the previous work of many scholars of Chekhov and Russian theatre, including David Allen, Vera Gottlieb, Ronald Hingley, Donald Rayfield, Konstantin Rudnitsky, Tatiana Shakh-Azizova, Anatoly Smeliansky, and Nick Worrall. I am particularly indebted to the work of Laurence Senelick, especially his magisterial study *The Chekhov Theatre*.

I would also like to thank my Russian teachers at the University of Texas, Curt Woolhiser, Tatiana Segura, and Elena Lifschitz. I especially want to thank Tom Garza and Elizabeth Richmond-Garza for their warm and constant support of my venture into Russian language and culture.

I want to give special thanks to the students of my 2004 Modern Drama in Performance class who worked with me on *The Cherry Orchard*: Sarah Bayne, Annie Bennett, Bob Jones, Suzanne Julian, Keiko LeMon, Siddhartha Mahanta, Graham Schmidt, Lauren Schultz, Joey Seiler, Avimaan Syam, and Kan Yan, along with Eunice Roberts, who joined us to play Ranevskaya. That class, and that performance, remains one of the most satisfying teaching experiences I have had, and it has proved invaluable for my understanding of Chekhov.

Finally, I thank my family for their constant encouragement, and my wife Laurel for her unfailing support and love.

INTRODUCTION

The Cherry Orchard is one of the landmark plays of the modern theatre, not only for its compelling subject matter and psychologically nuanced characters, but for its rich and revealing production history. In the century since its first performance, it has seen a wide range of conflicting interpretations: tragic and comic, naturalistic and symbolic, reactionary and radical. It has been performed as a lament for the dispossessed Russian gentry and as a call to revolution, as a vehicle for detailed psychological acting and as an abstract theatre-poem, as a somber family drama and as a cartoonish vaudeville. The seeds of these interpretive conflicts were present in the original production at the Moscow Art Theatre, where the playwright, Anton Chekhov, found himself repeatedly at odds with the theatre's co-founder and director, Constantin Stanislavsky. Indeed, these conflicts are woven into the structure of the play itself, which combines farcical and serious elements, clinical naturalism and visionary symbolism, a longing look to the past and a hopeful dream of the future.

The Cherry Orchard tells the story of a family losing its home. Lyubov Andreyevna Ranevskaya, together with her daughter Anya, her foster daughter Varya, and her brother Leonid Andreyevich Gayev, are forced by debt to give up their estate and its historic cherry orchard. From the beginning of the play, a family friend, a serf-turned-businessman named Yermolay Alexeyevich Lopakhin, has warned them of the impending catastrophe, and urged them to cut down the cherry orchard, subdivide the land, and lease it for summer cottages to achieve financial solvency. They refuse to entertain this idea, and prove incapable of coming up with a viable plan to save the estate. When the estate goes up for auction, Lopakhin buys it, and proceeds

1

with his plan to cut down the trees and build summer houses. The lives of all the characters are changed: Ranevskaya will return to Paris, to her wayward lover; Anya will start a new future with her suitor Petya Trofimov, a revolutionary student; Varya, whose possible marriage to Lopakhin falls through, will become a housekeeper; and Gayev will work in a bank. The servants – the eccentric governess Charlotta, the chambermaid Dunyasha, the valet Yasha, and the clerk Yepikhodov – adapt themselves to the changed fortunes of their employers. The old butler Firs, who has lived his whole life on the estate, is left behind, forgotten, locked in the house as Lopakhin's men begin to cut down the cherry trees.

The Cherry Orchard was written in the midst of a transformation of the European theatre, and just before a cataclysmic change in Russian history. Its basic story, of the pressures of change on a single family, resonates widely with the events of its time, both cultural and political. The characters easily take on symbolic dimensions – Gayev, the enervated aristocrat; Lopakhin, the millionaire peasant; Trofimov, the student radical; Firs, the ancient retainer. While the story emerges from a specific social milieu, one Chekhov knew well (he himself owned an estate with a cherry orchard at Melikhovo), it also has universal applications. These facts have combined to give it a full and complex afterlife in production, as over a hundred years of history have cast Chekhov's play and his characters in different interpretive lights.

When *The Cherry Orchard* first appeared on the stage, in the 1904 Moscow Art Theatre production directed by Stanislavsky and Vladimir Nemirovich-Danchenko, it served as an obituary for the nineteenth century and a harbinger of the twentieth. The loss of the Ranevsky orchard was a powerful metaphor for the decline of the Russian gentry in the face of inexorable historical pressures. At the same time, the MAT *Cherry Orchard* represented the culmination of a theatrical tradition that had finally reached its limits. The eerie sound effect of a breaking string that concludes the play represents not only a social and political rupture, but an aesthetic one. The naturalism pioneered in the nineteenth century by such figures as Henrik Ibsen, André Antoine, and the Duke of Saxe-Meiningen, and brought to its highest achievement by the Moscow Art Theatre, was giving way to the explosive theatrical experimentation of the early twentieth century. The subsequent performance history of the play has drawn on the tensions between past and future built into the structure of the play itself. A century of productions have explored its mixture of tradition and innovation, nostalgic longing and revolutionary change. One hundred years after its first performance, in another new century of instability and upheaval, *The Cherry Orchard* remains a poignant, potent myth of wasted opportunities, frustrated dreams, and fragile hopes.

The Moscow Art Theatre production established the basic interpretive questions about the play, setting up three main lines of conflict that have persisted throughout its performance history. The first is the question of genre: Stanislavsky called it a tragedy, Chekhov a comedy. The second is a question of style: the Moscow Art Theatre production was the epitome of nineteenth-century naturalism, whereas innovative directors like Meyerhold saw the play as a symbolist work belonging to a new theatre of experimentation and abstraction. The final question is one of politics: Stanislavsky's gravely sympathetic treatment of the Ranevskys made the play an elegy for twilight Russia, whereas more radical directors have seen it as a hopeful call for the "new life" sought by Anya and Trofimov.

The question of genre is probably the one that has most vexed directors, audiences, reviewers, and scholars over the first century of the play's existence. Every new production must take some kind of position with regard to the original Chekhov/Stanislavsky argument. It is clear that from the play's inception, Chekhov conceived of it as a comedy. As early as 1901, when *Three Sisters* had just opened, Chekhov wrote to his wife, Olga Knipper, "The next play I write will definitely be funny, very funny – at least in intention."[1] He later wrote, "There are moments when an overwhelming desire comes over me to write a four-act farce [*vodevil*] or comedy for the Art Theatre."[2]

When he had almost finished the play, he wrote to Stanislavsky's wife, Mariya Petrovna Lilina, "It hasn't turned out a drama, but as a comedy, in places even a farce."[3]

When Stanislavsky read it, he had a different reaction. He considered it Chekhov's best work, and wept during the reading. He wrote a long letter to Chekhov expressing his love for the play and making very clear his understanding of it:

> This is not a comedy, nor a farce as you have written, this is a tragedy, whatever escape toward a better life you open up in the last act . . . I wept like a woman, I wanted to control myself but I couldn't. I hear what you say: "Look you must realize this is a farce" . . . no, for simple men this is a tragedy. I feel a special tenderness and love for this play.[4]

The two men would never come into accord on the matter. After *The Cherry Orchard* opened, Chekhov wrote angrily, "Stanislavsky has ruined my play," and complained that it was being universally misunderstood: "Why do they so obstinately call my play a 'drama' in play-bills and newspaper advertisements? What Nemirovich and Stanislavsky see in my play definitely isn't what I wrote and I'm ready to swear by anything you like that neither of them has read through my play carefully even once. I'm sorry to say so, but I assure you I'm right."[5]

The question of style is a more complicated one. The Naturalistic movement in the European Theatre had dominated the last decades of the nineteenth century, spurred by the manifestos of Emile Zola, the experiments of Antoine and the *Théâtre Libre*, the social dramas of Ibsen, and the performances of the Meininger troupe on their tours around Europe. Naturalism aimed at a detailed recreation of life on the stage, life in all its social complexity and material density. Stanislavsky's early work at the Moscow Art Theatre was very much in this vein. For his Chekhov productions, he and his designer, Victor Simov, crowded the stage with real birch trees, worn furniture, working samovars, and the like. He also employed a wealth of atmospheric sound effects and prepared detailed production scores filled with incidental business to ground the characters in a convincing mundane reality. Stanislavsky admitted years later that his naturalistic techniques weighed down the poetic impressionism of *The Cherry Orchard*:

> The play is delicate, it has all the tenderness of a flower. Break its stem
> and the flower dries, its odor vanishes . . . In my great desire to help the
> actors I tried to create a mood around them, in the hope that it would
> grip them and call forth their creative vision . . . I took all the by-paths I
> could think of. I invented all sorts of *mises en scène*, the singing of birds,
> the barking of dogs, and in this enthusiasm for sounds on the stage I
> went so far that I caused a protest on the part of Chekhov.[6]

V. S. Meyerhold, a former member of the MAT company who would become a leading experimental director in the Soviet era before falling victim to Stalin's purges, wrote to Chekhov after the opening that Stanislavsky had destroyed the artistic effect of *The Cherry Orchard* through excessive naturalism. "Your play is abstract, like a Tchaikovsky symphony," he wrote, and subsequently published a polemical article on "Naturalistic Theatre and Theatre of Mood" in which he lambasted the Art Theatre for its inability to convey the artistic vision of Chekhov's play.[7] "To Chekhov the characters of *The Cherry Orchard* were a means to an end and not a reality," Meyerhold wrote. "But in the Moscow Art Theatre the characters became real and the lyrical-mystic aspect of *The Cherry Orchard* was lost."[8] The subsequent production history of *The Cherry Orchard* oscillates between abstract, symbolic productions of the play and regular returns to Stanislavskian naturalism.

As for the play's political meaning, it is almost impossible now not to read it as a precursor of the Russian Revolution of 1917. What Chekhov's attitude was to the "old life" of the Russian gentry and the "new life" represented by Trofimov and Lopakhin remains in dispute. Chekhov knew the play had subversive potential; he worried over the censors' responses to the revolutionary student Trofimov, and indeed was forced to alter two of his more inflammatory speeches. He also felt that the most important character in the play was the risen serf, Lopakhin, the man who ends up buying the orchard, and accordingly he wrote the part for Stanislavsky, the MAT's leading actor. When Stanislavsky instead played the aristocrat Gayev, and cast Olga Knipper, the theatre's leading actress, as a charming and glamorous Madame Ranevskaya, he may have tipped the balance of the play toward sympathy for the gentry and nostalgia for the past. The Marxist writer Maxim Gorky, who later replaced Chekhov as the MAT's house dramatist, certainly thought so. He expressed impatient disgust with the play's "egotistical," "flaccid" "parasites," reserving his sympathy for the foster-daughter Varya, "who works unstintingly for the benefit of these idlers" – and who, perhaps not incidentally, was played by the woman who would become Gorky's second wife. After the Revolution, both Soviet and Western productions often made the political dimensions of the play paramount, whether the interpretation was optimistic or pessimistic. The Revolution itself sometimes became a presence in the play; and contemporary productions have begun appending the play's politics to other, more recent historical upheavals.

In my account of the performance history of *The Cherry Orchard*, I will continually revisit the three main interpretive questions set out by the original production. In the opening chapter I examine the text of the play itself, and the many directorial and acting choices it presents, moment by moment, as it unfolds upon the stage. The next chapter considers the MAT production, still the touchstone for subsequent performances and the crucible for the play's conflicts. In each of the following chapters I focus on a few major productions that seem to me to embody a vital phase in the play's ongoing life. Sometimes these are within a particular national tradition; more often they are groups of linked productions from different countries, coinciding at key moments of cultural and theatrical history.

Chapter 3 considers Russian productions after the MAT opening, both within Russia and the USSR and on tours to the West. Of Chekhov's major plays, only *The Cherry Orchard* was regularly produced by the Soviets, who focused on its invocation of the "new life." This chapter also follows the history of the play at the Moscow Art Theatre, and considers how its tours influenced the perception of Chekhov's work in Germany, France, and the USA. Chapter 4 covers early English-language productions of the play in Britain and America. Although the initial London production failed in 1911, Chekhov eventually became so popular in England that a distinctive British style of Chekhov playing emerged, and *The Cherry Orchard* became a staple of the dramatic repertoire. Chapter 5 deals with a range of productions from mid-century. As the impact of the original MAT production began to recede, several prominent directors developed authoritative new productions in Europe and America. These productions heightened the director's role as interpreter while filtering Chekhov through different theatrical traditions. Jean-Louis Barrault in France, Michel Saint-Denis in England, and Giorgio Strehler in Italy all developed new productions removing the play from its specifically Russian context and reflecting the influence of modern playwrights like Pirandello, Brecht, and Beckett.

Chapter 6 considers a group of strikingly revisionist productions of the play that emerged from the theatrical radicalism of the 1960s and 70s. In Moscow in 1975, Anatoly Efros made his Taganka Theatre production a mixture of the farcical and the grotesque, with acting styles ranging from detached to hysterical. The Czech director Otomar Krejca deconstructed the play at Düsseldorf in 1976, while the Romanian Andrei Serban presented a visually striking and iconoclastic version of the play in New York a year later. In Nottingham in 1977, Richard Eyre presented a Marxist reworking by radical playwright Trevor Griffiths. In this version Trofimov was the hero, and the emphasis was not on the pain of the Ranevskys' dispossession but its "objective necessity."[9]

Chapter 7 examines the two most widely seen and influential productions of recent decades. Both undertook fresh and vivid explorations of the play's character relationships, eschewing a single interpretive focus in favor of complex, open-ended readings. Peter Brook's production, staged in Paris in 1981 and New York in 1988, used an international cast and a simple, elegant staging for a spare but humane production. Peter Stein's 1992 Berlin production, also seen in Moscow, Salzburg, and Edinburgh, was, by contrast, meticulously detailed in its setting and glacial in pace, but achieved comparable dramatic power.

The final chapter considers the present status of the play, and what new directions it is taking in the twenty-first century. One important trend has been to use the play to comment, directly or obliquely, on cultural crises far removed from Tsarist Russia. Race and ethnicity often play into reimaginings of *The Cherry Orchard*, as in Emily Mann's production at the McCarter Theatre in the USA, or Janet Suzman's South African version, *The Free State*. The play may be adapted to aesthetic and cultural modes far from any Chekhov could have imagined, as in the work of the Japanese director Suzuki Tadashi. I conclude with an account of productions in the former Soviet Union, including Adolph Shapiro's centenary production of the play at the Moscow Art Theatre in 2004. One hundred years after its initial production, *The Cherry Orchard* continues to inspire many new experiments, as directors, actors, and audiences confront Chekhov's themes of decay and upheaval in a changing cultural landscape.

CHAPTER I

THE CHERRY ORCHARD: TEXT AND PERFORMANCE

The Cherry Orchard is representative of Chekhov's dramatic method at its most fully realized. Like the other major plays, *The Seagull*, *Uncle Vanya*, and *Three Sisters*, *The Cherry Orchard* occupies four undivided acts, centered on a provincial household, following the fortunes of a large and varied group of characters over an extended period. The passing of time, the rhythms of arrival and departure, the dwelling on the past and philosophizing about the future: all are familiar devices from the other plays. In contrast to the well-crafted, plot-driven plays of Ibsen, Chekhov's dramas progress through apparently inconsequential dialogues, *non sequiturs*, and the trivialities of daily life. "People can be having dinner, just having dinner," Chekhov wrote in his most oft-quoted comment on his own work, "and at the same time, their happiness is being secured, or their lives are being destroyed."[1]

The rich texture of Chekhov's plays, their mixture of quotidian detail on the surface and powerful feeling underneath, allows wide scope for theatrical interpretation. Actors, directors, and designers are challenged to embody the overheard snatches of conversation, the quirky acts and habitual gestures, as poetic images or moments of human truth. To realize Chekhov's detailed stage actions requires hundreds of individual interpretive choices, each of which colors the meaning of the play as it unfolds. As J. L. Styan has pointed out, while Chekhov's plays seem narrow in scope in comparison to Shakespeare's, they offer the same kind of interpretive range, make the same kind of moment-to-moment demands, and refuse, in the same way, to yield definitive answers to the largest problems they pose.[2] And while

Chekhov certainly took issue with productions (including those of the Moscow Art Theatre) that he felt misrepresented his work, he built into that work a need for interpretation. His texts are deliberately left open, to be completed by reader, actor, director, and audience. He raised questions, but declined to give answers:

> You are right to demand that an author take conscious stock of what he is doing, but you are confusing two concepts: answering the questions and formulating them correctly. Only the latter is required of an author . . . It is the duty of the court to formulate the questions correctly, but it is up to each member of the jury to answer them according to his own preference.[3]

The discussion that follows tries to elucidate the performative decisions Chekhov makes himself, in his stage directions and in the implied action of his dialogue, as well as the points of interpretation that are left open to actors, designers, and directors. It also takes into account the development of Chekhov's text and the changes that were made in the course of its initial performance and publication. Finally, it tries to convey something of the way *The Cherry Orchard* functions in performance, as its action and its meaning unfold in real time on the stage.

ACT I

Chekhov's opening stage directions for *The Cherry Orchard* are detailed and evocative:

> A room which is still known as the nursery. One of the doors leads to Anya's room. Half-light, shortly before sunrise. It is May already, and the cherry trees are in blossom, but outside in the orchard it is cold, with a morning frost. The windows are closed.[4]

These directions immediately raise questions, both of practical stage-craft and of interpretation. Why "still known"? Is this a way of indicating that the house is stuck in the past? Or a suggestion that the family are in some form of retarded infancy? Or is it that Lyubov Andreyevna refuses to let her daughters grow up, perhaps as a way of staving off her own advancing age? Perhaps there is a hint of the dead Grisha, who after all would have been the last to occupy this room; has it been left unchanged as a sort of morbid memorial, like the nurseries in Ibsen's *The Master Builder*? In any event, how is the room's status as a nursery indicated, if it is, before Ranevskaya names it on her entrance? Child-sized furniture is a likely option, and would support a reading of the family as overgrown children. Toys are often included in modern productions, with rocking horses and toy trains among the most popular.

The stage directions suggest that the orchard, with cherry trees in blossom, is visible outside the windows of the house. This visual impression seems to have been important to Chekhov from the earliest stages of composition: before he had begun the play, he wrote to Stanislavksy, "It's called *The Cherry Orchard*, it has four acts and in Act One cherry trees can be seen in bloom through the windows, the whole orchard a mass of white. And ladies in white dresses."[5] As the play begins, it is the half-light before sunrise, but still the middle of the night, around 2 A.M. It is also very cold; the juxtaposition of the blooming trees and the morning frost may have symbolic associations. At any rate, all these elements – the nursery, the blossom, the frost, the half-light of a Russian summer night – provide challenging but suggestive material for set and lighting designers, and the opening image of *The Cherry Orchard* often makes a powerful impression.

The opening dialogue between Dunyasha and Lopakhin provides necessary exposition about the return of Lyubov Andreyevna, the owner of the cherry orchard, who has been abroad for five years. Lopakhin, the peasant-turned-businessman in white waistcoat and tan shoes, remembers her with a complex mixture of emotions. He recalls how as a boy he had been beaten by his drunken father, and Lyubov Andreyevna had brought him into the nursery to wash his bleeding face. This memory of her may include a tinge of

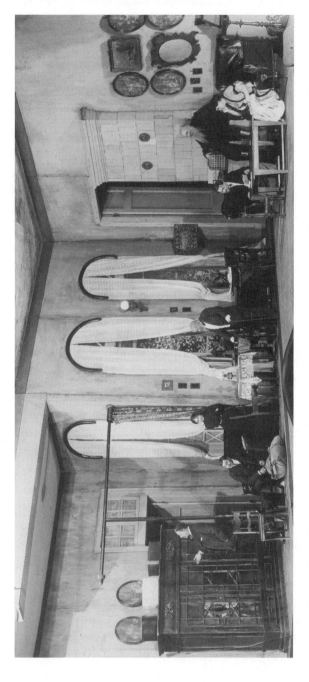

1. Victor Simov's design for the nursery in Act I, in Stanislavsky's original Moscow Art Theatre Production, 1904. (New York Public Library.)

desire – "such a slim young thing" – and class anxiety or resentment (the speech is reminiscent of the servant Jean's analogous memory in Strindberg's *Miss Julie*). The young Lyubov's kindly meant admonishment – "Don't cry, my little peasant, it'll heal in time for your wedding" – sets up the terms of the Lopakhin/Ranevskaya relationship, and also hints at the coming questions about Lopakhin's marriage to Varya.

Dunyasha's nervousness calls Lopakhin's attention to her upper-class pretensions; peasant-to-peasant, he chides her about getting ideas above her station. The moment can be played as one of solidarity between two working people, or of Lopakhin trying to hold down one of those he has risen above, or, perhaps most likely, as part of Lopakhin's recognition that he himself has failed to make a convincing transition from serf to gentleman – he is still, in his colorful metaphor, a pig in a pastry shop.

The clerk Yepikhodov enters in squeaking boots, drops the bouquet he has brought, and knocks over a chair, immediately introducing an element of farce to the play. He may be purely a figure of fun, or one of considerable pathos; at any rate his clumsy and hopeless wooing of Dunyasha extends the theme of unrequited love delicately suggested by Lopakhin's memory. But with the arrival of the travelers, the characters hurry to greet them, and the stage is left empty.

Chekhov had used an empty stage with vivid offstage sound effects at the climax of *Three Sisters*, during the Act III fire. Here he uses a similar technique to introduce Ranevskaya and her train. The noise of arrival gradually builds up offstage, then the surprising figure of Firs, an eighty-year-old servant in livery (comic, grotesque, pathetic?) hurries through leaning on his stick, muttering unintelligibly. This sets up a spectacular entrance as Ranevskaya, Anya, and Charlotta burst in, the last with a little dog on a lead, followed by virtually the entire company, all carrying coats, bags, umbrellas, and the like. Ranevskaya is clearly the center of attention; dressed for travel, presumably in Paris fashions, she does most of the talking and establishes an initial picture of her character for the audience. During this brief and busy passage across the stage Chekhov provides a range of character information, some essential, some apparently irrelevant: that this room was Ranevskaya's nursery, and that she "is like a little girl again"; that Gayev likes to complain when the trains don't run on time; that Varya habitually dresses like a nun – and that Charlotta's dog can eat nuts. Vladimir Kataev points out how these exchanges point up an important theme of the play: that, as Ranevskaya says of both Varya and Gayev, "You're just the same as ever" – that the characters are trapped in a kind of personal immobility while time rushes forward around them.[6]

The exchanges that follow among the three young women of the play provide useful exposition, as well as sketching out some of the class issues; each relationship, on the stage, can balance sisterly comradeship and submerged pecking-order power dynamics. While Dunyasha prattles about her proposal from Yepikhodov, Anya ignores her, so fatigued she is barely able to stand. Varya sends Dunyasha back to her duties and questions Anya about her embassy to retrieve Mama from Paris. Anya paints a brief and vivid picture of *émigré* squalor and decadence, ending with the hopeless realization that the interest hasn't been paid and the estate will be sold in August. At this moment of highest emotional tension, Lopakhin "*looks in at the door, and moos.*" This astonishing act can be played in a variety of ways. Is it simply a bizarre comic *non sequitur* revealing Lopakhin's oafishness with regard to Varya, or is Lopakhin intending some deliberate comment on the women's situation? David Magarshack argues that Lopakhin is teasing them for their frantic worrying over a problem he believes he has solved.[7] Whether Lopakhin moos like a cow or bleats like a sheep – the Russian word can mean either – may have bearing on how an audience interprets the exchange; Nick Worrall notes that "whether the girls are to be seen as 'silly cows' or 'lambs to the slaughter' might be a valid interpretive quibble."[8] At any rate, the episode gives the audience a first picture of the Lopakhin/Varya relationship, with its elements of surface teasing, repressed emotion, and painful absurdity. The exchange between Varya and Anya ends with another of Chekhov's uses of apparently inconsequential dialogue to reveal depths of shifting and overlapping emotion. In the midst of her despair over her prospects with Lopakhin, Varya suddenly notices, in a changed mood, that Anya has a brooch like a little bee. "Mama bought it," Anya says sadly, returning us to the theme of Ranevskaya's spendthrift ways, but then her tone suddenly changes to girlish excitement: "And in Paris I went up in an air-balloon!"

After Varya and Anya leave the stage, the Frenchified valet Yasha enters and begins his seduction of Dunyasha. How smooth or caddish Yasha is – how successfully he pulls off his air of continental suavity – depends on the actor, and Dunyasha may or may not be convinced at this point. She "*screams*" at his embrace and drops a saucer, which the superstitious Varya interprets as a good omen; nonetheless, it is the first of many breakages in the play. Donald Rayfield points out that *The Cherry Orchard* "smashes even more props than *Three Sisters*; Dunyasha's saucer is only the first symbol of a crashing world."[9] Criticizing Dunyasha for her ineptitude, Firs uses what will become his catchword throughout the play: "*Nyedotyopa.*" This word, apparently Chekhov's coinage though its source is debated, has long proved a challenge to English translators, variously rendered as "job-lot," "duffer," "nincompoop," and, in Frayn's version, "sillybilly."

Soon after, Ranevskaya appears in her Parisian clothes, with her circle of admirers fussing around her. Firs' deafness and devotion are made apparent as he gives her her coffee. Both Pishchik and Lopakhin pay her compliments, each perhaps animated by more fervent emotion. In response to Lopakhin's declaration that he loves her "more than my own flesh and blood," Ranevskaya ignores him, and gets up to start kissing the bookcase and the table. Is she deliberately avoiding an intimate conversation, or is she oblivious of Lopakhin's ardor, or does she simply take his devotion for granted? At any rate, the change in tone brings Lopakhin back to practical matters, and, checking his watch as he does repeatedly throughout the play, he introduces the subject of the cherry orchard. In Chekhov's manuscript, Lopakhin says, "To stop your estate running at a loss you must get up at four o'clock in the morning every day and work all day. For you of course this is impossible, I can see that."[10] In the final version Chekhov softens Lopakhin's tone, and merely has him propose his plan to cut down the orchard and divide the estate into lots for summer cottages. Ranevskaya and Gayev rally to the defense of the cherry orchard, which is even mentioned in the Encyclopedia. Firs, intruding surprisingly into the conversation, mentions how forty or fifty years before, the orchard was productive and profitable, and the dried cherries were "soft and juicy and sweet and scented" – but the recipe has been forgotten. All but Lopakhin are willing to let the subject drop, but he continues with a vision of the future in which the small-property owners will again farm their lots, and "this old cherry orchard of yours will become happy and rich and luxuriant."

At this point Varya interrupts to give Ranevskaya two telegrams from Paris; Chekhov specifies that she "*selects a key which clinks in the lock as she opens the antique bookcase.*" This moment serves several functions, associating Varya and her keys with the household management (and prefiguring her throwing them down in Act IV), introducing the powerful offstage pull of the lover in Paris, adding one more tiny detail to the play's soundscape (the key scraping in the lock), and introducing the famous bookcase. The reaction of Ranevskaya to the mention of Paris, and the tearing of the telegrams, will reveal much about where her relationship to her lover stands at this point. Gayev's bookcase speech can be played as a natural effusion of his loquacious and sentimental spirit, or as a deliberate attempt to distract Ranevskaya from her thoughts of Paris; if it is the latter, it gives his character a little more weight at this point in the play. Is the speech a *jeu d'esprit*, or a solemn oration, or one shading into the other? Chekhov says he is "*on the verge of tears*" by the end of it, though these could come from several sources, and that he is "*in some slight confusion*" afterwards, as he returns to his imaginary billiard-playing. It is certainly the actor's best opportunity so far in the play to characterize Gayev.

The tone of bizarre comedy returns with Pishchik swallowing Ranevskaya's pills and Charlotta making a strange and inconsequential pass across the stage. Lopakhin departs, leaving another reminder about the estate auction and prompting more teasing of Varya about the marriage. Ranevskaya and Gayev open the windows and look out into the orchard, remembering their childhoods. Suddenly Ranevskaya seems to see their mother. She "*laughs with joy*" though her emotions have also been stirred by painful memories of the past; Varya's "God save you, Mama" could be an expression of Varya's own superstitiousness, or genuine concern for her foster mother's sanity. This highly charged moment sets up the entry of Trofimov, who appears at the point in the act when Chekhov has wound things up to their most intense emotional pitch. Like Ibsen, Chekhov had learned from melodramas the power of the long-delayed entrance of the ominous visitor.

Trofimov is a surprising and probably disturbing presence in his shabby student's uniform and spectacles, with his thinning hair and mangy beard. John Gielgud, who played Trofimov in 1925, commented on "how effectively [the] part was placed to make the greatest effect in the simplest possible way – the first entrance of Trofimov, peering into the nursery in his spectacles, and Madame Ranevsky's emotion at seeing him again, because he was the tutor of her little boy who was drowned."[11] Trofimov may thrust himself heedlessly upon Ranevskaya, unconscious of the shock he will give her, or he may advance slowly and tentatively. At any rate, she dissolves in tears upon seeing him, so that Gayev remonstrates with her, out of either tender affection or exasperated embarrassment. She almost immediately begins commenting on Trofimov's appearance: "What's this Petya? Why have you lost your looks? Why have you aged so?" Whether her response to him is a comic *non sequitur*, or a way of continuing to mourn the past, or an attempt to put him in his place, depends on the choices of the individual actors and the general tenor of the scene. It leads him to comment on his status as a "perpetual student," with its suggestion, sometimes made more explicit, that he has been thrown out of the university for revolutionary activities.

As she leaves the stage Ranevskaya finally accedes to Pishchik's request for a loan, leading to a discussion between Gayev and Varya of her spendthrift ways. As this conversation slides into Gayev's condemnation of his sister's morals, Anya appears in the doorway. Gayev's attitude to Ranevskaya's sexuality can be played as one of puritan primness, fastidious distaste, or Freudian revulsion; Gayev's own sexual orientation may be implicated in the acting choice. Anya's entry turns the focus to Gayev's impulsive and irresponsible urge to talk, a habit that will afflict him through the remainder of the play. Though his nieces chide him, their attitudes soon turn to admiration as he spins out a three-pronged attack on the cherry orchard problem: a promissory note, Lopakhin, and their rich aunt the Countess in Yaroslavl are all proposed as sources of financial salvation. Whether Gayev, or the women, believe any of this is up to the actors, but Gayev's plan lifts the mood of the scene. He leaves, and Anya goes to sleep while Varya begins a long and apparently irrelevant story about how the peasants are saying that she has fed them nothing but dried peas (in Act II Ranevskaya herself is seen spreading this rumor). Trofimov is given another memorable entrance, standing silently as he watches the sleeping Anya being led away, then bursting into an effusion of happiness: 'My sunshine! My springtime!'

By the end of the first act, Chekhov has introduced us to all of the principal characters, and set up the main relationships: the youthful idealism linking Anya and Trofimov; the hypothetical betrothal of Lopakhin and Varya, with its attendant teasings and frustrations; the below-stairs triangle of Yasha, Dunyasha, and Yepikhodov; the web of relationships – of desire, duty, and dependence – centering on the magnetic Ranevskaya; and finally the bond of brother and sister to each other and to their ancestral home. The plot has been set in motion as well, and the clock is ticking toward the inevitable auction.

ACT II

Act II is the only exterior scene of the play, and takes place not in the orchard, as one might expect, but in the open fields, along a roadside near a shrine. The impression of outdoor space is vital; Chekhov wrote to Nemirovich-Danchenko, "you must give me proper green fields and a road, and a sense of distance unusual for the stage."[12] Chekhov's description of the scene, like the play as a whole, looks both into the past and the future. The shrine, "*old, crooked and long-neglected,*" stands next to "*large slabs which were evidently once tombstones.*" In the background, however, a row of telegraph poles represent the technologies of the twentieth century, and suggest the presence of the railway line Lopakhin so often mentions. (Stanislavsky wanted to show the train passing across the back of the stage.) A large town is just visible on the horizon, suggesting the urbanization and industrialization of Russia, and the city-dwellers who might one day occupy the cottages Lopakhin wants to build.

It is evening, and four characters are on stage, all, Chekhov specifies, "*in a reflective mood.*" Dunyasha and Yasha sit on an old bench, while Yepikhodov sets the tone with his plaintive guitar. The act begins with an autobiographical monologue by Charlotta. Chekhov intended this material for the end of the act, as part of a conversation between Charlotta and Firs, but Stanislavsky persuaded him to cut it and end Act II with the moon-drenched romanticism of Anya and Trofimov. Charlotta's speech makes a striking beginning, an isolated quasi-soliloquy of existential implications. "I haven't got a proper passport . . . where I come from or who I am, I don't know."[13] Charlotta's speech can be played for incongruous comedy – she cuts a strange figure with her peaked cap and gun, eating a cucumber while she talks of her early life as a circus-girl. But her rootlessness, and her odd self-questionings delivered to the baffled or bored servants, give her lines disturbing power: "Alone, always alone, I haven't got anyone. And who I am, and why I am, remains a mystery."

The scene that follows uses the traditional device of servants aping the manners of their masters, with Dunyasha powdering her nose and giving herself the airs of a lady. The singing of Yepikhodov and Yasha breaks the mood of Charlotta's speech – she says that they howl like jackals. The melancholy Yepikhodov, failing to get attention from Dunyasha, produces a revolver and mutters about suicide. This prop calls to mind one of Chekhov's tongue-in-cheek maxims of playwriting – that a gun shown onstage must be fired by the end of Act III – a principle Chekhov is here determined to violate. He wrote proudly that "there's not a single pistol shot in the whole play."[14] Chekhov throws in Charlotta's shotgun for good measure, to make the point all the more clearly.

All of the servants have social aspirations with associated poses: Yepikhodov's intellectualism ("Have you read Buckle"?), Yasha's cigar and Parisian *savoir-faire*, Dunyasha's delicate nerves. As J. L. Styan points out, the attention given to "such seemingly unimportant characters and their petty affairs" illustrates the larger social forces at work in the play.[15] The comic episode is rounded off effectively when the embrace of Yasha and Dunyasha is broken by the arrival of their social betters. Dunyasha's line "Your cigar has given me a headache," is perhaps one of her social-climbing pretensions – a man oughtn't to smoke in a lady's presence – or perhaps the result of a farcical bit of business, as she goes in for a kiss and gets a face-full of smoke.

Ranevskaya, Lopakhin, and Gayev arrive, in the midst of a heated discussion about the cherry orchard question. Lopakhin's opening speech communicates the passage of time, the urgency of the problem, and the failure of the Ranevskys to act: "It has to be settled once and for all – time won't wait. Look, it's a simple enough question. Do you agree to lease out the land for summer cottages or not? Answer me one word: yes or no! Just one word!" Ranevskaya, however, simply asks "Who's been smoking some foul cigar?" (mirroring Dunyasha in her tastes), while Gayev talks about billiards. Ranevskaya's money problems are given an explicit demonstration when, checking on the contents of her purse, she flings her money about the stage. Yasha collects the coins – possibly keeping some for himself – and is finally banished by the irritated Gayev.

Lopakhin tries to make them realize the immediacy of the sale by naming the potential buyer, the wealthy Deriganov – one of the play's many important offstage figures, along with the lover in Paris, the great-aunt in Yaroslavl, Pishchik's daughter Dashenka, and

Yasha's peasant mother. As the dacha proposal is once again rejected as "squalid," Lopakhin turns to go, but Ranevskaya stops him, "*frightened.*" After vehemently begging him to stay, she says off-handedly, "It's more fun with you here, at any rate." Is she trying to make light of her genuine need for him as the only practical man of business in her sphere? Is she exploiting, consciously or unconsciously, his more-than-flesh-and-blood devotion to her? How deeply is she frightened, and of what? She says she keeps waiting for something to happen, "as if the house were going to come down about our ears"; Chekhov counterpoints this ominous prophecy with Gayev's billiards jargon. Ranevskaya's mood of dread leads her to think about her life and her "sins," and she finally gives the background story, hinted at in Act I, of her drunken husband, drowned child, and faithless lover. As in Act I, she tears up a telegram from him; how do the two gestures compare?

Chekhov changes the mood again as Ranevskaya and Gayev suddenly hear the music of the "famous Jewish orchestra." Interestingly, the ordinarily perceptive Lopakhin does not hear it, and Chekhov gives no direction for its being audible to the audience. Ranevskaya brightens for a moment, and thinks of arranging a party (the Act III ball), but when Lopakhin catches her mood and starts talking about the theatre, she turns on him. Her rejoinder betrays her own lack of self-knowledge – unless it is deliberately directed inward – but it also makes a startling meta-theatrical attack on the audience: "There's nothing funny in the world. People shouldn't watch plays. They should look at their own selves a little more often. What grey lives they all lead. How much they say that should never be said at all."

Again, Lopakhin responds to Ranevskaya's mood (perhaps indicating the degree of his obsession with her), and turns on himself with surprising vitriol, recalling his brutal and illiterate father and reflecting that he is the same sort of stupid peasant himself: "I'm a pig." Ranevskaya's response – that he should marry Varya – receives only guarded acknowledgment from Lopakhin. Russian critic Vladimir Kataev suggests that Lopakhin's subsequent behavior in the scene is all conditioned by "his depressed state once he sees clearly that it does not even occur to Ranevskaya to take his feelings seriously."[16]

Gayev announces that he has been offered a job in a bank – an absurd employment for a man who, as he has just admitted, has wasted all his substance on candy – but his pride in the position is quickly undercut by the entrance of Firs. As he does in each act, Firs chides Gayev like a little boy for wearing the wrong clothing – here he has gone out without his overcoat. Firs' presence brings in some of the more serious material of the act, as he mentions the Emancipation of the serfs, a sweeping historical change that hangs over the whole play. "I didn't agree to have the freedom – I stayed with the masters," he recalls. "And I remember, everyone was glad. But what they were glad of, they didn't know themselves." Lopakhin also comments on the old days, presumably with bitter irony: "Lovely it was before. At least they flogged you." These lines raise the theme, prevalent throughout the play, of the different responses throughout the social hierarchy to the huge changes affecting Russian society in the late nineteenth century. The political dimension of the play now becomes central, as Trofimov enters with Anya and Varya, and the conversation turns to the present state of affairs in Russia.

Lopakhin and Trofimov immediately begin quarreling, although Harvey Pitcher points out that their use of the familiar second-person pronoun suggests an underlying affection.[17] Needled by Lopakhin about his "eternal student" status and his flirtation with Anya, Trofimov launches into a diatribe against the Russian intelligentsia and their failure to ameliorate the social conditions of the poor. Some of Trofimov's attacks are pointed and on target, to the extent that Chekhov was forced by the censor to change them: "And right in front of their eyes the whole time there are workers living on filthy food and sleeping without pillows to their heads, thirty and forty to a room – and everywhere bugs, damp, stench, and moral squalor." How far Trofimov becomes the mouthpiece of the play, in this speech and his speeches at the end of the act, is a critical question in determining the political impact of any production.

While his tirade certainly has force and reflects some of Chekhov's own views, it also comes from a questionable source. Just as in *Three Sisters* the exhortation to work rings false, coming from the idle Irina and Tuzenbach, so Trofimov's speeches mark him as just the kind of prating intellectual he has been condemning. When, at the end of his lengthy oration, he proclaims that it would be "better to be silent," the audience is unlikely to miss the irony.

When Lopakhin, who actually does work, takes up Trofimov's themes, his speech is likely to have more force. In an unusually reflective mood, he also comments on the poor state of Russia: "Sometimes, when I can't sleep, I think to myself: 'Lord, you gave us immense forests, boundless plains, broad horizons – living in it all we ought properly to be giants.'" The juxtaposition of these two men, and their attitudes to the future of their country, recurs throughout the play, and is one of the most important places where productions develop their political messages.

The scene is now set for one of the most extraordinary moments in all of Chekhov's drama. Yepikhodov strolls along the back of the stage playing his guitar, and the meditative tone is set by one of Chekhov's quasi-musical repetitions:

> RANEVSKAYA. (*Pensively.*) There goes Yepikhodov . . .
> ANYA: (*likewise.*) There goes Yepikhodov . . .[18]

It is sunset; Gayev makes a brief speech on Nature as the giver and destroyer of life, but is quickly hushed by his nieces.

> *They all sit lost in thought. Silence. All that can be heard is Firs muttering quietly. Suddenly there is a distant sound, as if from the sky: the sound of a breaking string, dying away, sad.*

This, along with its reprise at the play's end, is arguably the most significant sound effect in world drama; in few other works does an offstage sound have such symbolic and theatrical power. Evocative as Chekhov's description is, there is still a wide range of possibility for the director and sound designer: how loud the sound is, how sustained, how naturalistic, how localized, how distorted. Stanislavsky used three piano strings of different weights, strung from the flies behind the scenes, with a rumble of thunder on a drum to set the sound in relief. Modern productions often use artificially synthesized sounds, sometimes much expanded from Chekhov's description. The characters comment on the sound in various ways that help to define them (and also suggest the expressive range of the sound itself). Lopakhin, the practical man, guesses that a cable has snapped in a mine-shaft. Gayev suggests a heron, Trofimov an eagle owl: birds consistent with their personalities (and, perhaps, appearances). Ranevskaya, still in a foreboding mood, merely comments that it was "horrible, I don't know why." Firs reads it as a political portent, foreboding a catastrophe such as the Emancipation was to him: "It was the same before the troubles. The owl screeched, and the samovar moaned without stop."

Lopakhin's is the "correct" explanation, probably. The same sound occurs in Chekhov's 1887 story "Happiness," and there is no doubt as to its source; a bucket falling in a mine-shaft. Chekhov had heard the sound himself in his youth, and refers to it in his letters. Donald Rayfield notes that "This sound is associated with Chekhov's early work, with stories of the south of Russia, with the steppe undermined by mineshafts and hidden cables"; he goes on to link it to "the death of nature, industrialization, the crippling of human beings; this threat from an underground world to the frivolous gentry on the surface has something of the numinous horror of the Morlocks in H. G. Wells's *The Time Machine*."[19] Other Chekhov scholars have advanced a variety of readings. David Magarshack called the "dying melancholy sound . . . a sort of requiem for the 'unhappy and disjointed' lives of his characters."[20] Francis Fergusson argued that the sound "is sharp, almost a warning signal," while Maurice Valency associates it with Gayev's speech on the indifference of nature, which he takes to reveal "the essential theme of the play."[21] Harvey Pitcher, surveying these views, notes that Chekhov could not have intended that one specific meaning should be attached to the sound; he argues that the sound brings the play close to the world of the stories, and "the mysterious emotional relationship that exists between men and the world of nature."[22] Laurence Senelick adds a final, prosaically realistic explanation – Yepikhodov's guitar: "Might not the snapped string be one broken by the faltering bookkeeper? . . . Chekhov always overlays any symbolic inference with a patina of irreproachable reality."[23] Whatever meanings may be attributed to it, the sound of the breaking string creates a compelling theatrical effect; like the photograph in Act I of *Three Sisters*, it stops the play for a moment with the assembled cast onstage, giving the audience an opportunity to reflect on the characters' situation and their varied responses to it.

Immediately after the ominous sound, an ominous figure appears: the drunken passerby, who quotes revolutionary poetry and asks for money. In performance, this character can range from a comic stage drunk to a spectral herald of doom. Regardless, in his rootlessness and poverty he calls attention to the social disorder invoked by the speeches of Trofimov, Lopakhin, and Firs. His snatches of poems by Nadson and Nekrasov speak of a tired "suffering brother" and the weary moans of Volga workers. His presence frightens Varya and provokes another display of fiscal irresponsibility from Ranevskaya: startled and perhaps guilty, she gives him a gold coin.

As the other characters leave the stage, Anya and Trofimov are left alone on what promises to be a romantic moonlit evening. Trofimov, however, almost immediately declares that they are "above love," and speaks as though to a student rally: "On, on, on! In step together, friends!" Any production must determine how much this scene is a comic one, of an eager young woman and a distracted would-be revolutionary, or a serious reflection on property and oppression. The scene contains some of Trofimov's silliest rhetoric, but also some of his strongest; when Anya observes that Trofimov's revolutionary ideals have caused her not to love the cherry orchard as she used to, he replies, "All Russia is our orchard." The censors certainly took the scene seriously, and Chekhov had to remove the lines in which Trofimov indicts the Ranevsky family for having owned serfs: "The possession of living souls – it's changed something deep in all of you, hasn't it. So that your mother and you and your uncle don't even notice that you're living on credit, at the expense of others, at the expense of people you don't allow past the front hall."

The act ends on an upbeat note, with the moon rising, and Trofimov's premonition of happiness. Anya leads Trofimov to the river to avoid Varya; perhaps he is not above love after all. Chekhov's original ending was lower key, so much so that Stanislavsky persuaded Chekhov to change it. Chekhov had ended the act with Firs and Charlotta discussing their past lives: she recalling her circus youth and her dead parents, he thinking of a murder that occurred sixty years before. The present ending, with its focus on youth, idealism, and dreams of the future, may give the audience a fragile hope to carry beyond the end of the play; or it may merely set us up for the catastrophe that befalls the family in Act III.

ACT III

Act III begins with a burst of sound and movement: the *grand-rond* at the ball at the Ranevsky estate. The party is in full swing, and virtually the entire company dances through in pairs. Ranevskaya, interestingly, is paired with Trofimov, with whom she will share an emotional scene (and another dance) later in the act. Varya, who is dancing not with Lopakhin but with the supernumerary stationmaster, is "*quietly weeping, and wiping her eyes as she dances.*" The dancing makes a powerful theatrical statement, and it is hard not to read it metaphorically. Andrey Bely saw it as "a crystallization of Chekhov's devices: in the foreground room a domestic drama is taking place, while at the back, candle-lit, the masks of terror are dancing rapturously."[24] Meyerhold likewise found Act III a *danse macabre* representative of the entire play: "as in a nightmare," the characters "whirl around in a tedious dance without amusement, or fervor, or grace, or even lust, not knowing that the earth on which they are standing will be sold from under their feet."[25] Donald Rayfield, taking up Meyerhold's idea of the play as a symphony, discusses Act III as a kind of scherzo movement, with a frenzied mood that is "nightmarishly surreal in its mixture of trivia and horror, laughter and anguish."[26] In perfor-mance, the klezmer music of the Jewish band and the frantic actions of the characters can certainly support this reading.

The stage itself is divided, as in the first act of *Three Sisters*, into upstage and downstage rooms, which Chekhov uses for effects of irony and contrast. Following the pattern of *Three Sisters*, the public event takes place in the upstage ballroom, farthest from the audi-ence, whereas more private encounters occur in the drawing room downstage. J. L. Styan compares the staging to the dynamics of an Elizabethan theatre, where different parts of the platform have dif-ferent connotations: "In the drawing-room itself we shall be loaded with the anxieties of the present, while the action in the more for-mal ballroom beyond represents a parody of the gay past."[27] While Ranevskaya is agonizing over the fate of the orchard, Chekhov spec-ifies that "*In the ballroom a figure in a grey top hat and check trousers waves its arms and leaps about.*" This clownish figure, the governess Charlotta, can become a kind of presiding deity for the act, as she performs magic tricks, ventriloquizes, and leads the atmosphere of grotesque gaiety.

The juxtaposition of public festivity and private anguish was a staple of party scenes throughout Russian dramatic literature, as Laurence Senelick points out, citing Griboyedov's *Woe from Wit*, Pushkin's *Feast in Plaguetime*, and Lermontov's *Masquerade*.[28] The ironic tension of the act is built into its structure. Yet there remains space for theatrical interpretation. Is the party a symbolist nightmare, "Maeterlinck-like frightful" as Meyerhold wanted it, or a carefully observed study of a boring provincial evening, as Stanislavsky staged it?[29] Is the party lively or dull? Is the band good or bad? Are Charlotta's tricks convincing or absurd? How close to the surface are Ranevskaya's fears? How much emphasis is on the agitation of the family, how much on the tedium or hilarity of the ball?

After the dancing that opens the act, the sense of anxiety is established through Varya's concern about paying the musicians, Pishchik's momentary panic over losing his money, and Ranevskaya's explicit fears about the auction. Charlotta's card tricks seem to lighten the mood, though as Rayfield points out, Trofimov's card, the queen of spades, is "the harbinger of destruction in Russian literature ever since Pushkin's story of that name."[30] The conjuring of Anya and Varya out of thin air (from behind a rug) provides an opportunity to contrast the characters and attitudes of the two daughters. When Charlotta's magic show concludes, Ranevskaya's first lines indicate that she has not been diverted from her anxiety about the estate: "And still no sign of Leonid. I don't understand what he could be doing in town for all this time. It must be over by now. Either the estate is sold, or else the sale never took place." She is momentarily distracted by concern for Varya's potential marriage, for which, we learn, Varya has little hope: "Mama dear, *I* can't propose to *him*." But when Ranevskaya is left alone with Trofimov, she reveals the depth of her concern for the estate: "I love this house. Without the cherry orchard I can't make sense of my life, and if it has to be sold, then sell me along with it."

This statement is Ranevskaya's most passionate expression of her love for the orchard, her identification with it as a symbol of all that is best in her life. Yet the conviction of even this outcry can be questioned. In the introduction to his adaptation of the play, David Mamet argues that "nobody in the play gives a damn about the cherry orchard," including Ranevskaya.[31] Mamet sees the play as centered on a network of frustrated or distorted sexual relationships; for him Ranevskaya's primary concern is her lover in Paris. There is plenty of evidence in the play for this view. As Ranevskaya weeps over the orchard and her drowned son, a telegram from Paris falls out of her handbag onto the floor; and it is an argument over the lover that brings the scene to its highest emotional pitch. In the performance history of *The Cherry Orchard*, Ranevskayas can be divided into those most oriented toward Russia and the estate and those most oriented toward Paris and the lover.

Ranevskaya's scene with Trofimov is the longest two-person exchange in the play, and arguably the most emotional. It ranges across the deepest concerns of both of their lives: Trofimov's relationship with Anya and his professions of being "above love," his inability to finish at university, his idealistic vision of the future; Ranevskaya's concern for the past, for her estate and her dead son, and her desire to flee to Paris to look after her invalid lover. When Trofimov challenges her – "He's openly robbed you . . . he's a petty scoundrel, a nobody" – Ranevskaya responds with unprecedented venom, attacking Trofimov's masculinity: "It's time you were a man! . . . You're just a prig, a ridiculous freak, a monster!" The scene ends with Trofimov storming off in a rage. Immediately there is a loud off-stage crash, and Anya laughingly reports, "Petya's fallen downstairs!" This is probably the most extreme example in *The Cherry Orchard* of Chekhov undermining the quasi-tragic tone of the play with an injection of pure farce. Specifically, Chekhov undermines Trofimov's own desire to live theatrically; he has just made a deliberately stagey exit ("everything is finished between us!") and Chekhov literally pulls the rug out from under him.

Immediately after this scene comes one of the odd interjections of apparently inconsequential activity: the unnamed Stationmaster, a hanger-on representative of the *déclassé* nature of this party, begins to recite Alexey Tolstoy's "The Scarlet Woman." Chekhov doesn't specify how far he gets before a waltz draws the crowd away, but the recitation has significant theatrical potential. Both the Biblical subject matter of the poem – the conversion of a fallen woman by a holy prophet – and its first few lines, describing a riotous banquet, bear an ironical relation to the action of the scene. Ranevskaya and Trofimov soon appear to have made up, and dance together; then word comes that the orchard has been sold. While Ranevskaya endures an agony of waiting, a series of short, overlapping episodes heighten the feverish atmosphere: the clownish Charlotta leaps about in the ballroom, Yasha and Pishchik lay siege to Ranevskaya for favors, Dunyasha rejects Yepikhodov, who gets into an altercation with Varya. This last episode culminates in Varya raising Firs' stick threateningly at the door behind which Yepikhodov has gone. In another of Chekhov's moments of puncturing irony, it is Lopakhin who enters to face the blow.

Chekhov's stage direction doesn't specify that Varya actually hits Lopakhin, although she usually does in performance, and Lopakhin's lines about a "warm welcome" and a bump on the head encourage this choice. In the original manuscript, Chekhov specified that "the blow strikes Lopakhin," but he may have backed off from this action in order to avoid giving Lopakhin too much sympathy.[32] J. L. Styan points out, "by just missing him, in the same way that Vanya just misses the professor in Act III of Uncle Vanya, the incident is relieved of its more serious implications and turned into a joke."[33] On the other hand, Stanislavsky's production score indicates that Varya does strike him, and that "Somewhere in the depths of his soul he even feels that he has deserved the blow."[34] Certainly, the episode deflates Lopakhin's entrance, preventing it from being either the triumphant return of the victorious peasant or the dreaded appearance of the usurper. Magarshack suggests that the blow recalls Lopakhin's childhood beatings: "the stick is the symbol of the serf in Lopakhin."[35] The incident also provides an ironic snapshot of the Varya/Lopakhin relationship, like the Hamlet/Ophelia "Get thee to a nunnery" exchange in Act II. The threatened or actual beating, however inadvertently, expresses Varya's frustration with Lopakhin for failing to propose, and anticipates her anger when she learns of his purchase of the estate.

Lopakhin's return has prepared us for the climax of the play. Chekhov makes us wait a few more moments to learn the truth – initially neither Lopakhin nor Gayev will reveal what has happened. The latter, in a typically Chekhovian touch, tearfully produces some anchovies and herring he has bought in town. Then he hears Yasha playing billiards, and "His expression changes. He is no longer weeping." Whether he has been distracted and comforted by the thought of his favorite game, or downcast at being supplanted by the hated servant Yasha, is left to the actor. Gayev goes off, and the stage is set for the climactic revelation, expressed in dialogue of tremendous economy and power:

RANEVSKAYA: *Prodan Vishnyovy Sad?*
LOPAKHIN: *Prodan.*
RANEVSKAYA: *Kto kupil?*
LOPAKHIN: *Ya kupil.*

RANEVSKAYA: Is the cherry orchard sold?
LOPAKHIN: It's sold.
RANEVSKAYA: Who bought it?
LOPAKHIN: I bought it.[36]

Ranevskaya slumps against her chair; Varya throws down her keys and goes out. Lopakhin now enters into the long speech that is the apex of his role. Its mixture of triumph, shame, sympathy, and rage provides the actor with a great emotional range, and no two Lopakhins will be the same. "Great God in heaven – the cherry orchard is mine!" Exactly what this means to Lopakhin is complex and uncertain, although the element of triumph is unmistakable: "I have bought the estate where my father and grandfather were slaves, where they weren't even allowed into the kitchens." The purchase is partly a victory for Lopakhin over his class origins, partly, perhaps, an attempt to raise himself above his brutal peasant father. It is also unquestionably a shrewd business move. But it is likely also to be a decisive shift in the complex and almost entirely sublimated sexual relationship between Lopakhin and Ranevskaya, whom he has perhaps loved since she was a "slim young thing" washing his bleeding face. Since Lopakhin is convinced, because of his class status, that he can never have her, then perhaps despoiling her beloved orchard will yield him some measure of satisfaction: "Everyone come and watch Yermolay Lopakhin set about the cherry orchard with his axe! Watch the trees come crashing down!"

Almost as soon as he says these words, Lopakhin regrets them. When he addresses Ranevskaya personally he seems not only to regret the pain he has caused her, but to long for some way beyond their current impossible situation. Chekhov specifies that he speaks through tears: "Oh, if only it were all over. If only we could somehow change this miserable, muddled life of ours." Harvey Pitcher argues that these lines are central to the play:

> On a personal level, Lopakhin is trying to reach out to Ranevskaya emotionally, trying very belatedly to bridge the gap between them by looking ahead to a future where this kind of situation could never arise. But the remark is also striking because it is the only occasion in *The Cherry Orchard* where one of the characters manages very briefly to place himself outside the situation in which they all find themselves.[37]

Like Vershinin in *Three Sisters*, and with more conviction than Trofimov, Lopakhin tries to imagine a better life that would redeem their present suffering. But that life will come too late for them; Lopakhin knows it, so he resumes his attitude of triumph, now shot through with self-mocking irony. He orders the musicians to play:

> Let's have everything the way I want it! (*Ironically*) Here comes the new landlord, the owner of the cherry orchard! (*Accidentally bangs into an occasional table, and almost overturns the candelabra.*) I can pay for it all! (*Goes out with Pishchik.*)

It is Anya alone who can express hope for the future with conviction; she kneels by her mother and talks of a better life, of planting a new orchard, of the possibility of joy. Whether Ranevskaya or the audience can share that hope is one of the major interpretive questions of the play.

ACT IV

The setting for the final act makes a powerful visual impression that highlights the arrival/departure format of the play and the fate that has befallen the household. The set is the same as in Act I, but it is empty, stripped to the walls.[38] Chekhov specifies that "there are no curtains at the window, and no pictures. A little furniture remains, stacked up in one corner, as if for a sale. You can feel the emptiness." Suitcases and bundles of clothing are piled for the journey; during the act many of these will be cleared away, leaving a bare stage.

The act is the shortest in the play. Chekhov still felt it took too long in performance, complaining that Stanislavsky dragged a twelve-minute act out to forty minutes.[39] Chekhov is exaggerating; the actual playing time of Act IV is just about the twenty minutes that Lopakhin specifies they have before the departure to the station. So the act plays in real time, and the concern for catching the train places a real pressure on the scene and its few events: the packing, the farewells, the possible engagement of Varya and Lopakhin, and the final departure of the family from the house.

The beginning of the act reprises motifs we have encountered before in the play: Gayev's affectionate patronizing of the peasants, who have come to say farewell; Ranevskaya's foolishness with money, giving the peasants her purse; Lopakhin's social awkwardness (he has bought champagne for the occasion); Yasha's social pretension (he declares "This isn't real champagne"). The preparations for departure, with servants packing, moving, and carrying things, can be a powerful counterpoint to the emotional journeys of the characters.

The first substantial scene of Act IV is a long conversation between Lopakhin and Trofimov. The two men needle each other in familiar ways, but also seem to show some genuine affection and mutual respect. Though Trofimov warns Lopakhin that his hopeful plans for the orchard are merely "a form of arm-waving," he expresses real regard for the peasant-turned-businessman: "All the same, I can't help liking you. You've got fine, sensitive fingers, like an artist's. You've got a fine, sensitive soul, too."[40] Lopakhin seems to live up to Trofimov's regard when he comments on his poppy crop; on the one hand, it made him a lot of money, but its beauty seems to be what he valued most: "when my poppy was in bloom: what a picture!"

If a production wants to get the audience to believe in an optimistic ending for *The Cherry Orchard*, this scene is one place to do

it, as the two men of the future, in opposition to each other throughout the play, grope towards some kind of understanding. Donald
Rayfield calls this exchange "the only prolonged affectionate inter-
change between two characters in all of Chekhov's work."[41] As J. L.
Styan argues,

> By himself, neither Lopakhin nor Trofimov is so unequivocal a char-
> acter as to speak the whole truth, but somewhere between the prag-
> matism of the one and the idealism of the other the audience is given
> a glimpse of the need for human compromise. When in a moment
> Chekhov adds to this some of Anya's unaffected buoyancy and a good
> deal of Lyubov's warmth, he begins to furnish a sustaining image for the
> future.[42]

Yet there is plenty of material in this exchange that can lead us to
doubt, if not the sincerity of the two men, at least their effectuality.
Trofimov's futile search for his galoshes, an ongoing joke throughout
the act, rather diminishes his stature as a revolutionary. Lopakhin,
the practical man, seems to feel that all problems can be solved
with money; his pressing cash on Trofimov, and Trofimov's principled
refusal, show how far apart the two men are. Further, Trofimov seems
to recognize the limits of his own idealistic program, perhaps indicating a moment of doubt. After his most soaring rhetoric of mankind
"marching toward a higher truth," Trofimov acknowledges that he
himself may not achieve it: "I'll get there. (Pause.) Either get there
or else show others the way." Finally, Lopakhin shows an occasional
blindness to human feeling; the conversation is interrupted by the
shocking sound of axes striking the cherry trees, and Anya enters, on
Ranevskaya's behalf, to ask Lopakhin to wait to cut down the orchard
until they have gone.

The brief exchanges that follow return the play to a mood of haste,
expectation, and exasperation: both Varya and Anya ask about Firs,
who Yasha assures them has been taken to the hospital; Yepikhodov
accidentally crushes a hatbox; Yasha refuses to see his peasant mother,
and rejects the weeping Dunyasha, who in some productions is visibly

pregnant. Finally Ranevskaya enters, along with Gayev, Anya, and Charlotta, and announces that only ten minutes are left. Surprisingly perhaps, all the characters are in a good mood, or say they are; the tone of these exchanges must be determined in performance. Anya is radiant, looking forward to a "new life," and Gayev observes that they are all "quite cheerful" now that the question of the cherry orchard has been finally settled. He observes that "Charlotta's happy – she's singing," but he may speak too soon, as she performs one more grotesque trick: holding a bundle as though it were a crying infant, she abruptly throws it down and begs Lopakhin to find her a job.

Suddenly Pishchik charges in, full of excitement and elation – some Englishmen have found "some kind of white clay" on his land, and he is now rich enough to pay back all his debts. This ironic stroke of fortune keeps the mood elevated until Pishchik realizes they are leaving, and then his boisterous comic persona is subdued to deep emotion. Pishchik is a simply drawn, almost Dickensian character with just a few defining traits and catchphrases. It is indicative of Chekhov's achievement that he manages considerable emotional impact with this figure even while repeating those basic motifs (the enthusiasm, the self-regard, the horse-like qualities, the offstage daughter):

> Well, there we are . . . (*on the verge of tears.*) There we are . . . People of the most tremendous intelligence, these Englishmen . . . There we are . . . Be happy . . . God give you strength . . . There we are then . . . To everything in this world there is an end . . . (*Kisses Ranevskaya's hand.*) And if one day the rumour reaches you that the end has come for me, then remember this old . . . this old horse, and say: "Once on this earth there was a certain Simeonov-Pishchik, God rest his soul . . ." Most remarkable weather . . . Yes . . . (*Exits in great confusion, but at once returns and speaks from the doorway.*) Dashenka sends her regards! (*Goes out.*)

Ranevskaya again reminds the audience of the time – there are five minutes remaining – and once again raises the question of whether Firs has been taken to the hospital. Hurrying everyone else out of the room, she makes a final attempt to arrange the Lopakhin/Varya marriage. Lopakhin declares himself ready to propose, noting that they have champagne for the occasion (though it turns out Yasha has drunk the entire bottle). Lopakhin is left alone, then "*there is stifled laughter and whispering outside the door,*" and Varya enters. In one of Chekhov's most justly famous scenes, Lopakhin and Varya exchange a dozen lines of inconsequential small talk that determines the future direction of their lives.

Varya pretends to look for something in a trunk; they talk about their immediate plans, about the end of life in the house, finally about the weather.

> LOPAKHIN: This time last year we had snow already, if you remember. Now it's calm and sunny. The only thing is the cold. Three degrees of frost.
> VARYA: I didn't look. (*Pause.*) Anyway, our thermometer's broken . . .

Somehow the moment has passed, and when a voice calls for Lopakhin from outside, he hastily leaves, "*as if he has been expecting this call for some time.*" Lopakhin and Varya will not be married; she sinks to the floor, lays her head on a bundle of clothing, and sobs. Ranevskaya comes in, assesses the situation, and says simply, "We must go."

This little scene is an example of Chekhov's intuitive use of the Stanislavskian notion of subtext: there is nothing whatever in the words themselves to indicate the weight of emotion and intention behind them. Indeed, it remains up to the actors to determine at what points Lopakhin might be beginning a tentative overture, at what point he gets cold feet, at what point Varya finally gives up hope (although "Anyway, our thermometer's broken" has an irresistible sadness about it). Further, the emotional motivations behind the scene are left obscure, and must be fleshed out by the actors and director. How exactly does Varya feel about Lopakhin? The last time we saw them together, she was flinging the keys of the house at his feet. Why is he unable to propose? Is it unacknowledged love for Ranevskaya? Guilt over having ruined Varya's family? Sublimation of desire to business interests, as Varya believes? Or does he simply find her unattractive? Chekhov doesn't tell us; it is possible that Varya and Lopakhin don't know themselves; and it is perhaps not even necessary for the actors to know. The halting rhythms and impoverished dialogue of the scene, together with its climactic placement in the final act, give it devastating emotional impact on the stage.

By now it is time to leave, and the last few moments of the play are a series of farewells to the house. Ranevskaya, taking a last moment to look around the room, seems to see the walls and ceilings for the first time, just as Tuzenbach, going to his death in *Three Sisters*, saw the trees as he'd never seen them before. Gayev is prevented by his nieces from making a farewell speech, but he produces, in its place, a vivid and affecting memory: "I remember, when I was six years old, sitting up on this windowsill on Trinity Sunday and watching my father go to church." Chekhov leavens this potentially lachrymose moment with insistent and repeated comic touches. Yepikhodov has another misfortune, choking on a glass of water; Varya seems once again about to accidentally strike Lopakhin, this time with an umbrella; Trofimov finally finds his galoshes; and Gayev once again goes through his billiards routine. Finally they leave the house.

Harvey Pitcher points out that the characters exit in inverse order of their attachment to the estate.[43] Anya and Trofimov go first, eager to get to the new life. Varya takes a last look around the room and goes out "*without hurrying.*" Yasha and Charlotta leave with her dog, recalling the Act I entrance. Lopakhin follows, hurrying the others along, speaking authoritatively as the new owner. Finally Gayev and Ranevskaya are left alone together, but, as Pitcher says, "theirs was not the deepest involvement in the estate; that honour belongs to Firs."[44] These exits are interspersed with a repeated verbal motif, like the choric "They've gone" at the end of *Uncle Vanya*. In this case the repeated phrase is "Let's go," "*Idiom*" in Russian, spoken by several characters. Gayev and Ranevskaya share their final, tearful moment in the house – one Stanislavsky notoriously milked for maximum emotional impact – but they are summoned by Anya and Trofimov's

2. The final moments of the play, in Stanislavsky's original Moscow Art Theatre Production, 1904. (New York Public Library.)

eager, youthful cries from outside. "*My idiom!*" Ranevskaya replies, "We're coming!" And they go out; as far as the audience knows, the play is over.

The stage remains empty, perhaps for some time, as sound effects convey the exodus: doors are locked, carriages leave, an axe is heard on the cherry trees. Then footsteps come from offstage, and Firs shuffles in, looking ill. He tries the door handle – "Locked . . . They've forgotten about me" – and after his characteristic worries about Gayev's clothes, he sits and reflects on his existence: "My life's gone by, and it's just as if I'd never lived at all." As he lies down on the couch, he chides himself with the word he has used throughout the play on all those who met with his disapproval: "*Nyedotyopa!*"

> *A sound is heard in the distance, as if from the sky – the sound of a breaking string, dying away, sad. Silence descends, and the only thing that can be heard, far away in the orchard, is the thudding of the axe.*

CHAPTER 2

THE MOSCOW ART THEATRE
PRODUCTION, 1904

The original production of *The Cherry Orchard*, directed by Constantin Stanislavsky, with Chekhov's wife Olga Knipper as Ranevskaya, was one of the most influential productions of any play in the history of world theatre. Nonetheless, its author was never happy with it: "Stanislavsky has ruined my play," he famously complained.[1] The production was fraught with conflict from the beginning, even before the play was completed. Apart from the vexed question of the play's tone – Chekhov called it a comedy, Stanislavsky a tragedy – there were numerous conflicts over casting, setting, and details of staging. Knipper recalled that "The production of *The Cherry Orchard* was difficult, almost agonizing, I might say. The producers and the author could not understand each other and could not come to an agreement."[2] After Chekhov's death, the Moscow Art Theatre's co-director, Vladimir Nemirovich-Danchenko, wrote to Stanislavsky, "We had already lost Chekhov after *The Cherry Orchard*. He would not have written anything more."[3] Though the initial production of *The Cherry Orchard* was in many respects a painful one for all concerned, it developed an interpretation of the play that endured for half a century, had a widespread international impact, and launched Chekhov into the ranks of the world's great dramatists.

The Moscow Art Theatre was still a new institution in 1904, and its success was directly connected to Chekhov. Founded in 1897 by Stanislavsky and Nemirovich-Danchenko, the Art Theatre was dedicated to new aesthetic and social ideals. These included an ensemble system, a naturalistic approach to acting, long rehearsal periods, detailed realistic settings, accessibility to a wide range of audiences, and a commitment to raise the social value of the theatre. In its first season in 1898, the company performed Chekhov's *The Seagull*, which had failed disastrously in St. Petersburg two years before. The success of this production helped define the company's identity (it still uses a seagull for its logo), and made Chekhov essentially its house dramatist. Though he flirted with other theatres, all of his remaining plays – *Uncle Vanya* (1899), *Three Sisters* (1901), and *The Cherry Orchard* (1904) – had their Moscow premieres at the MAT.

By 1904 the company had been waiting a long time for a new Chekhov play. Chekhov was seriously ill with tuberculosis, and spending most of his time in Yalta. He communicated with Nemirovich and Stanislavsky mostly by letter, and through his wife, Olga Knipper, a MAT actress who had played leading roles in all her husband's plays. At the end of 1902 Nemirovich was pressuring Chekhov to produce a new play that would be a "trump card" for the theatre; by February 1903 he wrote to him, "We desperately need your play. Not only the theatre but literature as a whole."[4] In October, Knipper delivered the manuscript to the theatre; the directors were immediately enthusiastic, and Stanislavsky wrote Chekhov he thought it was his best work. According to Knipper, Stanislavsky found the first act "a comedy, the second he found thrilling, in the third act he was in a sweat and in the fourth he cried the whole time."[5] Nemirovich gave a balanced and perceptive critique; he found the second act slow, but thought "the most remarkable act in terms of mood, dramatic quality and toughness and courage is the last; in terms of grace and lightness of touch the first is outstanding."[6] Chekhov was disturbed, though, by Nemirovich's comment that "there is an overindulgence of tears." Stanislavsky likewise reported to Chekhov that the company wept at the reading. "What's this in your telegram about the play being full of people crying?" Chekhov wrote to Nemirovich. "Where are they? Varya's the only one, and that's because Varya's a cry-baby by nature, and her tears shouldn't depress the audience. You'll often find the stage direction 'through tears' in my text, but that only shows the mood of the characters and not their tears."[7] Chekhov's concern about the misinterpretation of his play as overly lachrymose was one he never forgot, and Stanislavsky's production did nothing to allay his worries.

The principal conflicts at this stage arose over questions of casting. Chekhov had conceived Ranevskaya as an "old woman," and felt the Moscow Art Theatre had no one to play the part. "You'll play the silly girl," Chekhov wrote to Knipper (meaning Varya), "but who's going to play the old mother?"[8] Later, he took Nemirovich-Danchenko to task over the inadequacy of his company: "for three years I've been telling you to engage an actress for the role of Lyubov Andreyevna. And now you're involved in a game of patience that has no chance of coming out."[9] Knipper was the obvious choice, as the theatre's leading actress; though by this time Chekhov wanted her to play Charlotta, which he considered the best part in the play. (Harvey Pitcher notes that there may have been elements of Charlotta based on Knipper, who was of German descent and who did Charlotta's baby ventriloquism trick as a party piece.) In the end, Knipper was cast as Ranevskaya, and Chekhov altered his original conception so that she could play it. "You will play Lyuba Ranevskaya since there's nobody else to," he wrote to her. "She's not dressed luxuriously, but with great taste. She's intelligent, very kind and absent-minded. She's nice to everybody and always has a smile on her face."[10] As reconceived by Chekhov for his wife, Ranevskaya was a woman of great beauty, vitality, and style. Chekhov wrote, "It's not hard to play Ranevskaya. It's only necessary to strike the right note from the very beginning. It's necessary to invent a smile and a way of smiling, and it's necessary to know how to dress."[11] In the end, Ranevskaya became the role most associated with Knipper; she played it for over forty years, and other actresses were invariably compared with her.

Chekhov wanted Stanislavsky to play Lopakhin, the role he felt was central to *The Cherry Orchard*: "If it doesn't come off the whole play falls apart."[12] Chekhov wrote to Stanislavsky, "Lopakhin is a merchant but he is a decent man, intelligent, not petty or a trickster, and it seems to me he is the central role of the play and that you would do it brilliantly." Chekhov specifically feared that Leonidov, who eventually played the part, would be too much of a *kulachok*, a money-grubbing peasant: "In choosing an actor for this role one must not lose sight of the fact that Varya loves Lopakhin and she is a serious, religious young woman; she wouldn't love a *kulachok*."[13] Stanislavsky balked at the role, fearing he couldn't pull off Lopakhin's peasant origins, though Stanislavsky himself, as a factory owner from a bourgeois family, was just the sort of artist-businessman on which Chekhov based Lopakhin. "It's true, I am wary of Lopakhin," Stanislavsky wrote. "The general view is I don't succeed in merchants or rather they come out stagey and calculated." Some critics have speculated that Lopakhin was too close to Stanislavsky's own merchant background for comfort.[14] Gayev he found easier to get hold of: "Gayev in my view should be light, like his sister. He doesn't even notice what he is saying. He understands after he has said it. It seems I have found the tone for Gayev. He comes out, as I do it, something of an aristocrat but a bit stupid."[15] Stanislavsky was highly successful, if sentimental, as Gayev. As Laurence Senelick has pointed out, the presence of Stanislavsky and Knipper in the roles of the gentry may have tipped the play's politics toward the conservative: "The audience's sympathy was to be pegged to Ranevskaya and Gayev from the outset, sacrificing Chekhov's ironic objectivity."[16] Though other critics have disputed whether this was Stanislavsky's intention, there is no doubt that these two performances were central to the play, and occasioned much sympathetic emotion from audiences.

Stanislavsky's wife, the 37-year-old Mariya Petrovna Lilina, took Anya; Chekhov observed that "Mariya Petrovna really does yearn for every role she's too old for."[17] He wanted her to play Varya, but she feared the character was too much like her earlier Chekhov roles. Chekhov bridled at this: "Varya does not resemble Sonya and Natasha. She's a figure in a black dress, a nun, a silly girl, a cry-baby, etc. etc."[18] Lilina did finally graduate to Varya, long after Chekhov's death. In the original production Varya was Mariya Federovna Andreyevna, who initially resisted the role, fearing she would seem too aristocratic

3. Victor Simov's design for the exterior setting of Act II, in Stanislavsky's original Moscow Art Theatre Production, 1904. (New York Public Library.)

for the servile foster daughter. Vasily Kachalov, a young star of the Art Theatre, was Trofimov. Elena Pavlovna Muratova was Charlotta; Chekhov agreed to her casting but worried she wouldn't be funny enough, saying once again that "This is a role for Mme Knipper."[19] Chekhov himself proposed the casting of Aleksandr Artem as Firs, Sofia Khalyutina as Dunyasha, and Nikolai Aleksandrov as Yasha, though ultimately he was unhappy with all three performances. Artem, he felt, acted "vilely," and the two servants failed to follow his stage directions, instead improvising their business.[20] Chekhov was more indulgent toward the MAT's great comic actor Ivan Moskvin, who, with Chekhov's permission, substantially embellished the antics of Yepikhodov, a part in which he gained international renown.

The scenery also provoked much discussion between Chekhov and his directors. Stanislavsky wanted to make the house appear run-down and dilapidated, but Chekhov insisted it be "large and solid . . . the furniture and the fittings haven't been affected by financial ruin and debts."[21] In Act II, Stanislavsky called for realistic detail, with a grave-yard setting, the sound of frogs and birds, and a little train passing in the distance during one of the pauses. "Konstantin Sergeyevich wants to bring on a train in Act Two, but I think he must be restrained," Chekhov wrote to Knipper. "He also wants frogs and corncrakes." To head off Stanislavsky, Chekhov invoked his own knowledge of country life:

> Haymaking usually takes place between 20 and 25 June, at which time I think the corncrake no longer cries, and frogs also are silent at this time of year. Only the golden oriole sings then. There isn't a cemetery. There was one a long time ago. Two or three gravestones lying around any old how, that's all that's left. The bridge is a very good idea. If you can show a train without any noise, without a single sound, then carry on.

Stanislavsky also suggested using the same set for Acts III and IV, partly no doubt for practical reasons of scene-shifting, partly to effect a stark contrast between the ballroom filled with life for the party and stripped bare for the departure. Surprisingly, Chekhov acceded to this request. However, production photos make it clear that by the time the play opened, Act IV was set in the Act I nursery, symbolically a more effective choice.

Chekhov was not present for much of the rehearsal period due to his ill health. When he did turn up, in December 1903, he felt out of place, and found his suggestions were going unheeded, so he stopped attending. His next visit to the theatre, for the premiere on 17 January 1904, was his last; he died a few months later.[22]

There has been much critical debate in recent years over how much the original MAT production actually violated Chekhov's conception of the play. One oft-raised criticism maintains that the production was slow, heavy, and mournful, based on Stanislavsky's misunderstanding of the text; Chekhov certainly seems to have believed this himself. Some recent scholars, however, have argued that the production's gloominess has been overstated. The chief evidence for these revisionist views has been Stanislavsky's own production score, a detailed notebook he prepared during the rehearsal process giving not only notes on movement and business but a moment-to-moment interpretation of the characters' inner lives. David Allen contends in *Performing Chekhov* that "if we examine Stanislavsky's production plan, we will find that the common view of the production is, in fact, a myth."[23] Allen argues that on the axis of comedy and tragedy, the production may have been farther toward the comic end than has been previously believed. Nick Worrall, also working from Stanislavsky's production score, makes a similar contention about the axis of realism and abstraction. "What would seem to emerge from the score . . . is an intuitive sense of the play's problematic nature, hovering between realism and symbolism," Worrall writes. "If Meyerhold and others are right, then what was acted on the stage of the Moscow Art Theatre in 1904 was an inaccurate reflection of the more abstract intuitions contained in the production score."[24] However, it is possible, and indeed almost certain, that the production evolved over the first few years of its existence; and that the company, as it grew more familiar and comfortable with the play, was able to take it further in the daring and original directions that Chekhov had intended, and which Stanislavsky had intuitively grasped in his score for the production but had been unable to realize onstage. Nemirovich-Danchenko wrote to the critic Efros in 1908, "Go and see *The Cherry Orchard* and you simply won't recognize in this lacy, graceful picture that heavy, mournful drama which *Orchard* was in its first year."[25]

The discussion that follows draws on Stanislavsky's score and the commentaries upon it by modern critics; on the letters and memoirs of members of the Moscow Art Theatre; on production photographs and drawings; and on comments by those who saw the production over the first several years of its existence. It is undoubtedly the case that the production changed over those years, just as it changed from the time Stanislavsky prepared the score, at the beginning of rehearsals, to the time it opened in January 1904. For example, the text used by Stanislavsky in preparing the score contains Trofimov's lines that were cut by the censor, as well as the Act II conclusion with Firs and Charlotta. None of this material made it into the opening production, although the censored lines were reinstated in MAT productions after the Revolution. The vicissitudes of theatrical production make the original MAT *Cherry Orchard* a hard entity to pin down. Nonetheless, the production appears to have had some consistency from its original rehearsal period to the influential European and US tours of the 1920s. For more than twenty years, Stanislavsky's direction, Simov's sets, and most of the leading performances were retained. As much as the production may have changed over time and evolved beyond the director's original conception, Stanislavsky's *Cherry Orchard* defined the play for generations, and remains one of the most influential theatrical productions in modern history.

ACT I

Simov's set design for Act I, which doubled for Act IV, was a particularly effective one. Simov used a traditional box set, with hard walls and ceiling and much three-dimensional detailing. However, he angled the walls for greater dynamism, thus creating diagonal movement patterns between the various entrances and around the furniture. The famous bookcase was a large and imposing structure stage right, partly obscuring the main door just upstage of it. The other door, to Anya's room, was stage left. To the middle and left of the angled upstage wall were three great windows, with high lunettes and sweeping white lace curtains that mirrored the cherry blossoms outside. The three-dimensional cherry trees figured prominently into the stage-picture, though Chekhov argued that they wouldn't be so close to the house: "But you know, there won't be much sunlight in the little patio formed by this garden room, and cherries wouldn't grow there."[26] The setting also played up the symbolism of the nursery. The great height of the room created a comic contrast with the miniature furniture, on which the characters sat awkwardly. Backstage light sources created the effect of sunlight streaming in through the large windows.

In the opening scene, Leonidov's Lopakhin cut a strikingly elegant figure in his white waistcoat and dark frock coat. Despite Chekhov's concern about Leonidov being too much of a coarse *kulak*, in production photographs he appears suave and dignified: well-cut suit, full goatee, hair swept back, penetrating but benign gaze, hands in pockets, feet wide apart. Chekhov had specified that Lopakhin "waves his arms about as he walks, takes long strides and meditates while walking about – walking in a straight line. His hair isn't short and so he often throws back his head. He absent-mindedly combs his beard from back to front – i.e. from his neck in the direction of his mouth."[27] In rehearsals, Chekhov told Leonidov not to shout – as a rich man he wouldn't need to – and he suggested that the actor portray him "like a cross between a merchant and a professor of medicine at Moscow University."[28]

While production photographs bear out this basically dignified image of Lopakhin, Stanislavsky's opening business worked against it. Lopakhin entered yawning, stretching, shuddering, disheveled from sleep. He smoked lazily on the divan, spat, picked his teeth with a matchstick, and so forth; he played with the book he had been reading as a meaningless object, juggling it in the air.[29] The business with the servants continued the vein of coarseness and comedy, with Dunyasha wiping her nose on her apron, and Yepikhodov launching into misfortunes in excess of those Chekhov had prepared for him. Moskvin's entrance as Yepikhodov developed into an elaborate set-piece that was hailed by the English novelist Hugh Walpole, who saw the MAT production in Russia:

> Who that has seen it will ever forget that first entrance of Yepikhodov with his nosegay, his squeaking boots, his short jacket, his staring, bulging eyes? Here, at the very first, is a figure to make the groundlings laugh, but Moskvin in that first entrance raises the character to the dignity of tragedy. As he drops his nosegay, you catch in the startled glance that he flings at the supercilious maid-servant his desperate appeal that she will understand that he is not really such a fool as he looks.[30]

Stanislavsky had Yepikhodov wipe the windows with a cloth and then wipe his face with the same cloth; he pulled over a chair by catching it with his coat, then accidentally overturned another while trying to set the first to rights.

The arrival from the station was given added commotion by Stanislavsky's introduction of two house servants, Polya and Yefimushka, who busied themselves with parcels and then remained to observe the scene. According to Yuri Zavadsky, a member of the company, Stanislavsky made the audience wait a full minute for the entrance of the Ranevsky family.[31] The buoyant Anya led the returning party, physically dragging Ranevskaya onto the stage. Though Stanislavsky's wife Lilina was too old for the teenaged Anya, she played the part with exuberance. She recognized that "the most important thing in it is youth," and wrote to Chekhov that she would undertake "to fool the public" with her youthful energy: "everything must be young, even the legs . . . To my mind they are quite different, a girl's feet and a woman's feet."[32] Lilina's Anya wore

4. Olga Knipper as Ranevskaya, in a Moscow Art Theatre publicity postcard. (New York Public Library.)

a white sailor-style dress such as a girl might wear, and kept her hair in a long plait down her back.

Knipper's Ranevskaya was a figure of glamour and charm; both Chekhov and Stanislavsky emphasized the importance of her Parisian dress and manners. As she aged with the part, Knipper moved closer to the "old lady" Chekhov had originally envisioned, and her performances became more sentimental and maternal. But the Knipper of 1904 was elegant and vital: Chekhov told Knipper, "I never wanted to make Mrs. Ranevsky a woman who has calmed down. Nothing less than death can calm a woman like that."[33] Knipper's Ranevskaya was a great beauty, with dark curls piled on her head, a soft pale face, and large dark eyes. Her emotional temperament was that of Knipper herself, of whom one contemporary wrote, "the main feature of her personality and her talent was always a love of life, with all its earthly joys, sorrows, interests and passions."[34] Harvey Pitcher, in Knipper's biography, notes that "Ranevskaya's capacity for giving herself wholeheartedly to the emotion of the moment, and for switching rapidly from one mood to another," was characteristic of Knipper.[35] So, too, was Ranevskaya's inability to cope with mundane realities like money, which she literally throws around the stage. Knipper found this trait part of a subtextual clue to Ranevskaya's nature. "When I was preparing Ranevskaya," Knipper wrote, "I kept wondering why she was always dropping everything. It was obviously more than just a realistic detail on Chekhov's part. She's in a state of inner confusion, she doesn't know what to do with herself, how to live."[36] Knipper conveyed this through her highly expressive hand gestures, which became a feature of the part: in Pitcher's words, "they were kindly, graceful hands that played delicately with a handkerchief, fluttered nervously and seemed incapable of grasping and holding onto anything."[37] After her Act I entrance, Knipper expressed Ranevskaya's heightened emotional state by leaping onto the sofa like a child, running around the room, kissing the furniture, and then melting into tears.

Stanislavsky's Gayev entered carrying a lady's hatbox and a luncheon basket, suggesting his dandified character. Stanislavsky was a tall, powerfully built man, not at all a natural physical match for the effete Gayev; his previous stage role had been Shakespeare's heroic Brutus in *Julius Caesar*. Knipper commented that as Gayev "his bulky figure, look[ed] so absurd, and yet so elegant, too."[38] Stanislavsky communicated the character largely through costume, gesture, and facial expression. He let his right hand dangle at the wrist "like a dog's broken paw."[39] He wore a tailored double-breasted jacket that slimmed his imposing frame, with a floppy silk bow tie that suggested effeminacy. He carried, and frequently gestured with, a large handkerchief, with which he fastidiously cleaned his nails. His goatee was neatly trimmed, his large, upturned moustache expressive. He carried a walking cane, which he manipulated like a billiard cue.

Gayev eagerly participated in the impromptu picnic which Stanislavsky created from the scene of Ranevskaya's coffee. The characters sat at the miniature tables and chairs while Firs served them "as if at a formal dinner," wearing white gloves. As Gayev tucked into cold chicken and Ranevskaya drank her coffee, Lopakhin explained his plan for saving the estate. Stanislavsky's score goes on:

> Lopakhin is determined, but very concerned about the fate of the inhabitants of the house. He tries to persuade them by the force of his words. The others . . . are outraged by Lopakhin's barbaric idea, but they avoid addressing the real issue, for they know full well that none of them would allow such a thing.
>
> They find wine in the basket and drink it. Lopakhin does not decline a glass.[40]

This episode, with its connotations of a children's tea party, became a feature of the production; a 1919 photograph of the Kachalov group of the MAT shows exactly the same business, with the group sitting on their undersized chairs, Kachalov as Gayev holding his coffee cup with little finger extended.

Gayev's bookcase speech follows, a celebrated moment in Stanislavsky's performance. Knipper thought this speech, and Stanislavsky's emotional journey within it, a keynote for the character and the play:

> I loved him tenderly in *The Cherry Orchard*. The whole performance acquired a much greater significance when he played in it. I always tried to catch the extraordinary ease with which he would slip from one mood to another – it was a great help to me in the part of Mrs. Ranevsky. His famous speech before the bookcase. "It was only when I finished it," he soon tells [Anya], "that I realized how silly it was." And to be sure, he finished the speech with his favorite billiard terms, looking highly embarrassed, as though he himself realized how silly it was.[41]

In his score, Stanislavsky observes, "A sad note can be detected. It is the sadness that he is an empty and irredeemable person."[42] This sad note, coming at one of Gayev's most absurd moments, hints at the tragic dimension many observers found in Stanislavsky's performance of the role. Stanislavsky likely felt personal empathy for Gayev in subtle ways. He based the Ranevsky household on his own estate, Lyubimovka, where Chekhov had begun writing the play. The arrangement of furniture in the Act I set mirrored that in Stanislavsky's own living-room.[43] Stanislavsky came to identify so much with Gayev that it was the last part he played before his retirement in 1928.[44]

While the tea party and the bookcase speech were generally light-hearted moments, the play's tragic aspect surfaced in Knipper's performance of Ranevskaya. In her vision of her mother at the window, Stanislavsky felt she experienced a kind of ecstasy: "God knows why she has imagined this. She has entered the past so vividly that she has forgotten she is no longer a child."[45] When she subsequently saw Trofimov, Knipper's Ranevskaya embraced him "as if he were her drowned child, Grisha, come back to life"; she then spoke to him "as if bewailing her lost youth."[46]

Stanislavsky's Gayev returned the play to comedy through a bit of byplay with Alexandrov's haughty Yasha (this characterization, a study in smarminess, became even more repellent as the actor grew older, with a puffy body and round, unctuously smiling face under his Parisian cap). As Gayev took out his pipe, Yasha superciliously offered him a light, which Gayev rejected; in response, Yasha rudely threw the match on the floor.[47] Gayev went away to sulk on a child's divan. When Anya later chided him about his coarse remarks about her mother, Gayev seemed "pitiful, like a child that has done something wrong."[48] The moment established again the childishness of the whole family, according to Nick Worrall: "[Anya] accompanies her reproach by kneeling in front of him and thoughtfully settling his tie, while Varya stands behind her and plaits her hair before bedtime."[49]

Gayev's confident assertion that the orchard will be saved changed his mood; Stanislavsky noted that both Gayev and Ranevskaya are subject to wide swings of emotion. As he tried to reassure the girls, Stanislavsky's Gayev spoke so confidently and optimistically "that it is possible to imagine that he really could be a bank manager."[50] Stanislavsky noted that the girls don't actually believe him, but they choose to do so, in order to make their predicament bearable for the moment. But Gayev undermined his prophet-like authority by putting a sweet into his mouth at the end of his speech. Stanislavsky noted, "That is a wonderful touch, and instantly demolishes everything he has said. All trust in him is undermined."[51]

The act ended with Trofimov, watching Anya being led off to bed, exclaiming passionately, "My sunshine! My springtime!" Stanislavsky made this a poignant and poetic moment. Along with the chirping of birds in the orchard and the distant sounds of livestock, Stanislavsky played a sound effect he had personally recorded on a wax cylinder, a shepherd playing on a reed pipe. It was a haunting sound that Chekhov had admired when he heard it at Stanislavsky's estate, and he agreed that "It's just what we need" for the atmosphere at the end of the opening act.[52] Trofimov sat alone onstage listening to these sounds, shielding his eyes from the glare of the rising sun as the stage was flooded with light.

ACT II

For the outdoor scene of Act II, Simov and Stanislavsky created an effective landscape that placed the characters' conflicts in the context of nature. The reflections on nature within the act – Gayev's apostrophe to its beauty and indifference, and Lopakhin's belief that living in the awesome Russian land, "we ought properly to be giants" – were supported by a setting that was both realistic and symbolic. For all Stanislavsky's quarrels with Chekhov over the degree of naturalism to strive for, the final setting was quite simple, and suggested a landscape by the Russian painter Levitan, Chekhov's close friend.[53]

Simov gained the effect of distance and openness by eliminating masking flats and using a semi-circular cyclorama, painted to suggest the haziness of atmospheric perspective. Stage left was an old wayside shrine, made of rough wood and capped with a small onion dome. In the center was a rustic bench, down right were two low haystacks. At the back were a few real birch and fir trees. Stanislavsky's sketch for the set includes a central ravine with a bridge over it, but this is not evident in the production photographs, which show a setting simpler and sparer than Stanislavsky's original conception. The photos also show that Chekhov successfully restrained Stanislavsky from having a small model train cross the stage in the distance.

While Chekhov argued against the use of frog and corncrake sound effects, a natural soundscape was liberally employed nonetheless. Chekhov pointedly said in Stanislavsky's hearing, "I will write a new play, and it will begin like this: 'How wonderful, how quiet! No birds, no dogs, no cuckoo, no owl, no nightingale, no clock, no jingle of bells, not one cricket can be heard!'"[54] In April 1904, an acquaintance of Chekhov's went to see a production of *The Cherry Orchard* in Yalta that was advertised as being "in the style of the Art Theatre production." What this meant, in practice, was that "the assistant director whistled, cawed, cuckooed, rattled, croaked and squeaked throughout the entire play, drowning out the words of the actors with the sounds of birds and frogs."[55] Evidently offstage sounds were an ineradicable part of Stanislavsky's practice and the MAT's reputation.

Here are the opening directions for Act II from Stanislavsky's score:

> It is nearly evening. Sunset. Summer. Hay-making. Heat. The steppe. The town cannot yet be seen in the mist. Some kind of bird calls persistently, monotonously. Now and again a gust of wind brushes the leaves and causes a rustling. In the distance a field of rye sways, like waves (the reflection of a spotlight on a metal sheet). Occasionally a withered branch falls to the ground. There are people walking through the wood, and we hear the sound of snapping twigs.
>
> A corncrake, frogs, songs, mist from the trap-door.
>
> Dunyasha and Yasha sit on the steps and Yepikhodov on a gravestone. There are many mosquitoes and flies. Dunyasha and Yasha swat mosquitoes on each others' hands and faces. It's their way of flirting . . . As the curtain rises, Yasha and Dunyasha sing a duet, and Yepikhodov tries to join in, but he doesn't succeed. They sing very badly, as none of them has an ear for music.[56]

David Allen points out that "The lyricism of the setting forms a majestic backdrop to the comic fooling of the characters in the foreground," calling this the dominant note for Stanislavsky's staging of the act.[57] Stanislavsky certainly didn't stint on the fooling, particularly with Moskvin's Yepikhodov, who got his foot caught in his hat and then fell with a crash just after his dramatic exit, cheaply anticipating Trofimov's fall down the stairs in Act III. Yasha likewise had his share of farcical business, dancing the cancan while sitting down, then blowing smoke in Dunyasha's mouth as she tried to kiss him.[58]

When Knipper's Ranevskaya entered, it was evident that "she might be happy walking on a boulevard in Paris, but not among Russian villages."[59] She and Gayev sat to rest as though they had been walking for miles; they poked each other with cane and parasol "like grown-up children." They established the heat and atmosphere by fanning themselves and swatting mosquitoes, which plagued the characters throughout the act. Chekhov hated this business; in a variation of his comment on sound effects, he told Leonidov, who played Lopakhin, "In the next play I shall make the character say, 'What a wonderful place, there is not a single mosquito here.'"[60] Leonidov might well have been sympathetic, as Stanislavsky had him wear a handkerchief with knotted corners on his head as protection against the imaginary insects. This costuming further eroded Lopakhin's dignity. Stanislavsky had worn such a handkerchief as Astrov in Act I of *Uncle Vanya*, leading Nemirovich to complain, "I can tell you for certain that Chekhov won't like it; I know his tastes and his creative nature extremely well."[61] Yet the photos attest that Lopakhin wore the handkerchief in production, looking very absurd, as Stanislavsky perhaps intended. When Lopakhin was remonstrating with the Ranevskys about the need to sell the orchard, he lost even more dignity in his exasperation, spitting on the ground in dismay: "This speaks of the peasant in him," Stanislavsky wrote.[62] He got on his knees, tore his hair, beat his breast; Stanislavsky wanted "some kind of very strong, but absurd, expression of temperament."[63]

Stanislavsky called for added business in the act, some of it telling, some superfluous. A bicycle messenger went past, riding to the house with a telegram from Paris, which Ranevskaya failed to intercept. Yasha appeared "as if out of the ground" to pick up Ranevskaya's dropped purse, surreptitiously helping himself to a coin in the process. Ranevskaya and her daughters got into a protracted romp in one of the haystacks, with much flinging of hay, shrieking with laughter, kissing, tickling, fussing with hair and clothing, and so forth.

The general effect of the business was to emphasize the frivolity and idleness of the gentry, as they purposefully ignored both Lopakhin's practical suggestions and Trofimov's speech attacking the intelligentsia. This speech was a big set-piece for V. I. Kachalov, who was the up-and-coming star of the Art Theatre. Knipper reported to Chekhov, during rehearsals, that Kachalov was making a mark in the role, "although Kachalov is now so much in fashion people like everything."[64] Kachalov began the speech calmly, smoking a cigarette, then built to fiery declamation. Stanislavsky had the sounds of the Jewish orchestra become audible in the distance during Trofimov's speech, perhaps creating a mournful or ironic counterpoint to the corrosive rhetoric. A production photo shows Kachalov, in belted tunic and high boots, raising his hand in a revolutionary gesture, his whole body tensed in passionate oratory. Chekhov had toned down his speeches for the censor, but still worried over his subversiveness; he had written to Knipper, "Trofimov is in exile off and on and gets chucked out of university every so often, and how is one to depict that sort of thing?"[65] Kachalov had himself been something of a young firebrand, and "infused the role with his memories of his own student days in Petersburg, when he attended left-wing demonstrations and carried a volume of Plekhanov in his pocket."[66]

Gayev ignored Trofimov's speech, absorbing himself in his newspaper. He began his apostrophe to nature while lying prone on one of the haystacks. "When reprimanded, he rapidly places his hands over his mouth, covers his face with his hat, and lies back with arms folded."[67] The characters then sat lost in thought, swatting at mosquitoes. The repeated line "There goes Yepikhodov," added by Chekhov during rehearsals, created a sense of tension and eerie expectation. The sound of the breaking string, created by wires stretched backstage and backed by a rumbling drum, was overdone, in Chekhov's view. He wrote to Knipper in March of 1904, "Tell Nemirovich that the sound in Acts Two and Four of *The Cherry Orchard* must be shorter, a lot shorter, and must be felt as coming from a great distance. What a lot of fuss about nothing – not being able to cope with a trifle like this, a mere noise, although it's so clearly described in my play."[68] The sound struck Ranevskaya deeply, who shuddered, along with Anya; Varya seemed less affected, and the others showed no significant reaction. The tramp's entrance was heralded by the offstage cracking of twigs and the muttering of a hoarse voice. Played by M. A. Gromov, Solyony in the MAT *Three Sisters*, the tramp was an imposing figure, carrying a large stave. The women were frightened by him, though the men

were unmoved; Stanislavsky's Gayev was even friendly in giving directions to the station. When the tramp advanced on Varya, Lopakhin
shoved him back, and even Firs got involved, threatening the tramp
with his stick.[69] Gromov was memorable in the role; one contemporary critic, Yuly Aikhenvald, praised the "chance nameless passerby
with a tree-limb in his hand; he appears to the spectators for only a
moment with unsure steps, with verses of Nadson and Nekrasov on
his drunken lips, – but his face flashed before us a complete drama, a
whole life, wasted, bitter, pitiful."[70]

Stanislavsky rehearsed Chekhov's concluding scene with Firs and
Charlotta, but felt he could not make it work onstage. "Such a
lyric ending lowered the atmosphere of the act and we could not
lift it again," Stanislavsky wrote in *My Life in Art*. "I suppose that
it was mainly our own fault but it was the author who paid for
our inability."[71] Instead of this "meeting of two lonely people,"
Stanislavsky ended the act with the duet of Anya and Trofimov. Anya
sat on the steps of the shrine in her white dress, while Trofimov
shared his visions of the future. According to the critic Nikolai Efros,
Kachalov was very moving in this scene: "Through the funny outward
appearance of the old student Trofimov, there shone out in Kachalov's
acting the whole beauty of that character, his young optimism, his
stiffness combined with tenderness."[72] In the atmospheric moonshine
created by the Art Theatre's spotlights, Kachalov and Lilina closed the
act on a note of romantic idealism and young love.

ACT III

The party scene of Act III was one Stanislavsky prepared with special
care. He developed an elaborate supporting cast of characters and
complicated business to create a singularly dreary and boring provincial party. Stanislavsky used this background of faded gentility and
rural ennui as a backdrop to the emotional climax of his production:
Ranevskaya's loss of the cherry orchard.

Simov's setting for Act III was his least original; the flimsy-looking walls, parallel to the footlights, made the stage pictures flat and static. On the stage left side, Simov placed the doors to the ballroom, which was visible behind, distinguished by a chandelier. Keeping the two-room depth on the relatively shallow MAT stage resulted in a very broad and flat acting space. Large pillars, both stage left and upstage right center, were wrapped in some sort of decorative garlands. The most distinctive feature of the set was the wall treatment; the flats were painted in a leaf pattern, suggesting the orchard just outside.

Though Stanislavsky began the act with Chekhov's *grand-rond*, the overall effect was not boisterous excitement but enervation. Stanislavsky's description of the atmosphere at the beginning of the act is telling: "The ball is a complete failure. There are few people. Despite all efforts, it has not been possible to get more people to come. They have barely managed to drag out the Station-master and the Post Office Clerk . . . Half of the dancers do not know the figures for the quadrilles, never mind the *grand-rond*." Between dances, the party guests sat bored and listless, as though at a funeral, around the edges of the room. Stanislavsky introduced a whole host of dreary guests: a shop-assistant in a jacket and red tie, a priest's wife and her unattractive daughters, including a tall, skinny one dancing with a very young boy, a retired military man and his wife, an old lady dressed in black, a billiard-playing German with a goatee and pipe, "a fat land-owner and his thin wife wearing the old-fashioned dress she got married in," and so forth.[73] Stanislavsky even brought Pishchik's daughter Dashenka, one of the play's great offstage presences, into the scene. Some, but not all, of the supernumeraries are visible in a production photo of Act III, in which the characters are awkwardly attempting to dance in a line across the flat, shallow stage. Besides the dancing, much party business involved the inadequate refreshments: fruit and nuts on the tables, and seltzer water, which had run out.

In the first scene after the *grand-rond*, Trofimov and Pishchik turned over all the empty bottles, desperate for a drink. Gribunin's Pishchik was a well-drawn characterization that remained with the production for at least twenty years. He wore a bald pate, with white hair in back, a long white beard down his chest, and a peasant smock belted at the waist under a dark frock coat. He stood with a peasant's open stance, hands on hips, and could fall asleep while standing up, or even while eating, "chewing more and more slowly."[74] He was the butt of elaborate party tricks by Charlotta: she produced odd sounds by tapping him on the cheek and the top of the head, and later ensnared him with the rug she had used for the tricks with Anya and Varya. Charlotta's magic show – a few lines of dialogue in Chekhov's text – occupied pages of notes from Stanislavsky and several minutes of stage time.

Chekhov was never happy with Muratova as Charlotta. He had based the character on an eccentric English governess he had met on Stanislavsky's estate, and he always wanted Knipper for the role; he declared Charlotta his favorite character. Muratova was quite tall and thin, and wore a long white skirt with a sash, a white blouse, and a man's necktie. She recalled asking Chekhov whether she should cut her hair short like a man's: "After a long pause he said reassuringly: 'You may.' Then after some silence he added caressingly: 'Only you should not.'"[75] She makes a striking figure in the production photos, with strange accessories for each act: lorgnette and dog in Act I, peaked cap, rifle, and cucumber in Act II, and the highly theatrical get-up of top hat, frock coat, checked trousers, and monocle for the party scene. Stanislavsky seems to have had doubts about her abilities as a ventriloquist; he suggested using a phonograph offstage.

The elaborations of the party business were a major sticking point with symbolist critics, who saw Act III as a bizarre dance of death and felt Stanislavsky mired it in extraneous detail. Meyerhold, writing to Chekhov in May 1904, argued that Stanislavsky had failed to communicate the horror:

Your play is abstract, like a Tchaikovsky symphony. The stage director must feel it above all with his ear. In the third act, against the background of the stupid "stomping" – this "stomping" must be heard – Horror enters unnoticed by anyone.

"The cherry orchard is sold." They dance. "Sold." They dance. And so to the end . . . Gaiety in which sounds of death are heard. In this act there is something Maeterlinck-like frightful . . . In the Moscow Art Theatre one did not get such an impression from the last act. The background was not concentrated enough and at the same time not remote enough. In the forefront: the story with the billiard cue and the tricks. Separately. All this did not form a chain of "stomping." And in the meantime all the "stomping" people are unconcerned and do not sense the harm. The tempo of this act was too slow in the Art Theatre. They wanted to convey boredom. That's a mistake.[76]

Meyerhold is not always lucid in his complaints about Stanislavsky's production, but the thrust of his objection is clear enough: the Art Theatre's naturalism obscured what Meyerhold thought was the crucial musical or symbolic rhythm of the act. Rather than a *danse macabre*, Stanislavsky had presented a grab-bag of unconnected details, losing the governing idea. Meyerhold expanded his ideas in his famous essay "Naturalistic Theatre or Theatre of Mood," first published in 1906. Meyerhold felt the leitmotiv of the act was Ranevskaya's premonition of coming disaster, which should be set against "monotonous strumming of the provincial orchestra and the dance of living corpses. The scene with the tricks is only another discord in the melody of the tedious dance."[77] This musical structure was lost in Stanislavsky's production through the elaboration of background elements like Charlotta's magic show:

The director of the Art Theatre showed how the harmony of this act can be destroyed. He created a scene with many details which proceeded slowly and laboriously. For a long time the spectator concentrated his attention on this scene and lost the leitmotiv of the act. And when the act had finished, only the melody of the background remained and the leitmotiv had disappeared.[78]

Some recent critics have argued, based on the production score, that Stanislavsky was fully aware of the symbolic dimensions of the scene and that "the staging is clearly intended to go beyond realism."[79] David Allen calls the characters "puppet-like" and Nick Worrall describes Stanislavsky's party scene as "conceived in a spirit of grotesquerie akin to Chekhov's one-act comedy *The Wedding*."[80] However, whether or not Stanislavsky's party business conveyed any symbolic meaning, there is no doubt that it significantly protracted the act, and caused some problems of focus. The Ukrainian critic Nikolaev assessed the situation after the eighth performance:

> The whole third act of the play is portrayed so that you cannot for a second concentrate and investigate carefully the subject being unveiled before you by the stage picture. All those dances, card tricks, recitations, games, all this kaleidoscopically changing bustle of a ball improvised on a country estate grips you with its striking picturesqueness, its striking likeness to reality, and, becoming its involuntary participant, you, as in reality, lose the ability to follow the changes in the interactive characters of the play, i.e., you lose the most substantial thing, the reason you came to the theatre. I had to exert really incredible violence to tear myself away from the wonders of the director's talent to listen to the dialogue between Ranevskaya and Trofimov.[81]

The scene Nikolaev refers to, a long and emotional exchange between Knipper and Kachalov, was played with a self-conscious element of exaggeration. Stanislavsky wanted Knipper to emphasize Ranevskaya's Parisian leanings through a performance of Gallic femininity. Of the moment when she tells Trofimov she was "beneath love," Stanislavsky wrote:

> Either from coquettishness or nervousness, she sinks her head on the table, and stands there in a coquettish pose. You can sense the French woman in her. (Anyway Olga Leonardovna [Knipper] must find the tone of a French woman.) . . . She half-laughs, half-cries, or rather, she does both at the same time. This mood must be played with a nervous dissoluteness.[82]

Similarly, Nemirovich Danchenko urged her to play up Ranevskaya's French side, rather than dwelling solely on her personal sufferings:

> you must understand above all the two contrasting aspects of the role or, rather, of Ranevskaya's soul: Paris and the cherry orchard. Outward lightness, grace, the brio of the overall tone are in evidence every time we skim over trifles which do not go deep into the soul. Even more clearly giggles, gaiety, etc. Such brightness will make the switch to drama more acute.[83]

At the emotional climax of this scene, Stanislavsky had Knipper throw herself at Trofimov's feet "as if she were acting in a French boulevard melodrama."[84]

Although Stanislavsky stressed Ranevskaya's histrionic side, he did not neglect her inner anguish. One famous bit of business revealed her abstraction and fragility. Firs poured her a cup of tea, and in her self-absorption she allowed the hot water to burn her fingers; she dropped the cup with a sudden spasm of pain. According to Michel Saint-Denis, who spoke to Stanislavsky about this moment, the director used real boiling water in rehearsals to give Knipper the necessary physical memory to make the business convincing.[85]

Stanislavsky would not begin to develop his famous "method" of actor training until 1906; in *My Life in Art*, he acknowledged that during rehearsals for *The Cherry Orchard*, "Our inner technique and our ability of reacting on another's creative soul were very primitive."[86] Stanislavsky was clearly beginning to think about internal motivation and psycho-physical actions, things that would become the cornerstones of his system. As Jean Benedetti has noted, *The Cherry Orchard* is the first of Stanislavsky's production scores to contain substantial notes on motivation, both psychological and social, as well as stage business.[87] The most detailed interior narrative in the score is for Lopakhin's announcement of his purchase of the cherry orchard:

> RANEVSKAYA: Has the cherry orchard been sold?
> LOPAKHIN: (*Guiltily, examining his handkerchief. Looks down. Doesn't answer at once.*) It has.
> RANEVSKAYA: (*Pause. Barely audible.*) Who bought it?

LOPAKHIN: (*Even quieter and more embarrassed.*) I bought it. (*Agonizing pause. Lopakhin feels badly and this arouses the beast in him. The awkwardness of his position starts to make him angry. He nervously pulls at his handkerchief. Ranevskaya just sinks down and remains in that position for some time. She takes nothing in, understands nothing. It is as if she has suddenly grown old.*)[88]

Stanislavsky's notes go on for pages, and are full of arresting psychological and physical details. He suggests that during Lopakhin's account of the sale, when he is at some physical distance from Ranevskaya, "the feeling of pleasure and commercial pride" overcomes his embarrassment and Lopakhin begins to boast "with artistic enthusiasm over his skill and efficiency. It is essential in order to justify Lopakhin that there should be precisely this 'artistic enthusiasm.'"[89] By the time Lopakhin shouts "The cherry orchard is mine," the emotions have become unchecked:

Gross guffaw. He clowns, leaning his head on the table, ruffles his hair, butts Pishchik who is sitting next to him in the chest. Stands up, raises his arms and beats his chest. He continues his speech as he does so. All this clowning is explicable by the force of his character, his unbridled nature, his ecstasy.[90]

And later in the speech:

Now he is stern, imperious . . . he knows no mercy. The drink has gone to his head. He cannot feel Ranevskaya's sorrow and misery. Darkening malice and resentment towards the humiliations and trials of his childhood have been aroused in him. All this will be accepted if the actor goes at it boldly, powerfully, like a warrior not a bruiser.[91]

Stanislavsky emphasizes the range of Lopakhin's emotions and the violence of his character, something Leonidov apparently had difficulties with in practice. Nemirovich wrote to the actor just before the performance, complaining that he was "half-hearted" in the way Lopakhin "plays the stroppy peasant" in Act III; he urged Leonidov to "get to know every trait of this complex character more deeply" and eschew "theatrical tricks."[92]

At the end of the speech, Lopakhin grows sentimental, but Stanislavsky read his emotions somewhat cynically. As Benedetti notes, there is enough contempt in Stanislavsky's understanding of Lopakhin's psychology to explain why he didn't want to play the role.[93]

> He drops to his knees, kisses her hands and skirt like a little puppy dog (the fact that he is drunk helps). He weeps. The more sincerely and tenderly the better. Why then, if he is so tenderhearted, didn't he help Ranevskaya? Because he is a slave to merchants' prejudices, because they would have made him a laughing-stock. *Les affaires sont les affaires.*[94]

What observers most remembered from the Moscow Art Theatre version of this scene was not Leonidov's performance of the speech but its effect on Knipper. Her desolation was one of her most famous moments. Cheryl Crawford, one of the founders of the Group Theatre, saw Knipper perform in Moscow in the twenties: "when she sat at the table opposite Lopakhin and learned that everything had been lost due to her improvidence, she was extremely touching. The truth hit her slowly; her hands fluttered on the table, her face grew immobile as she faced reality for the first time."[95] Anya and Trofimov led Knipper's Ranevskaya offstage in tears. The party continued in the other room, though the doors were closed to muffle the sounds of music and merriment. In a music cue representative of the changeover of power, the "trite little polka" the band had been playing was replaced by a lively Russian folk dance. The thumping beat of the dancing shook the glasses on the tables, and just before the curtain fell on the empty stage, a piece of plaster broke off from the ceiling and shattered in pieces over the floor.[96]

ACT IV

For the many observers who found Stanislavsky's production of *The Cherry Orchard* a heavy, mournful affair, Act IV was largely to blame.

Both the direction and Stanislavsky's own acting as Gayev created an atmosphere drowning in sorrow. Chekhov was furious; after hearing reports of the production, he wrote to Knipper, "they say that in act IV Stanislavsky plays disgustingly, that he drags it out painfully. An act which should last 12 minutes *maximum* takes 40 in your production. All I can say is that Stanislavsky has ruined my play."[97]

The bleak atmosphere began with the setting. The Act I "Nursery" set was stripped bare; on Nemirovich-Danchenko's suggestion, Simov even painted the walls with darker patches, to show where pictures and lamps had once hung. The imposing bookcase was removed, making the space seem much larger. The curtains were gone, the windows partly shuttered from outside. A number of furniture pieces were shoved together stage left; two large packing crates stood upstage, covered with hatboxes, bundles, and the like.

The staging reinforced the sense of loss. Stanislavsky began the act with the sound of wooden boxes being nailed shut; as Nick Worrall notes, the sound had "fairly obvious associations."[98] That sound was then ironically counterpointed with a cork popping, as Lopakhin opened his painfully inappropriate champagne. Two peasants came down the stairs carrying a mattress, which they took outside; the business of removing the family furniture would continue throughout the act. Through pantomime, all the characters established the cold in the unheated and desolate house.

Even in his grim final act, Stanislavsky did not proscribe comedy entirely. Moskvin still had free rein for Yepikhodov's misfortunes, repeatedly breaking things and doing himself injuries with a hammer. Oliver Sayler praised his "heedless disregard of his hands while he nails up boxes and watches the departure of the family in the last act, – always he brings the smile which is the reward of high comedy, never the uproarious laughter which is the boon of farce."[99]

Lopakhin made his farewell to Trofimov "in a minor key," impressed by the latter's refusal of his money. Stanislavsky suggested that Lopakhin is "in some confusion" during the act. Stanislavsky's Gayev was himself heavy with emotion; though he tried to appear cheerful, he was deep in thought, fiddling with keys on a ring. Knipper also conveyed a sense of deep mourning, wandering among the cases, touching the furniture, "kissing some of the beloved chairs and other items."[100] Stanislavsky's treatment of these characters seems to go against Chekhov's text, where Gayev declares "cheerfully" that "everything's all right now" and Ranevskaya admits that her nerves are better and she is sleeping well now that the question of the estate is settled.

Just before the non-proposal scene with Varya, Lopakhin checked his watch and went to look out the windows, keeping his back to Varya as she entered. He remained looking out while she pretended to look through the trunks. Lopakhin's reticence was understandable in the MAT production: Varya was a dour figure in a shapeless black dress, her hair done up severely in a bun and usually covered with a tightly wrapped headscarf. Stanislavsky's notes include little on the psychological state of the characters in this scene, though these are implied by their physical actions. Varya sat sadly on a bundle on the floor; Lopakhin spent much of the scene turned away to the windows, drumming on the windowsill and the glass with his fingers. Finally, after some painful moments, a peasant appeared outside the window and tapped on the glass to get Lopakhin's attention; he exited hurriedly while Varya broke down in tears.[101]

While Stanislavsky's production score does not extend to the end of the play, the final exit of Ranevskaya and Gayev was one of the production's most celebrated and well-documented moments. A production photograph shows them standing in the deserted room, several feet apart. Knipper has her hands crossed over her chest in an image of saint-like suffering. Stanislavsky is pressing his handkerchief into his mouth in anguish. In the production, Knipper exited first, leaving Stanislavsky onstage for the emotional climax of his performance. He turned to speak to Ranevskaya, but she was gone. Racked by uncontrollable grief, he held the handkerchief in his mouth to stifle his sobs, then slowly turned to leave. One spectator recalled, "As he turns his back and goes out we see the big shoulders twitch, and it is almost more than an impressionable playgoer can bear."[102] Over the years,

Stanislavsky's exit became legendary, moving audiences to tears both in Russia and on the MAT's European and American tours. As Sharon Carnicke has argued, "By allowing Gayev to remain after his sister left, Stanislavsky takes centre stage, focuses the audience's full attention on his reaction to the loss of his home, and creates the potential for a heart-rending moment that is not found in Chekhov's script . . . Such a directorial choice gives the stage fully to the play's star and unambiguously asks the audience to empathize."[103]

Stanislavsky left no notes on Firs' scene at the end of the play, but there is no reason to doubt that it was also played for full pathos. A MAT photo of the final moments shows how Stanislavsky and Nemirovich-Danchenko ended *The Cherry Orchard*. Firs lay slumped on a large chair stage left amid the jumble of furniture. His right arm hung limply over the arm of the chair, where he had leant his stick. His legs sprawled out to his left. The chair was half-draped in a blanket, mirroring the diagonal of Firs' unconscious body: the image connected Firs visually with the old unwanted lumber left behind in the house. The stage was dark. A few bars of light from the shuttered windows ran across the floor and up the stage left wall, while the axes rang in the orchard and the protracted sound of the breaking string filled the theatre. This haunting image brought home the powerful impact of Stanislavsky's essentially tragic reading of the play.

The MAT production of *The Cherry Orchard* was not, at first, a particular success. Stanislavsky himself felt the actors were not ready, and rather cynically decided to make the opening night a celebration of Chekhov's literary jubilee in order to distract attention from the production. "Our reckoning was simple," he admitted in *My Life in Art*. "If the actors were not able to put the play over, its failure of great success could be blamed on the unusual conditions of the jubilee evening which would not fail to draw the attention of the spectators away from the actors to the author."[104] At the jubilee there was a large and adulatory crowd, but Chekhov had to be dragged to the theatre under protest. After the third act, the author was brought onstage to be honored, but Chekhov was so ill he could barely stand. One of the speeches, a ponderous address to "Dear, honored Anton Pavlovich," sounded so much like Gayev's bookcase speech that Chekhov and the actors shared a private laugh over it.

Chekhov was unenthusiastic about the production, and the reviews were mixed. Many critics dwelt on the social aspects of the play, and seemed unable to grasp Chekhov's ambiguous portrayals of the student Trofimov and the merchant Lopakhin, who did not correspond to expected types. There was some unqualified praise for the "tender, sensitive responsiveness" of the MAT actors, and a recognition that they were the supreme interpreters of Chekhov.[105] Stanislavsky himself carried off the main acting honors, and reviewers recognized the balance of humour and tragedy in his portrayal; Aleksandr Amfiteatrov found him ". . . a figure whose humour causes the heart to contract, like the humour in Gogol's *Overcoat*. There are unforgettable stage performances, however many years pass since their appearance. I am certain that I shall never forget Stanislavsky-Gayev, how, when the cherry orchard having been sold at auction, he enters carrying two small packages [of anchovies] in his hand."[106] At least one critic, A. Kugel, saw the play as the comedy Chekhov intended, noting that "the comic angle on the play was followed through with wonderful subtlety and great skill."[107] More often, observers saw the production as a naturalistic slice of life, crowded with psychological and material detail. The criticisms of Meyerhold and Nikolaev, that the artistic shape of the play was lost in its material and emotional clutter, constituted one perspective. Another came from Vasily Torporov, who saw the MAT performance as an artistic breakthrough for naturalism:

> These weren't actors! Living people were conversing in sleepy voices. Whether it was good or bad – I had no time to understand . . . Of the usual arsenal of acting techniques [Stanislavsky] used none – no effective intonations, no coups of any kind, no deft gimmicks to evoke applause. None of it. I could not even tell if it was any good from our actors' point of view. I simply couldn't take my eyes off him. He seemed to have bewitched me.[108]

Not everyone was moved by the fate of Gayev and Ranevskaya. Maxim Gorky took a harsh dislike to the characters the production made its protagonists: "Here are the tearful Ranevskaya and other former owners . . . egotistical like children, and as flaccid as old folks. They have failed to die promptly and so pine, seeing nothing around themselves, understanding nothing – parasites, devoid even of the strength to batten on life."[109]

Gorky's stern attitude toward the gentry was one that was spreading in the country; a year after *The Cherry Orchard*'s premiere there would be a significant uprising in Russia. Laurence Senelick has pointed out that at its first performances, no critic or journalist read *The Cherry Orchard* as portending a revolutionary cataclysm, but the association would be made soon enough.[110] In 1917, on the eve of the October Revolution, the Moscow Art Theatre presented *The Cherry Orchard*. The actors were nervous, uncertain how the audience would respond to the play in such a charged atmosphere. According to Stanislavsky, the spectators sat spellbound:

> It seemed to us that all of them wanted to wrap themselves in the atmosphere of poetry and to rest there and bid peaceful farewell forever to the old and beautiful life that now demanded its purifying sacrifices. The performance was ended by a tremendous ovation, and the spectators left the theatre in silence, and who knows – perhaps many of them went straight to the barricades. Soon shooting began in the city.[111]

At any rate, the conflict between the new life and the old, between laughter and tears, between visionary symbolism and naturalistic detail, would be played out through the text of *The Cherry Orchard* throughout the first century of its existence. And the Moscow Art Theatre production, the original battleground of those conflicts, would remain as memory, touchstone, and legend in the ongoing history of the play.

CHAPTER 3

RUSSIAN AND SOVIET
PERFORMANCES, 1904–1953

The first decades of the twentieth century saw cataclysmic changes in Russian history and culture. The Russo-Japanese War of 1905, the Great War of 1914–18, and a series of popular uprisings culminating in the Bolshevik Revolution of 1917, followed by civil war, political strife and the aggressive social restructuring of Stalin's First Five-Year Plan, transformed the country completely. In the world of the theatre, there was an explosion of experimentation by innovative directors like Vsevolod Meyerhold, Evgeny Vakhtangov, and Aleksandr Tairov; by authors like Vladimir Mayakovsky and Nikolai Evreinov; by constructivist designers like Lyubov Popova and Vladimir Tatlin; and by groundbreaking actors like Mikhail Chekhov, the playwright's nephew. In this atmosphere of turbulent change, actors began to hear premonitions of revolution in *The Cherry Orchard*, and in Tuzenbach's lines about the coming storm in *Three Sisters*. But as Olga Knipper noted with some sadness, "it was not of such a storm that Chekhov's fine soul had dreamed."[1] Surprisingly, though, despite the vicissitudes of time, Chekhov's work in general and *The Cherry Orchard* in particular survived through all these upheavals in theatre and society. In the fifty years between the first rehearsal of *The Cherry Orchard* and the death of Stalin, the play was performed in a wide range of styles and venues, while the MAT production remained, essentially unchanged, as the most important, influential, and enduring product of the Russian theatre.

THE CHERRY ORCHARD AND THE REVOLUTION

The 1904 Moscow Art Theatre opening of *The Cherry Orchard*, though fraught with conflict and not universally applauded, was successful enough to encourage productions of the play all over Russia. Chekhov's death a few months later would give the play even greater public notice. Nemirovich observed that "an affection for Chekhov has been revealed in Russian society which we could never have suspected. Never in his life was he set alongside Pushkin and Tolstoy and above Turgenev and now that is almost universally the case."[2] Stanislavsky speculated that "perhaps, because of Chekhov's death, [*The Cherry Orchard*] will finally be understood."[3] Whatever Stanislavsky meant by this, Chekhov's death shortly after the premiere ensured both the playwright's permanent association with the MAT and the play's atmosphere of pathos and loss.

The first rival production, staged just weeks after the MAT opening, was directed by Vsevolod Meyerhold, Stanislavsky's protégé and rival. Meyerhold had left the MAT in 1902 to form the "Fellowship for a New Drama," which toured the provinces in a repertory based on the MAT's. Meyerhold's *Cherry Orchard*, in Kherson, seems not to have differed drastically from Stanislavsky's, which Meyerhold saw only after his own had opened. Though Meyerhold later wrote a polemical article criticizing Stanislavsky's naturalism and complaining that "the lyrical-mystic aspect of *The Cherry Orchard*" was lost at the MAT, his own production was still far removed from his later theatrical experiments.[4] According to Edward Braun, Meyerhold's promptbook reveals a production very much in the MAT vein, with "little trace of the symbolist influence."[5] One critic called *The Cherry Orchard* "an ordinary sort of play with farcical lackeys, chambermaid and governess."[6] This account suggests a fairly conventional production, but also indicates that Meyerhold had successfully brought out the comic side of Chekhov. Apparently Meyerhold's own performance as Trofimov was conceived (or received) in such a comic vein that his "Hail, new life" speech got a laugh from the audience.

Meyerhold himself wrote to Chekhov that he "wasn't ashamed" of his production after seeing the Art Theatre's, which he plainly disliked.[7]

Not all of the regional productions met with success. Mariya Savina, a *grande dame* of the Petersburg theatre who had turned down the role of Nina in the original production of *The Seagull*, toured to Odessa as Ranevskaya in 1904. She had never been enthusiastic about Chekhov, but was persuaded to take the role by her director, Anatoly Dolinov, who admired the Art Theatre production and tried to reproduce it as a vehicle for Savina. Her disdain for the play doomed the production from the start: "This 'orchard' is worse than a fairy-tale pantomime: such a mass of things and such a lot of noise . . . [Dolinov] is awfully stuck on the play, its 'ideas' etc., but yesterday I pointed out that 'nothing will come of nothing.' . . . Be as hypocritical as you like, audiences are still audiences and boredom is still boredom."[8] Despite some effective moments in rehearsal, Savina failed in the role, mixing up the lines and blocking. She only played it twice, and dismissed her failure as the fault of the play: "everyone expected something special from me, even the author according to Knipper, but there was no material."[9]

The plethora of regional productions of *The Cherry Orchard* exposed the play to a wide range of audiences, including some who quickly grasped its revolutionary implications. V. N. Baranovsky, a student in Kazan, wrote passionately to the author:

> What a fool our censor is to allow such a thing to be performed and printed! All the salt is in Lopakhin and the student Trofimov . . . Lopakhin and the student are friends, they march hand in hand "to that bright star, blazing there . . . in the distance." All the characters in the play are allegorical . . . *The Cherry Orchard* is all Russia.[10]

Baranovsky's letter must have disturbed Chekhov, who had worried about how far he could push the play's political dimensions. According to Baranovsky, the Kazan production had an enthusiastic audience who accepted the play as an optimistic appeal to the new life. This response reveals that even during Chekhov's lifetime, *The Cherry*

Orchard was subject to a variety of stagings that generated an even wider range of audience interpretations.

In the Russian provinces, one of the leading proselytes for Chekhov, and for an optimistic reading of *The Cherry Orchard*, was the actor and director Pavel Gaideburov. With his Itinerant Theatre, Gaideburov staged *The Cherry Orchard* all over Russia, playing Trofimov more than 300 times. Gaideburov found new and receptive audiences for the play, including the future director Evgeny Vakhtangov, then a young man in the remote region of Vladikavkaz.[11] Gaideburov's productions, necessarily stripped down for touring, provided an alternative to the cluttered naturalism of the MAT production. The nursery was suggested by bare white walls, the open fields by a broad cyclorama, the Act III party by the shadows of offstage dancers.[12] One reviewer noted that such an approach "condenses the power of experience, economizes and sharpens the spectator's attention, focusing it on the essentials," while at the same time minimizing the nostalgic appeal of "the ancient, moribund, sweet-smelling 'cherry orchard.'"[13]

While provincial productions of the play were responding to the dynamic political and artistic climate, the MAT production was growing stale. Though *The Cherry Orchard* remained a pillar of the repertory during the pre-revolutionary years, the production was out of step with the times. During these years, Stanislavsky was developing his acting "system" and focusing on the inner life of the actor; the externals of the production remained unchanged. While the MAT had some leftist credibility through its intermittent association with Maxim Gorky, it was primarily a theatre of the bourgeois intelligentsia, and it remained detached from the political and aesthetic upheavals of 1905–17.[14] Next to the theatrical experimentation led by Meyerhold and Vakhtangov at the MAT's studios from 1912 onward, and the political ferment in the streets, the productions in Stanislavsky's MAT seemed conservative and tradition-bound.[15] As the October Revolution loomed, the MAT made an effort to open itself up, politically if not stylistically.

Nemirovich-Danchenko recognized that the MAT's Chekhov productions were developing "notes of sentimentality and preachiness";

he also saw clearly in which direction the political winds were blowing. Two weeks before the October Revolution of 1917, the MAT offered performances of *The Cherry Orchard* for the Soviet of Workers' Deputies and other revolutionary organizations.[16] Stanislavsky's anxiety at performing *The Cherry Orchard* during the Revolution was understandable, but in the end, it was unwarranted: *The Cherry Orchard* actually helped the MAT weather the political storm. Laurence Senelick notes that "of Chekhov's full-length plays, it was the only one considered adaptable to Soviet circumstances."[17]

By government decree, all of the MAT's tickets in the first two years after the Revolution went free of charge to Soviet workers. Stanislavsky did his best, on the one hand, to accommodate himself to his new audience; he was also at pains to accommodate the audience to his vision of theatre. Many had never been in a theatre before, and Stanislavsky had to instruct them not to smoke, talk, eat, or interrupt the performances by calling the actors before the curtain. This he did using program notes, pre-performance lectures, and occasional angry harangues from the stage during the performance. According to his autobiography, he became such an authoritarian figure in the minds of the worker-spectators that whenever he appeared in the foyer, small boys would scamper through the crowd warning, "He is coming!"[18]

In this atmosphere, *The Cherry Orchard* was not well received, though Stanislavsky reports that audiences were respectful and attentive. When the theatre opened again to a wider range of spectators, it became a focus of nostalgia for the dispossessed gentry, according to a European observer, André Van Gyseghem: "numbers of people, artist and audience, clung to the theatre as the last remnants of their beloved past. Sitting in the audience, many a Madame Ranevsky must have wept her heart out while away across the broad Russian acres her *Cherry Orchard* was being confiscated by the new 'landlords,' the sons of the proletariat."[19] The MAT quickly came under attack for its supposed traditionalism. "Chekhov and Stanislavsky stink," the Futurist poet Vladimir Mayakovsky stated bluntly in 1920.[20] *The Cherry Orchard*, after all, concerned itself with a society that had been swept away. Leftist critics felt Chekhov could be consigned to the same dustbin of history: "You have to be phenomenally obtuse to dredge *Ivanov* and *Seagull* out of the bin and endlessly stage *Cherry Orchard* and *Three Sisters* . . . It's time to abandon to their own eras down-in-the-mouth, grief-stricken Chekhov, bourgeois Ostrovsky, smugly virtuous Dickens etc. . . . The theatre must now present bright, gripping spectacles, joyful and powerful experiences, and not staged funerals."[21] Implicit in this criticism is the image of Chekhov as a gloomy pessimist, and *The Cherry Orchard* as a tearful lament, that Stanislavsky's productions had encouraged and that Chekhov himself had always tried to dispel. Another Soviet critic, Petr Kerzhentsev, was perhaps the first to condemn the MAT for "museum-piece" theatre: "What else can you call a theatre but a museum where the performers seriously act and the audience seriously watches plays by Chekhov about gloomy people, who don't know how to struggle with life, who weep over their vanishing past and are powerless to do anything to hold on to it?"[22]

To the younger members of the MAT and its studios, and to the new generation of Soviet theatre artists, *The Cherry Orchard* was at best moribund, at worst reactionary. Vakhtangov wrote in his notebook that "Stanislavsky's theatre is already dead and will never be resurrected. I am happy at this. Strange, but I now find it unpleasant to recall even *Three Sisters* and *The Cherry Orchard*." Vakhtangov complained that the MAT sentimentalized Chekhov, allowed his characters and audiences a dreamy emotional lassitude. In a conversation about Stanislavsky's Chekhov productions, he summed up the characters' general attitude as "Let's have a cup of tea and dream":

> "Vakhtangov said this deliberately in an exaggerated 'Chekhovian' tone. He sighed, raised his eyes to the sky, and imitated with startling accuracy the excessively sentimental tones of someone playing Anya in *The Cherry Orchard*: 'Don't cry, dear mama, don't cry! We will build a new orchard, more beautiful than the old one.'. . . No, I would stage Chekhov's plays as very cruel works, whose living reality is not softened by any 'moods' or by the melodious intonations of the actors, but shown exactly as it is."[23]

Vakhtangov's remarks suggest a new approach to Chekhov, but one that wouldn't be applied to *The Cherry Orchard* for several years. When the new generation of directors turned to Chekhov, they concentrated on his farces and vaudevilles, which allowed greater departures from realism in acting, design, and direction. Meyerhold's *33 Swoons* (a compilation of three Chekhov farces) and Vakhtangov's *The Wedding* were energetic, satirical, colorful, almost cartoonish works far removed from the sobriety of the MAT *Cherry Orchard*. Aleksandr Tairov, the visionary director of the Kamerny Theatre, never staged a Chekhov play until his experimental *Seagull* of 1944.

Despite this kind of criticism from the Soviet left, the Moscow Art Theatre and its Chekhov productions survived. The Commissar for Education, Anatoly Lunacharsky, protected the MAT, along with several other well-established bourgeois theatres, by giving them the title of Academic Theatres. The MAT even had the patronage of Lenin, who believed it was important to protect the best of pre-revolutionary culture for historical reasons: "If there is a theatre from the past which we should at all costs save and preserve, then it is, of course, the MAT," Lenin stated.[24] So in a sense, the MAT *Cherry Orchard* was condemned to be a museum piece; that was its function in Soviet culture. As an officially sanctioned exemplum of the Russian theatre, Stanislavsky's production not only survived, but became a significant cultural export. In the 1920s, the MAT *Cherry Orchard* avoided the hostile milieu of radical Soviet theatre and criticism largely by getting out of the country.

THE MOSCOW ART THEATRE ON TOUR

The MAT had a successful history of touring from pre-revolutionary times; a German tour in 1906, which did not include *The Cherry Orchard*, gained them international prestige. In 1919, a substantial body of MAT actors, including Knipper and Kachalov, took *The Cherry Orchard* and several other plays into the Russian provinces.

Unable to return to Moscow due to the advance of White Russian forces, they toured around Eastern and Central Europe for three years, playing in Germany, Austria, and Czechoslovakia. In 1922, Knipper, Kachalov, and others returned to the MAT in Moscow, but several others remained in exile, continuing to perform and tour as the Prague Group of the Moscow Art Theatre. This company was led by Mariya Germanova, who played Ranevskaya in their *Cherry Orchard*. Her fame and position at the MAT were almost equal to those of Knipper and Kachalov, according to Sergei Ostrovsky; however, she was mainly a protégée of Nemirovich-Danchenko and was not liked by Stanislavsky.[25] The production of *The Cherry Orchard* seems to have been a near-exact copy of the original version at the MAT, and it was through this production that much of Western Europe came to know the play. It was the only MAT *Cherry Orchard* seen in London (in 1928 and 1931), where James Agate hailed it as a "masterpiece," praising the "feats of acting" and excusing the "miserable scenery."[26]

The main body of the MAT also toured in the 1920s, most notably to America, but also to Paris, Berlin, Prague, and Zagreb. The tour of 1922–24 was planned, with the consent of Soviet officials, to get the theatre away from attacks by leftist critics and to help it restore its finances by earning foreign currency. It was also Stanislavsky's attempt to unite the company, bringing the Kachalov exiles back into the fold of the new generation who had lived through the Revolution in Moscow.[27] In all of these endeavors the tour was a failure. The MAT actually lost money on the venture, and rather than being protected from criticism, it was under continual attack in the Soviet press for toadying to the capitalist West.[28] The company was riven with conflict, and several members remained behind in America at the tour's end. The tour was also physically grueling, with the company giving nine or ten performances a week and constantly moving from place to place for almost two years: apart from their European stops, the company played in New York, Washington, Philadelphia, Boston, Chicago, Pittsburgh, New Haven, Newark, Hartford, Cleveland, and Detroit. In spite of its many challenges, the tour was outstandingly successful in one aim: presenting an "authentic" Russian Chekhov, and the methods of Stanislavsky's Art Theatre, to the West. In this regard its importance cannot be overstated.

The Cherry Orchard was the flagship of the MAT tour. While the company took a large and diverse repertory of more than ten plays and concert pieces on the tour, over a quarter of their 380 performances were of *The Cherry Orchard*. When the MAT actors were asked to perform special Friday matinees for working theatre professionals, *The Cherry Orchard* was the play they chose.[29] John Barrymore went to one of these and called it "the most amazing experience I have ever had by a million miles in the theatre." He accordingly arranged a special performance of his *Hamlet*, then on Broadway, for the Moscow players.

The MAT were greeted with adulation everywhere they went. Stanislavsky wrote back to Russia, "We have never had such a success in Moscow or anywhere else. No one seems to have had any idea what our theatre and our actors were capable of."[30] In Paris, André Antoine, the founder of the Théâtre Libre and the leading figure in the theatrical revolution of the late nineteenth century, proclaimed that "our theatre still has a great deal to learn from the Russians":

> The wonderful perfection of their *mise-en-scènes*, the splendid truth of their scenery and costumes, where everything has been thought out to the last detail, the high level of their acting, the self-denying discipline of the actors and their love of the theatre make us acutely conscious of how much our theatre still has to do to restore its old prestige.[31]

Though the production of *The Cherry Orchard* which the MAT played in the West was nearly twenty years old, it had been carefully preserved. All of the scenery and business, and most of the principal players, were the same as they had been in the 1904 premiere. In an English translation of the play published to coincide with the American production, Oliver Sayler noted, "The Moscow Art Theatre holds *The Cherry Orchard* almost as holy ground . . . Its various roles have been guarded jealously by the actors who first embodied them."[32]

Stanislavsky and Knipper, of course, played Gayev and Ranevskaya, while Leonidov still played Lopakhin, Moskvin Yepikhodov, Gribunin Pishchik, and Alexandrov Yasha. Simov's sets, with much trouble and expense, were transported along with the company, assembled and struck at theatre after theatre. Both the production and the company were showing their age, and this fact occasioned the only negative press the MAT received. John Corbin of the *New York Times* (28 January 1923), while acknowledging that "the realism of scenic paintbrush and stage carpentry is a negligible thing compared with the realism of the spirit," noted that "the two interiors are far below the standard of Broadway." Percy Hammond of the *New York Tribune* (23 January 1923) wrote the "dire" Act II scenery was "in the early grand opera manner, full of canvas hummocks and chromo forestry." Corbin was especially critical of the cherry trees themselves: "these spindling trunks of five to ten years' growth with flowering twigs tacked on, should be gnarled and ancient boles beneath a bridal veil of blossoms." Apparently the celebrated naturalism of the MAT did not impress the New York critics. Corbin even took a shot at Stanislavsky's famous sound effects: "the song of birds in the orchard, which pipes up when a window is raised, presently ceases, though the window remains open."

The critics were more enthusiastic about the acting, though they recognized the difficulty of assessing foreign performers playing characters alien to their audience's experience. In excepting Moskvin, Hammond damned him with faint praise: "Now and then we feel at home, as when Mr. Moskvin, as the blundering clerk, engages us in some of the excesses of the so-called American type-actor." Corbin felt that the leading players, after nearly twenty years in their roles, were too heavy and solid. The "Junoesque form and demeanor" of Knipper overweighed the flighty Ranevskaya, and Stanislavsky was far too imposing a figure for Gayev: "it is fairly obvious that the Herculean presence of the director and his vigorous vibrant voice, so eloquent of an orderly mind and an unshakeable will, are ill-adapted to suggest the will-o'-the-wisp brain and uncontrolled moods of this attenuated aristocrat." Nonetheless, the acting of the Moscow players made an impression, particularly on the American theatre community. Lee Strasberg, for one, did not object to the production's status as a twenty-year-old warhorse, seeing it as an opportunity to appreciate the whole history of the Moscow Art Theatre: "We were fortunate in seeing not productions, but works of art . . . We saw at that time . . . not just the success of that year; they brought to us the successes of their entire career. We were privileged."[33] Strasberg and other young actors, together with MAT expatriates like Richard Boleslavsky, would go on to carry their version of Stanislavsky's method throughout the American theatre. Numerous repertory groups sprang up across the United States based on the MAT model. Notable among these was Eva Le Gallienne's Civic Repertory Company, discussed in the next chapter, which became the primary vehicle for Chekhov in America.

The production was not without political controversy. Before the MAT arrived in the USA, the Washington division of the American Defense Society alleged that the actors were Soviet spies and would use the income from their performances in the cause of world communism.[34] At the same time, Stanislavsky came under fire in Moscow for pandering to White Russian émigrés and the enemies of the Revolution. The political balance of *The Cherry Orchard* production helped it navigate these perilous waters. While on the one hand, the MAT were serving as cultural ambassadors for the "new life" of Soviet Russia, the production's nostalgia for the old life helped disarm a potentially hostile American press. As Sharon Carnicke notes, "the centrality of the [Ranevsky] family made the production appear to side with a Russia that had been swept away by revolution."[35] Yet *New York Times* critic John Corbin read the production as optimistic: "It is as if Chekhov saw in the new middle class the hope of a disenchanted yet sounder and more progressive Russia. The war has halted that movement, but indications are not lacking that it is already resuming."[36] As proved to be the case throughout the play's history, people were able to find in Stanislavsky's *Cherry Orchard* the political message they were looking for.

The initial New York run sold out before it opened, and while the primary audience consisted of *émigrés*, intellectuals, and theatre professionals, the MAT had a popular success as well. A tongue-in-cheek piece published by John Weaver in *The New York Times* effectively conveys the political atmosphere surrounding the *Cherry Orchard* production, and much about its style and impact. Entitled "A 100 Per Cent. American Speaks," the piece is in the voice of a very skeptical playgoer who expects nothing good from these "Bolshevicky." The first act of *The Cherry Orchard* he finds puzzling:

> A lot of people runnin' up and down
> In a great big room, carryin' suitcases and trunks,
> And whisperin' in the corners.

But later, he is drawn in by Stanislavsky's performance:

> . . . And – listen, I can't make out how it happened,
> But when that great big goof looked out at the orchard
> And I could hear the axes cuttin' the trees,
> And all of a sudden this six-foot bird breaks down,
> And stuffed his handkerchief right in his mouth,
> And real tears in his eyes – can y'imagine?
> I just set there and blubbered like a baby.
> Just think of a bunch of low-down Bolshevicky
> That can't talk even a word of English, makin'
> A hard-boiled egg like me cry like a kid!
> And me not understandin' what they said![37]

Stanislavsky's handkerchief business, just before Gayev's final exit from his ancestral home, was the moment most often remembered by American critics and audiences. Harold Clurman, a founder of the Group Theatre, wrote years later, "I shall never forget the heartbreak – not without its humor – when Stanislavsky, as Gayev in the original production, reached ineffectually for his handkerchief."[38] Given the language barrier, it was the pathos of Gayev, Ranevskaya, and Firs that made the biggest impression, rather than the speeches of Trofimov or Lopakhin.

Successful as *The Cherry Orchard* was in the USA, the MAT's directors were concerned about the fate it would meet back in Russia. Nemirovich-Danchenko wrote a stern letter warning that if the company were to return and "perform the earlier productions in the same old way, then in three months the MAT will never recover from the lambasting it will receive . . . *The Cherry Orchard* will not be allowed. That is, mourning for gentlefolks' estates will not be allowed. But the play can't be staged from any other angle (such as the 'Greetings, new life!' angle)."[39] Stanislavsky was more sanguine, and outlined a new approach to the play that would become dominant throughout the period:

> Give even Lopakhin in *Cherry Orchard* the wide-ranging scope of a Chaliapin, and young Anya the temperament of a Yermolova, and let him chop down with all his might whatever has outlived itself, and let the girl, who with Petya Trofimov forecasts the advent of a new era, shout to the whole world: "Greetings, new life!" – and you will understand that *The Cherry Orchard* is alive for us, a close, contemporary play, that Chekhov's voice resounds in it cheerfully, provocatively, for it looks not backward but forward.[40]

Accordingly, the play was refitted for the Soviet era, and reopened in 1928 at the Moscow Art Theatre in a more hopeful version. "Everything that could be done to somehow freshen up the play was done," reported Yury Sobolev, Nemirovich-Danchenko's biographer. "This was especially true of the first act where there is now much more laughter than before . . . The elegiac mood of the last act was somewhat toned down."[41] With the protection of its Academic status and the upbeat tone of its *Cherry Orchard*, the MAT could safely move forward into the era of Stalin.

FROM SOVIET RADICALISM TO SOCIALIST REALISM

In presenting a more optimistic, forward-looking version of *The Cherry Orchard*, the MAT was merely following a trend begun while

5. The servants from the Moscow Art Theatre production, from a publicity postcard: Charlotta (Muratova), Dunyasha (Khaputina), Yasha (Alexandrov), and Yepikhodov (Moskvin). (New York Public Library.)

they were abroad. Pavel Gaideburov's Itinerant Theatre had taken a "bright and joyous" production of the play on tour through civil-wartorn areas in 1922. Several critics promoted the idea that the way to update the play to a revolutionary world-view was to follow the author's precept and treat it as a comedy. As I. Bachelis wrote, "Chekhov wanted the break with the past to be cheerful and merry . . . He almost literally followed Marx's precept – a precept everybody knows! – that laughter allows people to break easily with their pasts. The Art Theatre lagged behind Chekhov. *It didn't want to laugh.*"[42] Once again, the argument about genre in *The Cherry Orchard* had become an argument about politics.

In any event, several theatres did attempt more comic, and politically radical, productions of *The Cherry Orchard* during the 1920s. Konstantin Kholkov, at the Leningrad Comedy Theatre in 1926, directed a farcical production that ridiculed all of the characters except Lopakhin and Anya; according to Kholkov, "They are the ones who chop down the old, unnecessary cherry orchard, which lets no sunlight penetrate the window of the cold and arid house."[43] In Nizhniy-Novgorod in 1929, the play was staged as an outright farce.[44] Gaideburov directed the play at the Bolshoy Dramatic Theatre in Leningrad, using an over-the-top scenic effect to drive home the Soviet message. As Trofimov delivered his Act II harangue to Anya, in the background "an industrial landscape began to glow with kindled fires."[45] Andrei Serban would use a similar effect in the USA some fifty years later.

The more radical productions of the play were a part of a broader movement in Russian theatre to challenge the hegemony of the Moscow Art Theatre and all it represented. Throughout the teens and twenties there was a recognized fissure between the "Theatre of Stanislavsky" and the "Theatre of Meyerhold." In place of the former's naturalistic acting and staging, the latter offered bold experimentation, dynamic new approaches to acting, constructivist scenery, garish costumes, radical manifestos. Meyerhold's theatre was politically as well as aesthetically radical: he wanted to put the Revolution in the theatre, to proclaim a "Theatrical October."[46] The production that went farthest in bringing this kind of theatrical approach to *The Cherry Orchard* was directed by Andrey Lobanov in 1934 at Ruben Simonov's Theatre-Studio, attached to the Vakhtangov Theatre in Moscow.

Lobanov and his designers set out to show the decadence of the Ranevskys, the corrupt world that had to be cleansed and purified. N. V. Kuzmin's costume designs are cartoonish and bizarre, making the characters look like circus performers or George Grosz caricatures: the effect is similar to that of Meyerhold's *33 Swoons* and Vakhtangov's *The Wedding*. The set designer, Boris Matrunin, made the Ranevsky estate a cold and angular place, filled with outmoded furniture, to which the audience could attach no sentimental nostalgia. There was no orchard, and even the Act II landscape was replaced by a series of squalid interiors. According to Laurence Senelick, the act "was set in a claustrophobic cheap eatery, from which a drunken Petya Trofimov was ejected by waiters, and then in a stuffy, darkened bathhouse where he conspiratorially addressed his harangue to a bunch of gymnasium students."[47]

The servants were comic grotesques, their farcical antics foregrounded. Lopakhin was a money-grubbing *kulak* of the sort the Soviets were busy liquidating.[48] A. I. Delektorskaya's Ranevskaya was a svelte creature in a kimono, making up at her dressing table, a woman of "epicurean egocentrism"; her relationship with Yasha was developed suggestively.[49] Gayev was especially decadent, obviously a figure of contempt. Lobanov made notes on Gayev's reaction to the sale of the estate:

> Suddenly seems knocked for a loop: can't mooch around the house any more or loll on the sofa, there won't be his favorite junk, the bookcase with its spiders, those old walls. With the sale of the estate the ground's shot from under his feet and it's obvious his game is up. His house is tumbling down to the last rafter and him along with it. He goes to the job at the bank in town like a captive bear, taken from his native forest to a zoo, where he will soon drop dead.[50]

This brutal indictment of the character represents the radical Soviet reading of the play at its most ruthless.

The year of Lobanov's production, however, also marked the end of the radical Soviet theatre. 1934 was the year that Andrey Zhdanov propounded the doctrine of "Socialist Realism" at the First All-Union Congress of Soviet Writers. This doctrine, inspired by Stalin's First Five-Year Plan, called for artists to be "engineers of the soul" in indoctrinating workers into Soviet ideology, and it condemned as "formalism" the theatrical experimentation of the previous decades. The Moscow Art Theatre was upheld as the model for all Soviet theatres. Playwrights and directors who failed to fall in line with Socialist Realism were putting their jobs, and their lives, at risk. Theatres were closed, productions banned, arrests made, and all the innovative artists of the teens and twenties warned to change their ways.

By an astonishing historical irony, the Theatre of Meyerhold, which burned with Communist fervor and looked outward and to the future, was condemned, while the Theatre of Stanislavsky, which avoided politics and looked inward and to the past, was approved. The MAT enjoyed government favor as Stalin's favorite theatre. Stanislavsky's production of *The Cherry Orchard*, suitably retooled to emphasize the optimistic message of "the new life," became an enduring icon of the Soviet theatre throughout the Stalinist period. Stanislavsky himself, who had always been uncomfortable with the changes wrought by the Revolution, was named a "People's Artist of the USSR" and publicly mourned at his death in 1938. Shortly afterwards, his student and rival Meyerhold, whom Stanislavsky had spent his last years trying to protect, was arrested, imprisoned, tortured and killed.[51]

The MAT kept Stanislavsky's production of *The Cherry Orchard* in its repertory until after the death of Stalin in 1953. In Russia at least, the ascendancy of Socialist Realism, and the authoritarian policies of Stalin, had trapped *The Cherry Orchard* in a time capsule from which it would not emerge for many decades.

CHAPTER 4

THE CHERRY ORCHARD IN ENGLISH:
EARLY PRODUCTIONS

Just as *The Cherry Orchard* became the flagship play for the Moscow
Art Theatre, symbolizing Chekhov's work both within the Soviet
Union and on the company's tours abroad, so it became the most
prominent play in early English-language performances of Chekhov.
Though audiences, actors, and critics were initially bewildered by it,
The Cherry Orchard soon came to be regarded as the most accessible of
Chekhov's plays. For the first few years critics viewed it as a naturalistic
drama, of interest primarily for what it revealed about social conditions in Russia prior to the Revolution. Frequent revivals, however,
showed the play in different lights. Productions experimented with
its tone, style, and politics. In both England and America, mournful
realistic productions gave way to more optimistic comic ones. Specific actors and directors became associated with the play and with
Chekhov: John Gielgud, Charles Laughton, and Tyrone Guthrie in
England; Eva Le Gallienne and Alla Nazimova in the USA. Before
1920, there had only been a single production of *The Cherry Orchard*
in English, given for two performances; by 1933 there had been a
dozen productions and their revivals, including long runs in the West
End, at the Old Vic, and on Broadway.

FIRST PERFORMANCES

The Cherry Orchard was the first full-length Chekhov play to be
produced in London, in a 1911 performance by the Incorporated
Stage Society. It was in many ways an auspicious opportunity for

the introduction of Chekhov to the British theatre-going public. The Stage Society, which produced private performances of unlicensed or non-commercial plays, was the primary venue for challenging new drama, championing foreign playwrights like Ibsen, Hauptmann, and Brieux, as well as Harley Granville-Barker and George Bernard Shaw. It was Shaw himself, an admirer of Chekhov, who persuaded the Society to perform Constance Garnett's translation of *The Cherry Orchard*; he heralded the event as "the most important [production] in England since that of *A Doll's House*."[1] As was usual in the independent theatre movement, the Society staged the play only twice, on a Sunday and Monday (28 and 29 May 1911), in the Aldwych Theatre, rented for the occasion.

The performance was a failure, later compared by many critics to the disastrous St. Petersburg premiere of *The Seagull* in 1896.[2] A Russian who attended wrote, "It was unutterably sad to witness this charade."[3] The director, Kenelm Foss, had had very little time to rehearse, the sets and costumes were crude makeshifts, and the actors had little understanding of the play and no experience of working as an ensemble. Ranevskaya was played by the novice Katherine Pole, dismissed by the *Pall Mall Gazette* (30 May 1911) as "a pretty young lady with a refined personality and within its limits, an effective little gift for acting." J. T. Grein of the *Sunday Times* (4 June 1911) felt she lacked the stature required for the central role, which needed "a magnetic woman, a *grande dame*." Grein found Herbert Bunston's Lopakhin merely a "forcible . . . rough-and-ready merchant"; most audience members took him for a brutish villain.[4] Nigel Playfair hammed up his role as Pischchik, and Ivan Berlyn's Yepikhodov was simply incomprehensible: "What he was doing in the household of an apparently sane woman like Madame Ranevsky was only one of the many hopeless puzzles with which the Stage Society presented us," according to Hugh Walpole.[5] Yet there were bright spots in the production, which featured several distinguished or soon-to-be-distinguished actors. Grein, a leader of the independent theatre movement, praised several performances in the *Sunday Times* (4 June 1911):

A fine performance was given by Mr. Franklin Dyall as the unmarried brother of the heroine, the kind of Russian so well known on the boulevards, a man of the world, great talker, great idler, sucking pastilles all day long, and playing the prince with empty pockets . . . Mr. Harcourt Williams rendered the student in that reflective and effective manner which we are wont to associate with Russian revolutionists in the bud. Miss May Jerrold was a restrained and almost pathetic milksister, who chooses to remain a pauper because the rich parvenu had not the courage to claim her willing "yes."

A few details of the direction can be gleaned from the notes of George Calderon, a leading proponent of Chekhov in Britain, in his own 1912 translation of the play. Apparently, the actors took turns making "points" in the traditional Victorian/Edwardian style, rather than maintaining a constant image of life on the stage through ensemble acting; Calderon complained that "Chekhov's disjunctive manner is defeated of its purpose unless the whole company keep continuously alive."[6] Franklin Dyall made a sentimental set-piece of Gayev's bookcase speech, thus undermining the effect of Ranevskaya's subsequent apostrophe to the orchard.[7] In the party scene of Act III, the background action overwhelmed the foreground: the dancing, magic tricks, and comic recitation were "forced unmercifully on the audience" so that "Ranevskaya, left unsupported, ceased to exist upon the stage at all; what Meyerhold calls the leitmotiv of the scene was drowned in ornaments and variations."[8] Lopakhin's triumphant monologue was diminished, since Bunston played him as a typical stage drunk.[9]

Many left before the final curtain. "At the end of the second act signs of disapproval were very manifest indeed, and the exodus from the theatre began," wrote Arnold Bennett. "Certain it is that multitudes preferred Aldwych and the restaurant-concerts, or even their own homes, to Chekhov's play."[10] As Jan McDonald has argued, part of the problem may have had to do with the expectations of the Stage Society audience; nourished on Ibsen and Shaw, they looked for timely social critiques and clear political arguments.[11] George Calderon observed that "While our Western playwrights, confined within the boundary of the attainable, wage a heavy-handed polemic with social institutions and conventions, the Russians are at grips with the deepest cravings of their inward nature."[12] In any event, the audience was bored and confused by the play, and many reviewers felt its essential foreignness was impenetrable for English playgoers. The *Telegraph* (30 May 1911) commented, perhaps ironically, that "to be plunged, without any preparation whatsoever, into an atmosphere, a social life, a set of characters, so different from those we habitually meet, was, and must be, a shock to a well-regulated and conventional English mind." As A. B. Walkley reflected in an unsigned notice in the *Times* (30 May 1911),

> Though Anton Chekhov's comedy may be a harmonious work of art, presented at home in its own atmosphere by people who know all about, if they do not actually live, the life it depicts, Mrs. Edward Garnett's 'Cherry Orchard' cannot but strike an English audience as something queer, outlandish, even silly . . . [The characters] all seem children who have never grown up. Genuine comedy and scenes of pure pathos are mixed with knock-about farce.

These comments suggest that the Stage Society had managed to bring across some of the basic qualities of *The Cherry Orchard*, but that the audience was not yet ready for them; as Grein remarked, "it is nobody's fault that you cannot make Muscovites of Englishmen." Yet Arnold Bennett, among others, noted the special merits of the play, which he called "intensely original and interesting":

> It has a theme, and it has a perfectly plain theme – the break-up of an estate and of a family. It has a plot, and the plot is handled throughout with masterly skill. It is simply crammed with character. Indeed, it has so much characterization, and unfamiliar characterization, that an unimaginative audience could not project itself beyond the confusing externalities of the characterization into the heart of the play . . . It is one of the most savage and convincing satires on a whole society that was ever seen in the theatre.[13]

Most defenders of *The Cherry Orchard* took the play for an exercise in theatrical naturalism, assuming its principal virtue was its accurate picture of pre-Revolutionary Russian society, and that its principal difficulty was the unfamiliarity of that society. Yet some recognized the innovations of Chekhov's dramatic method. H. W. Massingham defended Chekhov's complex mixture of genres against Walkley's charge of haphazard confusion. "It does vary between harsh and delicate effects . . . a cause or a social class that falls by its own folly is by turns pathetic, merely unwise, and wildly ridiculous."[14] Massingham characterized *The Cherry Orchard* as "a comedy and a farce and a tragedy in the sense in which life is all these things, being made up of change and loss, and a certain sparkling recovery, and a grimly ludicrous, ironic, riotous play of unknown forces over it all."

In general, while the critics recognized that *The Cherry Orchard* had flopped with the Stage Society's audiences, they expressed interest in the play and in Chekhov's unfamiliar and challenging style. J. T. Grein called it a play that every student of the drama should know, and a picture of Russian life "which cannot fail to be interesting to anyone except people whose horizon is bounded by the Channel."[15] Commenting on the play's controversial reception, Bennett remarked, "This row is a fine thing. It means that something has been done. And I hope that the directors of the Stage Society are proud of the reception of *The Cherry Orchard*. They ought to be."[16]

The next London performance of *The Cherry Orchard* was at the St. Martin's Theatre in 1920. By this time there had been several attempts to stage Chekhov in London, all for only one or two performances. *The Seagull* (Little Theatre, 1912) was poorly received, but *Uncle Vanya* (Aldwych, 1914) garnered positive reviews and some enthusiasm from Stage Society audiences, who were perhaps embarrassed at their failure to understand *The Cherry Orchard*. In the years after the war, audiences became more receptive to Chekhov; in a society that had been shaken to its foundations, Chekhov's world-view resonated better than it had amid the certainties of Edwardian London. Several Chekhov plays were staged by the Art Theatre of Russian *émigrée* Vera Donnet: *The Seagull* in June 1919, *Three Sisters* in March 1920, and finally *The Cherry Orchard*, 11 and 12 July 1920. This time the play was approved by critics and audiences, who were slowly warming to Chekhov's understated style. As St. John Ervine commented (*Observer*, 18 July 1920), "One looks on at the performance of this play, a little befogged perhaps, by the first act, with a sensation that one is witnessing a vague and incoherent and trivial thing . . . Everything is inconclusive, invertebrate, supine, and yet how amazingly satisfying it is!" The *Morning Post* (13 July 1920) found the play better acted than in 1911: "the actors seemed to be more resigned to their characters; at less pains to score points of their own." Actors singled out for praise in the reviews included the young Edith Evans as a richly comic Charlotta, Felix Aylmer as a genial Pishchik, and Ernest Paterson as Firs, a part he had also played in the 1911 production. Ervine called his "the finest performance in the play . . . as rich a study of faithful senility as I have seen."

Leyton Cancellor was alternately amusing and depressing as Gayev; Joseph Dodd, as Lopakhin, came across as intelligent and not unsympathetic. Ethel Irving, as Ranevskaya, divided the critics: the *Morning Post* praised her "charming and ineffectual" characterization, whereas Ervine thought she "seemed to be puzzled by the swift alterations of hope and despondency, of deep emotion and trivial gaiety, perhaps because she tried to think of Madame Ranevskaya in an English way." Virginia Woolf likewise found her too much of a "British matron in extremity," noting that "her mere presence on the stage was enough to suggest that all the comforts and all the decencies of English upper-class life were at hand" (*New Statesman*, 24 July 1920).

A frequent criticism of the production was that it was too slow and somber; the *Daily News* (13 July 1920) called it "a kind of ritual . . . a very solemn performance," while Frank Swinnerton complained of "the horrifying solemnity of all productions of Chekhov in this country" (*Nation*, 17 July 1920). Swinnerton felt the Art Theatre's *Cherry Orchard* "showed intelligent actors grappling without imagination with a poetic and realistic play which slipped continually through their understanding." In a perceptive essay, Swinnerton advocated a lighter, more detached approach to acting Chekhov:

> He has no need to be solemn; and his interpreters have no need to be solemn; because while we are all serious about our own emotions we may expect from actors detachment exceeding mere absorption in their assumed roles, and perception of the needs of the general picture. The general picture should be created in the color of life, and not in that of an essay in decadence. Until this fact is grasped, and Chekhov is played with some lightness and naturalness of deportment, we shall always lose the true quality of his dramatic work.

Some of the daily newspapers still found the play obscure, trivial, or hopelessly foreign; J. Middleton Murry, exasperated by such philistinism, wanted to make a time capsule of their views "and drop it into literary London in 1930, when *The Cherry Orchard* will have become a classic."[17] Yet many reviewers acknowledged that the play was a masterpiece, but that it presented challenges that a one-off independent theatre production would be hard-pressed to overcome. Sydney Carroll (*Sunday Times*, 18 July 1920) thought Donnet's Art Theatre production a "perversion of a great man's work . . . miscast, mishandled from a scenic standpoint, and misproduced"; he was particularly vexed by the low-budget scenery, "a hideous freak background resembling . . . Rotherhithe laid waste by the Hun." Virginia Woolf complained of the actors' unnatural speech, lack of ensemble playing, and crude "points" made to the audience; she was disturbed by "the consciousness that hung about them of being well-trained English men and women ill at ease in an absurd situation, but determined to make the best of a bad business." Woolf particularly objected to Dunyasha's shocked reaction to Charlotta's observation that her parents might not have been married. Nonetheless, by the end Woolf was deeply moved by the production: "I do not know better how to describe the sensation at the end of 'The Cherry Orchard,' than by saying it sends one into the street feeling like a piano played upon at last, not in the middle only but all over the keyboard and with the lid left open so that the sound goes on" (*New Statesman*, 24 July 1920).

The production was enough of a success for critics to call for a West End run of the play. While recognizing the commercial pressures involved, Ervine urged producers to take the risk, not only for the sake of audiences but to expose young playwrights to an important new dramatist: "Fifty performances for a masterpiece – is that too much to ask when 'Chu Chin Chow' seems likely to run for fifty years?"

J. B. FAGAN AT THE LYRIC, HAMMERSMITH, 1925

It would be five years before a producer risked an extended run for Chekhov, once again with *The Cherry Orchard*. This was not a West End production, but one that originated at the Oxford Playhouse and was invited to move to the Lyric Theatre, Hammersmith, by its producer Nigel Playfair, who had been Pishchik in the Stage Society production of 1911. The play was directed by J. B. Fagan, an Irish manager-playwright and the first director of the Oxford Playhouse. In his first season at the theatre, Fagan invited the Russian *émigré* director Theodore Komisarjevsky to stage *The Cherry Orchard*, but Komisarjevsky got a better offer in Paris; his own *Cherry Orchard* would follow in the wake of Fagan's in 1926.

Margaret Webster described Fagan's production as having "a charming laughter-and-tears quality" that was "probably more Irish than Russian."[18] Several critics had noted that "there was much of Ireland in the atmosphere and the people of *The Cherry Orchard*," although Dublin productions by the Irish Theatre Company in 1917 and 1920 had not met with great success.[19] As an Irishman, Fagan felt a strong affinity with the play, which he determined to make "the most interesting" of the 1925 season, and he talked to the company at length about it. Nonetheless, the young John Gielgud, who played Trofimov, admitted that "at the first reading it mystified us all considerably."[20] Fagan's talented young company also included his wife Mary Grey as Ranevskaya, Alan Napier (later the butler on television's *Batman*) as Gayev, the Irish actor Fred O'Donovan as Lopakhin, Glen Byam Shaw as Yasha, and James Whale, the director of the *Frankenstein* films, as Yepikhodov and set designer.

For Gielgud, the production was a turning point in his career and the beginning of a lifelong association with Chekhov: "It was the first time I ever went on the stage and felt that perhaps I could really act."[21] Gielgud found he could submerge himself in the character, and lose the self-consciousness that had hampered him in other roles: "As Trofimov, for the first time I looked in the glass and thought, 'I know how this man would speak and move and behave.'" Part of the key for Gielgud was a complete physical transformation. As Trofimov, he adopted a thin black wig, scruffy goatee, and steel glasses, creating a shabby-student appearance inspired by his brother Val, who later understudied him in the role.[22]

Though Gielgud thought Fagan's production "was somewhat clumsy and tentative, for we were a young and inexperienced company, though sincere," the play was a hit in Oxford.[23] It won positive comment in the national press, with the *Morning Post* praising its "sure grasp of the Chekhov method of portraiture which makes each character extraordinarily alive and interesting, yet allows none to dominate the play."[24] It received an ovation that, according to the student paper, "would not have disgraced a football match."[25] The London transfer was less immediately successful; initial houses were small, and reviews divided. Basil MacDonald Hastings, in the *Daily Express* (26 May 1925), attacked it as "fatuous drivel," remarking brutally that "Lenin achieved something after all. He wiped out of existence all of the characters in Chekhov's plays." James Agate, by contrast, called it the best play in London and "one of the great plays of the world" (*Sunday Times*, 31 May 1925). The producer, Nigel Playfair, posted their assessments side by side to stir public interest, and the socialite Lady Cunard wrote an influential letter to the *Express* calling

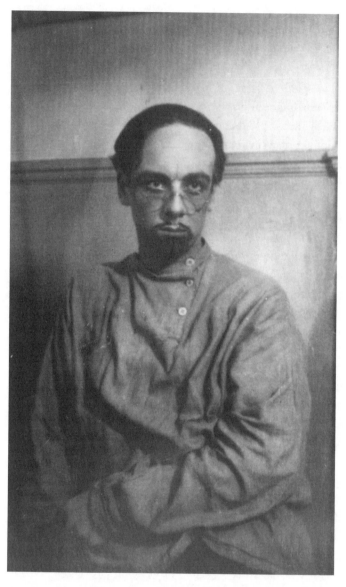

6. John Gielgud as Trofimov, in the first West End performance of *The Cherry Orchard*, Lyric, Hammersmith, 1924. (New York Public Library.)

The Cherry Orchard the most perfect work of the modern theatre and contending that "the haunting beauty and life-sense of this master-piece can only be fully appreciated by those who have seen it on the stage."[26] Attendance improved, a decision to close was reversed, and the play eventually transferred to the West End's Royalty Theatre for over 100 performances – the first successful run of a Chekhov play in London.

Like the other attempts at British Chekhov, Fagan's production was a somber affair. Critics spoke of its "splendid gloom" and "miasma of misery," and observed that "the general atmosphere . . . is one of the futility of life."[27] The settings were somewhat meager, with drawing-room windows looking onto a blank wall, and a curtained backdrop for the outdoor scene of Act II.[28] The stage groupings, to one critic, "suggested tableaux from the lamented Tussaud collection" (*Star*, 26 May 1925). In spite of the dour tone of the production, it lacked emotional impact; audiences giggled at Lopakhin's non-proposal to Varya because of "the inability of the actors to render the poignancy of the situation."[29] But the ensemble was praised, and many individual performances noted, especially O. B. Clarence as Firs, who "must have drawn tears from the policeman in the gallery," according to James Agate. Agate considered Gielgud's Trofimov "perfection itself," but thought Napier's Gayev "a trifle too seedy for a remnant of the old nobility," and O'Donovan's Lopakhin "a wee bit too brutal," trailing "clouds of Abbey Theatre boorishness" (*Sunday Times*, 31 May 1925). Mary Grey's Ranevskaya was merely "large and slow and kind."[30] She met the usual fate of English actresses in being found too English for the role: "The feckless, irresponsible, passionate Mme. Ranevsky . . . has absolutely nothing in common with the English temperament. . . . As Miss Mary Grey comes on to the stage, so gentle, so motherly, so considerate, we feel that it is impossible she should have experienced the disasters that have overwhelmed Mme. Ranevsky. 'She is much too sensible,' we say instinctively."[31]

Responses to the production did reflect a deepened understanding of Chekhov, whose works were now generally available in translation and held in high esteem by the literary establishment. The question of the play's tone was intelligently debated in the journals. "Should Chekhov's 'Cherry Orchard' be played lightly, satirically, almost in the farcical manner?" asked one reviewer, observing that the Fagan production was "dreamy, drifting, against its background of symbolic poetry; rather than alive, alert, under the implied criticism of irony."[32] Another critic felt the production too "heavily sentimentalized," adding, "the atmosphere of the play should be almost farcical in its brightness and quickness."[33] While many critics still believed Chekhov to be a dour naturalist, depicting with sadness the passing of a particular way of life, some began to view him differently:

> Chekhov was for a long time considered a sort of master photographer, but we are now beginning to see the absurdity of this description. He was more an expressionist than a photographer, and by his enormous use of the monologue played the devil with theatrical realism. The minor characters in "The Cherry Orchard" with their whimsies and their *idées fixes* remind one rather of Ben Jonson and the comedy of humours.[34]

Such revaluations of Chekhov's method would eventually have their effect in the British theatre, but the success of Fagan's production established him in a sentimental role as "the voice of twilight Russia."

THEODORE KOMISARJEVSKY, BARNES THEATRE, 1926

This view of Chekhov reached its epitome in the brilliantly directed Chekhov season of Theodore Komisarjevsky at the Barnes Theatre in 1926. Komisarjevsky, a Russian *émigré*, was aware of the dangers of treating Chekhov too somberly. He recalled seeing a 1925 production of *The Seagull*, and never having "laughed so heartily as . . . when the nonsense to which this simple play had been reduced by a 'meaningful,' monotonous and dreary production was accepted by the audience as a 'highbrow' affair."[35] Still, Komisarjevsky was not above playing down to the tastes of the British theatre-going public, whom he rather despised: "to suit the public taste," he wrote, "life on the English stage had to be shown through a mist of loveliness."[36] The consequence of his shrewd assessment of his audience, and his own theatrical mastery, was a series of beautifully staged, lit, and acted Chekhov productions that bathed the plays in an atmosphere of romantic nostalgia.

Komisarjevsky had come to England from Russia in 1919. His sister, Vera Kommissarzhevskaya, played Nina in the first production of *The Seagull* in 1896 (while the production failed, her performance deeply impressed Chekhov). In Russia Komisarjevsky never directed Chekhov, and was twice turned down for employment at the Moscow Art Theatre.[37] He saw the MAT Chekhov productions and acknowledged their unique achievement:

> Although the visual side of Stanislavsky's production [of *The Seagull*] was still devised in the old naturalistic manner of the "Meininger," the acting in this play was quite different from that in the preceding Moscow Art Theatre productions. Stanislavsky found that an actor must act "from within" and that the ensemble on the stage should be based on the "inner contacts" between the actors. When Stanislavsky tried later to "systematise" and to analyse what he had discovered intuitively, he misinterpreted himself.

Komisarjevsky admired Stanislavsky as an actor and director but rejected the "system," which he felt misrepresented the intuitive approach of a great theatre artist.[38] Nonetheless, he became associated with Chekhov and Stanislavsky in the mind of the British public, and was indeed the means by which many aspects of Stanislavskian acting came into British theatre practice.[39] John Gielgud, for instance, recorded that Komisarjevsky "influenced me greatly, teaching me not to act from outside, seizing on obvious effects and histrionics; to avoid the temptation of showing off; to work from within to present a character; and to absorb the atmosphere and general background of the play."[40]

Komisarjevsky's Chekhov season, in a small converted cinema in the London suburb of Barnes, established the author's reputation in England, but it defined British Chekhov as romantic, atmospheric, and elegiac. The most popular and influential production of the season was *Three Sisters*. Notoriously, Komisarjevsky transformed Baron Tuzenbach from the homely and awkward character Chekhov describes into a handsome romantic lead. When Gielgud, who played the part, questioned this decision, Komisarjevsky responded, "My dear boy, the English always demand a love interest."[41] Komisarjevsky's method with Chekhov, as exemplified in *Three Sisters*, was to highlight the main romantic story line, create a beautiful visual picture through his mastery of lighting and design, edit the text to keep the story moving, and reduce specifically Russian references. Robert Tracy has observed that Komisarjevsky provided British audiences with "a selectively anglicized Chekhov, who would not startle them by being exotically Russian or by sympathetically anticipating the October Revolution."[42] Yet his productions also were sensitive to the richness and subtlety of Chekhov's dramaturgy, and the need for complete orchestration of verbal and non-verbal effects. He was the inventor of what he called "Synthetic Theatre," which attempted to unite all the elements of a production to support a total artistic vision: an approach ideally suited to Chekhov.[43] He attributed his success to "the fact that I evolved the way to convey Chekhov's inner meaning and made the rhythm of the music of the play blend with the rhythm of the movements of the actors, giving the necessary accents with the lighting and the various outer 'effects.'"[44] Productions of *Ivanov*, *Uncle Vanya*, and *Three Sisters* were all hits, and Desmond MacCarthy held that the acceptance of Chekhov by the British public could be attributed, "above all, [to] the delicate, imaginative expertness of M. Komisarjevsky as a producer."[45]

The Cherry Orchard was the last play of the Barnes Chekhov season, and the least well received. As Patrick Miles has suggested, the disappointing results may have been a consequence of Komisarjevsky's exhaustion, or his company's.[46] The production design was beautiful as ever, but "could not make up for the general lifelessness of the actors, who seemed petrified by exhaustion or terror."[47] Critics who had loved the earlier productions were unsatisfied: "something was missing – a deep content – that gentle excitement of the soul – which recollection of *Three Sisters* can still evoke" (*Observer*, 3 October 1926). Komisarjevsky certainly succeeded with atmospheric design, from the opening, with "mingled lamplight and moonlight on white walls, already flushed with the roseate hues of dawn, the distant tinkle of sleigh-bells warning the sleepy watchers of the *émigrés'* return," to the close, which "bathed that last scene in a glow of afternoon sunshine filtering through the shutters."[48] Some critics felt Komisarjevsky succeeded in his attempt to create a "synthetic" performance; Charles Morgan, noting that Chekhov's plays "depend for their effect upon a slow and delicate gathering together of minor impressions into a perfected whole," praised the company collectively for "subject[ing] themselves to the play and to M. Komisarjevsky's very beautiful production of it."[49]

Numerous other critics, however, sensed that the production elements and performances were out of harmony. Komisarjevsky had tried to balance the atmospherics of his *Cherry Orchard* with moments of farce and humor, in accordance with Chekhov's intentions, but the result lacked emotional weight. The ensuing critical discussion replayed the terms of the Stanislavsky/Chekhov controversy over the play's genre and tone. Desmond MacCarthy, who criticized Fagan for overplaying the tragedy in 1925, felt that Komisarjevsky now went too far in the other direction: "the pathos of the characters was lost in their absurdity." Dorothy Dix conveyed only Ranevskaya's light-headed irresponsibility; she was "too silly a woman to touch us as much as she ought to do." Lawrence Hanray was a more absurd figure as Gayev than Allen Napier had been for Fagan – he was particularly effective in his billiard moments – but while this performance was closer to Chekhov's conception, it meant that Ranevskaya had to carry the emotional weight of the play. "If our sympathies for Leonid are checked by his being played as a contemptible, sniffy little man, then we must believe more than ever in the large heart of Lyubov," MacCarthy observed. The *Observer* critic praised her "fashionable effectiveness" and Parisian charm, but conceded, "perhaps it was foolish to expect this feckless sleeping beauty to dominate the play" (3 October 1926).

As evidence of Komisarjevsky's over-comic take on the play, MacCarthy pointed to the "amusingly drunk" Tramp in Act II. "The effect of his passage across the stage should be sinister . . . He is a sort of spectre from the underworld. On the stage at Barnes he was one more addition to the long list of comics." Pishchik's farewell, likewise, was merely absurd rather than poignant. The one deeply moving moment, apparently, was the non-proposal scene between Lopakhin and Varya. The final departure of the Ranevsky siblings from their home, so famously milked by Stanislavsky, lacked pathos in Barnes: "at that moment we should forget that Leonid is an absurd elderly duffer," MacCarthy wrote. "Excellent as Mr. Hanray's performance otherwise was, he did not make us forget it." Evidently the critics, seduced by the elegiac tone of Komisarjevsky's other productions and his beautifully atmospheric staging, were put off by the director's "mocking and at times caustic attitude" toward the characters of *The Cherry Orchard.*[50]

One comic figure who made an impression in Komisarjevsky's *Cherry Orchard* was the Yepikhodov of the young Charles Laughton, who also played Solyony in *Three Sisters*. Ernest Short reported that "he makes the moonstruck clerk an unforgettable mixture of pathos and fun." Alan Dent recalled that after seeing the production, "I went round Bloomsbury telling everyone I had got to know about an astonishing, new, young, plump comedian I had happened to see . . . I have never since beheld a funnier or more melancholy performance of this peculiarly difficult because intensely Russian character."[51] Laughton's performance gained him immediate notice, which he would soon increase in motion pictures. As a legitimate star, he was the dominant figure in the next attempt to redefine *The Cherry Orchard* as a comic play: Tyrone Guthrie's 1933 production at the Old Vic.

TYRONE GUTHRIE, OLD VIC, 1933

Laughton and his wife Elsa Lanchester, together with Flora Robson, were the lead actors of Guthrie's 1933 Old Vic season. Guthrie, a young Anglo-Irish director influenced by William Poel, Harley Granville-Barker, and Bernard Shaw, wanted to break with the Old Vic's tradition of rather worthy and pictorial Shakespeare productions and inject the theatre with new life, both in classical and modern plays. Laughton was now an international celebrity on the strength of his performance in Alexander Korda's film *The Private Life of Henry VIII*; he had also played a Chicago gangster in the West End. Accordingly, he had a larger-than-life aura with an edge of danger and a reputation for scenery-chewing excess. Guthrie cast him as Macbeth, Prospero, Angelo, and Henry VIII, as well as Lopakhin in *The Cherry Orchard*.

Guthrie had already directed the play once, at the Cambridge Festival Theatre as part of a weekly repertory. Conscious of Chekhov's reputation for somberness, he commissioned a new translation from his brother-in-law, Hubert Butler, which he hoped would help audiences perceive the play differently: "There must be a translation in manners as well as in language," he wrote in a program note. "I hope we have not so botched the attempt as to substantiate the conception that Chekhov is 'morbid' or foster the idea of 'Russian gloom.'"[52] In the cavernous Old Vic Theatre, with the stage separated by a yawning orchestra pit from the audience, Guthrie directed the play with broad strokes of staging and an accelerated pace. "If the production be keyed down to a pitch that would make the behaviour of the characters compatible with custom in our country there is a danger of its being stodgy and restrained indeed compared with a performance by the Moscow Art Theatre," he wrote.

Critics and audiences welcomed this energetic *Cherry Orchard*, which played for twice the Vic's customary run. Desmond Mac-Carthy hailed the production as "the best which has been put upon the English stage," noting that "the big audience laughs and is touched and admires."[53] The *Times* critic felt that "Mr. Tyrone Guthrie has not repeated the mistakes of Mr. Fagan, but in his determination to bring out the farcical extravagance of the dialogue and to dispel the notorious Russian gloom he has swung perilously near the other extreme and abated somewhat the deep pathos of the play" (10 October 1933). Leslie Rees concurred that Guthrie's approach, in which "Every character is made to yield fun," gave the audience "a somewhat wrong notion of the play at the outset."[54] This *Cherry Orchard* prompted much more laughter than any previous English production; though W. A. Darlington commented approvingly that "they laughed in the right places, and with the right tone."[55] Nonetheless, at least some audience members adhered to the notion of Chekhov as a somber dramatist. At one performance, Flora Robson's Varya tripped over a rug and fell on her face while pursuing Yepikhodov. No one laughed at the mishap; James Whale, a former Yepikhodov who was in the audience, reported, "We all thought, how very Russian."[56]

Laughton's Lopakhin received the most critical discussion, though his was not one of the more broadly played roles. James Agate wrote that he "made more of Lopakhin than has ever been made in this country," but also praised Laughton for a surprisingly restrained performance.[57] The *Times* critic remarked that this "loutish fellow, with head held on one side and flapping hands, is a very precise study of character, and though his practical mind brings him a sense of triumph, we are made to feel the self-distrust that lurks within." Likewise, MacCarthy wrote, "What he conveys better than any of his predecessors is Lopakhin's muddled inconsistent emotional attitude toward the family he supplants." Laughton was both resentful and adoring of Ranevskaya, frustrated with and in awe of her apparent indifference to her fate. In his triumph in Act III, Laughton's

Lopakhin "conveyed this mixture of emotions, and in so doing he succeeded in being more 'Russian' than any English actor I have seen in the part . . . He was both soft and hard, humble and overbearing, ruthless and sympathetically upset; he was triumphant and yet he felt somehow that it was all wrong."[58]

Laughton seems to have had some broadly comic moments as well; production photographs of him with Elsa Lanchester's Charlotta indicate that he made much of Lopakhin's self-effacing mock-flirtation with the governess. But the keynote of his performance was Lopakhin's inner turmoil. Guthrie himself found Laughton's performance "extremely subtle and interesting."[59] Ivor Brown called him "a tortured creature" who doubted whether he had truly risen above his peasant origins: "There is only one scene in which Lopakhin declares his strength, and Mr. Laughton suddenly flares out of the man's torpid self-questioning to play it with magnificent ferocity. Then back to his flabbiness, his flapping of uncertain, if wealthy, hands."[60]

The flapping hands were a distinctive feature of the characterization, as was the Yorkshire burr Laughton used for the role. Agate described it as "a superb study of character in the best sense of the word," and "the finest piece of acting in town."[61] W. A. Darlington concurred that "If Mr. Laughton has given a better performance than this, I have not seen it."[62]

The production's comic tone hinged not on Lopakhin, but on Ranevskaya. Athene Seyler, a celebrated comedienne, was an unlikely fit for the role; James Agate wondered, "What would Miss Athene Seyler, a soubrette after Moliere's heart, do with Mme. Ranevsky, that part normally drenched with Dido-esque grace, nostalgia, and what-not?" Seyler's performance was a polished piece of high comedy, "witty, wise, and exquisitely skillful," according to Guthrie. Seyler eschewed the weepier strains of the role in favor of the cosmopolitan woman of the world. Ivor Brown contrasted her performance with that of Olga Knipper. With Knipper, the overall effect was "exquisitely grey and autumnal; the music discoursed was the funeral march of a way of living, gracious, kindly, foolish, doomed to fade." Seyler, by contrast, "reminds us of the gay and durable spirit of Madame; she deeply feels the wrench of leaving the orchard, but we know that, in a month or so and while the money lasts, Madame will be happy again in Paris." Guthrie believed Seyler fell short of perfection through a want of lyricism: "She looked, she moved, she felt so truly and sensitively; the gaiety, elegance, and poignance were all hers, but not the power to delight by the sheer sensuous quality of the voice."[63] Desmond MacCarthy thought Seyler conveyed the charm of the character better than any other actress he had seen: "She plays it so lightly, so gaily, so sentimentally, so elegantly."[64] MacCarthy sometimes found her a little too calculated in her effects, without the "complete naturalness in inconsistency" on which he felt the character's comedy depends. His descriptions of the performance are telling:

> When she gives a piece of gold to the tramp – though she has not paid her servants' wages and there is nothing to eat in the kitchen – the essence of the comedy lies in her dismay on realizing what she has done, not in a laughing or easy acceptance of her generous gesture. And when, in the middle of giving the most serious advice to "the perpetual student" and telling him how noble and brave he is, she suddenly says: "And you really must do something about your beard," this should be spoken not as though a tender admiring friend had suddenly switched into being a woman of the world, but spoken with exactly the same sympathetic earnestness as the rest of her advice. There lies the comedy: to her trivial and important things are on exactly the same level.

That such subtle and penetrating criticisms are possible shows both how effective the Old Vic performance was, and how sophisticated and knowledgeable English critics were becoming in the techniques of Chekhov's dramaturgy.

Besides Seyler and Laughton, the most noteworthy performance was Flora Robson's Varya. She, along with Laughton, gave gravity to the production. Most roles were treated very lightly, and Ivor Brown noted (*Observer*, 9 October 1933) that "most of the characters in the play are really happy," and will go on being so even after the orchard is lost:

> But Varya? No, there is no happiness for her. For she is the eternal shadow of all these happy ones, the somber truth behind the gay illusion, the woman who works and tries to pay reality's bills. Miss Flora Robson plays Varya superbly; her unquiet spirit broods over the whole play. Really the emotional pivot of the piece is altered by the casting of Miss Robson and Miss Seyler. Madame, with all her incompetence, will look after herself, or be somehow looked after. It is Varya who here carries tragedy's robe and wears that sable to perfection. In this rendering it is Miss Robson who is doing Olga Knipper's work and driving at the very heart of darkness.

Guthrie was pleased with Robson's "unique quality of poignancy"; he had directed her as Varya in Cambridge, and she had been the first actor he cast for the Old Vic season.[65] MacCarthy praised the "unexaggerated intensity" of her "harried and pathetic Varya"; the *Times* critic thought she evoked "the hardness of the aging spinster and the hopeless passion from which that hardness springs." Only Agate found her less moving than he expected, but he felt the subtlety of her performance suffered in as large a theatre as the Old Vic: "you cannot enlarge the self-effacing."[66] Stung by this criticism, Robson underwent private vocal coaching to expand her performance for the remainder of the run.[67]

Others in the uniformly strong cast included Leon Quartermaine, "quietly effective" as a "deliciously played" Gayev; Roger Livesey, who played Pishchik "with a lively sense of his humanity and his foolishness"; and Dennis Arundell, a comically conceived "prattling" Trofimov, "that undisguisable if invaluable bore."[68] Then-unknown young actors notable in minor roles were James Mason, who "leered his way successfully through Yasha," and Marius Goring, a "gloomy Yepikhodov."[69] Elsa Lanchester's Charlotta, "in her zeal and forgivably, wandered off into Strindberg," according to Agate; Guthrie thought she "made a haunting impression of loneliness." Production photos highlight the quirky, glassy-eyed intensity she brought to such film roles as the *Bride of Frankenstein*; she certainly made a vivid visual impression, and MacCarthy thought her "demeanour and gestures . . . admirable."

Guthrie's direction was widely lauded, though some thought the pace too fast or the comic tone too unrelieved. The *Times* critic felt that Trofimov's fall down the stairs in Act III lost impact because the preceding quarrel with Ranevskaya lacked depth and intensity: "because the scene itself has been played at a pace which slurred over its emotional significance, the anti-climax has no more than its pure farcical value."[70] At the time Guthrie was, by his own account, "in full reaction against naturalism," and some of his staging was felt to be "too deliberately mannered for a realistic play," notably a pyramidal grouping of the characters in the second act.[71] His party scene in Act III was praised for its "remarkable wit, period sense, detail, colour, and exactitude of timing."[72] Several critics did complain at not being able to see the cherry orchard outside the windows of the house. But the consensus agreed with Leslie Rees:

> to show how amusing Chekhov, the gloomy Russian Chekhov, can be, is plainly the uppermost intention in Mr. Guthrie's mind, and, assuming this to be a valid aim, he succeeds very well.[73]

Future British productions of *The Cherry Orchard* would no longer have to justify treating the play as a comedy.

Guthrie revived the play in 1941, again with Athene Seyler but with an otherwise new cast. The play took on a more somber tone in wartime, and critics saw it as a parable "in a world resounding to the blow of the axe in a thousand cherry orchards."[74] This production was not as influential as the earlier one, but it is worth mentioning because of a review by Graham Greene that gives evidence of Guthrie's skillful direction:

Watch the eternal student (interestingly made up to look like Chekhov himself and very well acted by Mr. Walter Hudd) scratch his bottom while he boasts about mankind. See the tired broken Gaev lift his nose like an old war-horse at the click of billiard balls, and in the last scene the absurd governess, Charlotta, sprawl like a ventriloquist's doll in the corner of the about-to-be-abandoned room. It is these little moments, flashes of individual insight, which make a play fresh however often we see it.[75]

Such comments reveal not only the sophistication of Guthrie's production, but the extent to which *The Cherry Orchard* had become a classic in the British theatre, along the lines of Shakespeare, that could be made fresh "however often we see it."

CHEKHOV IN AMERICA: EVA LE GALLIENNE, 1928–1968

In the American theatre, perceptions of *The Cherry Orchard* were long colored by its initial presentation, by the Moscow Art Theatre with Stanislavsky, Knipper, and Leonidov, in 1923. The impact of that production, discussed in Chapter 3, made it difficult for the first English-language performance to succeed in comparison. This was actually an English import, Fagan's Lyric production, which played at the Bijou Theatre in 1928. It was largely re-cast, but had Mary Grey (under her married name, Gemma Fagan) still playing Ranevskaya, Fagan himself as Gayev, and Glen Byam Shaw elevated from Yasha to Trofimov. Alexander Woollcott, the notoriously acerbic critic for *The World*, called *The Cherry Orchard* the finest new play in world theatre in a hundred years, but declared that "since the New York stage was absurdly willing to let a quarter of a century pass before producing 'The Cherry Orchard,' it might better, I think, have waited a little longer and done it well."[76] Brooks Atkinson called it "lamentably inadequate," "drenched in boredom," "the cadaver of The Cherry

Orchard from which the breath of life has departed." Atkinson felt the English company failed because they lacked the ensemble cohesion the MAT performers had demonstrated. Woollcott found them simply too English: "I vow there were times when I thought that all Madame Ranevsky's household would fall to playing cricket and then drift over to the vodka shop for a perfectly ripping lemon squash."

The first native production fared better, and began the play's association with the woman who would own *The Cherry Orchard* on the New York stage for forty years: Eva Le Gallienne. Le Gallienne was an actress, director, and producer who was instrumental in creating the repertory theatre movement in America. Brought up in England and Paris in an accomplished literary family, Le Gallienne had high ideals for the American theatre. Her Civic Repertory company, at the 14th Street Theatre in New York City, was an attempt to create a working ensemble to present classical and modern plays of literary distinction, to oppose the Broadway model of commercial managements, star-centered productions, and long runs. Chekhov was a staple of her repertory: she produced not only *The Cherry Orchard* (1928), but *Three Sisters* (1926), and *The Seagull* (1929). Inspired by the Moscow Art Theatre, which she had seen, she considered Chekhov's plays perfectly suited to an ensemble such as hers: "A group of people, intimately related to one another by a sincere and affectionate attitude toward the work to be expressed, have a better chance of projecting the true essence of Chekhov's plays, than, let us say, an all-star cast of superlative actors, all intent on projecting themselves as individuals."[77]

Le Gallienne took an upbeat approach, subscribing wholeheartedly to Trofimov's idealistic faith in the future. In her edition of the Garnett translations, she quotes Trofimov's Act II speeches at length, equating his perspective with Chekhov's own:

> How can such an idealist be called a pessimist? . . . Chekhov had a profound faith in the eventual success of Man in the fullest sense of the word . . . And what a mighty and accurate vision he had of the future. In

Trofimov's wonderful lines at the end of the second act of "The Cherry Orchard" it is as though the Russian Revolution had been foreseen as inevitable and its essence laid bare: "All Russia is our garden."[78]

Brooks Atkinson, the *New York Times* critic, was convinced – not only that "it is indeed, a comedy, as Chekhov always maintained," but that its message was not of tragedy but of hope: "Its unobtrusive symbolism becomes articulate in Anya's joyous enthusiasm for the 'new life' and the contented death of the 'old life' in Firs' muttering resignation while the woodsmen hack at the cherry trees, singing at their labors, and the servants firmly close the shutters from the outside." That rather alarming juxtaposition of Firs' "contented death" with the off-stage workers' song was an innovation of Le Gallienne's that she maintained in her productions of the play right through to 1968.

Le Gallienne appears to have succeeded in building a unified company: Richard Watts, Jr., thought *The Cherry Orchard* "an ensemble performance of extraordinary skill," adding that the production was "an authentic tribute to a first rate dramatic organization." Le Gallienne's achievement in creating the ensemble is doubly remarkable given the presence in the company of Alla Nazimova, a celebrated Russian *émigrée* actress brought in to play Ranevskaya. The Civic Rep actors had been working closely together for three years; Nazimova was something of a *grande dame* and had her own working methods. Though she had played with the Moscow Art Theatre and is often credited with introducing Stanislavskian methods to America, her performances were often mannered and external. "I always thought of her as a marvelous technician, like a beautiful trapeze artist," Le Gallienne later recalled. "But she never moved me . . . Everything was well-faked."[79] Although Nazimova "required careful handling," according to Jo Hutchinson, who played Anya, Le Gallienne was able to maintain an atmosphere of professionalism and dedication throughout the company (this despite Le Gallienne's former romantic involvement with Nazimova and ongoing relationship with Hutchinson).[80] Nazimova eventually left in a dispute with Le Gallienne over billing,

7. Alla Nazimova as Ranevskaya, with Harold Moulton as Trofimov, in Eva Le Gallienne's 1928 production at the Civic Repertory Theatre, New York. (New York Public Library.)

but was persuaded to return for a revival of *The Cherry Orchard* in 1933.

Nazimova's performance was strong and distinctive, drawing on her Moscow Art Theatre background and her personal knowledge of the play's milieu. She was not intimidated by the MAT's reputation or its legendary players, declaring, "I was a much better actress than Knipper, but she was Chekhov's wife and got all the parts."[81] Nazimova's Ranevskaya was a glamorous figure, wearing a vintage black silk dinner gown and stark white makeup. She was "beautiful, elegant, *witty* – and turn-of-the-century Russian," according to one observer; another found her "wayward, sexually attractive, careless of her precarious situation, glamorous."[82] Her performance had something of her trademark exoticism and "sphinxlike quality of mystery," according to John Mason Brown, who thought her "the best Madame Ranevsky to have been seen in an American production."[83] The *Times* critic felt she was not as good as Knipper, "but gave the [role] more beauty, and a deal of fitful charm in her sudden moods."[84] Nazimova brought a full range of emotion to the part; George Cukor remembered particularly her reaction when Trofimov brings to mind her dead son Grisha: "Usually actresses play this moment rather sentimentally, but Nazimova gave you the impression the boy had only just been drowned. She had this beautiful, rather fragile voice, and she sobbed as if [Trofimov] was actually carrying the body of the child. It had a terrible stab of immediacy."[85]

The Cherry Orchard played in repertory with Molière's *The Would-Be Gentleman* and Barrie's *Peter Pan*, so production values were necessarily limited. The set by Aline Bernstein used the full depth of the theatre's small stage, back to the scene dock, so that all entrances had to be made from the wings. Le Gallienne had the actors rehearse with all of the furniture, properties, and costume pieces from the beginning in order to try to create a sense of felt life. Referring to a *chaise-longue* in which Gayev spent most of the first act, Le Gallienne wrote that it "has become molded to his body . . . he is familiar with every threadbare spot in its upholstery, every detail of its carving." Her consciousness of this kind of meaningful detail extended to the symbolic value of costume. She herself played Varya; as she noted, it was one of three "women wearing black" that she played in Chekhov, along with the Mashas of *Three Sisters* and *The Seagull*:

> Just as in painting there is a note of black somewhere in the canvas, so Chekhov in his plays has nearly always that note of black in one of his female characters. It seems to bring the other figures into relief in a curious way; from a director's angle it is immensely intriguing; of course it is true, too, that the wearing of black is an outward manifestation of an inner state of mind, especially when worn by young women, and these three women of Chekhov's are all quite young.[86]

Le Gallienne's presence in the role gave Varya unusual prominence. The non-proposal scene in Act IV included a distinctive directorial touch. As Lopakhin stood behind her groping for words, Varya knelt before a trunk, pretending to look for something, as the text suggests. Once Lopakhin's inability to propose became apparent,

> Eva as Varya kept her hands in the trunk as if searching, but her eyes revealed the truth. She looked over the top of the trunk, calmly but sadly. She knew there would be no marriage proposal. At the same time, Lopakhin crossed quietly behind her, held out his hands as if wanting to touch her, and looked as if he desperately wanted to speak. Lacking courage, he crossed back to the window in silence.[87]

Le Gallienne was also noted for the way she threw Trofimov's galoshes: "her whole frustration, her anger, everything was in that one gesture," recalled Robert Lewis, a company member.[88]

The production was politely but not rapturously received; John Mason Brown thought it "self-respecting even if it was uninspired; excitingly indicative even if it was incomplete," but definitely "Grade C milk as far as the Stanislavsky production was concerned."[89] When Le Gallienne revived the production, again with Nazimova, in 1933, it had "advanced to Grade B Chekhov." Brooks Atkinson, by contrast, praised the "limpid, modulated performance," and especially Nazimova, whose acting had a "flowing rhythm that catches every evanescent mood and intonation in this character."[90]

The Cherry Orchard was a legitimate hit, selling out all performances twenty-four hours after opening night. Le Gallienne resisted the urge to move the play uptown, feeling this would be a betrayal of her principles for the Civic Rep. She did extend the play's run to sixty-four performances in the season. She continued to revive the production off and on, usually with Nazimova, until 1933, when she transferred it to the New Amsterdam Theatre on Broadway in an attempt to raise enough money to save the financially troubled Civic Rep. Though the production was popular, the theatre was forced to close after that season.

The next Broadway production of the play, in 1944, was also led by Le Gallienne, who played Ranevskaya and co-directed with Margaret

Webster. Webster, an influential popularizer of Shakespeare whose manifesto was entitled *Shakespeare without Tears*, evidently believed in Chekhov without tears as well. One critic noted that "the players did not go strictly by the book and weep as often as Chekhov ordered in the stage directions."[91] Under Webster's influence, the play took on a more comic tone than in Le Gallienne's earlier production. In the opening moments of the play, for instance, two servant girls ran across the stage carrying a wicker hamper; one of them tripped and took a comic pratfall. As George Jean Nathan complained, "almost every old vaudeville device . . . was introduced: the slap on the maid Dunyasha's backside, the stumbling over the furniture, the slapping of the forehead too forcibly and the resulting comic staggers, the bumping into the door on an exit, etc."[92] The farcical tone was especially pronounced in the party scene of Act III. Leona Roberts, who had played a crudely comic Charlotta in Le Gallienne's earlier production (she entered riding in a baby carriage), went even farther in 1944, playing vaudeville turns directly to the audience.[93] Rex O'Malley, as Yepikhodov, was made up in "a sort of comic mask resembling Hitler" and used an exaggerated cockney accent together with an array of clumsy physical gags.[94]

The production used a new translation prepared by Le Gallienne and Irina Skariatina. Le Gallienne's performance mostly avoided the comic demeanor of the rest of the production. She was a tall, authoritative, intellectual actress, most successful in roles like Ibsen's Hedda Gabler; her Ranevskaya was a figure of elegant dignity and tragic stature, "reed-thin . . . with pale, cameo features and enormous, heavy-lashed blue eyes."[95] For some critics her performance did not fit the play:

> There is a sharpness and intelligence about Miss Le Gallienne's Mme Ranevsky that makes her feckless conduct inexplicable as well as inexcusable . . . She moves with authority, with a kind of spirited grace, even though she does not at any point capture the elusive, mercurial essence of that temperament which can move with lightning speed from tears to laughter, which can compass joy and despair in a single breath.[96]

8. Eva Le Gallienne as Ranevskaya and Joseph Schildkraut as Gayev in Le Gallienne's Broadway *Cherry Orchard* from 1944. (Photofest.)

On the whole Le Gallienne won positive notices for her "radiantly assured . . . eloquent and moving performance."[97] Joseph Schildkraut, with whom Le Gallienne had worked frequently for years, was a distinguished Gayev. Walter Kerr described his "delightfully languid, incompetent, billiard-playing Gayev" as "a richly styled and immensely attractive fool. Not an object of pity; a likeable, even an admirable, ass." Rosamund Gilder felt Schildkraut's "detailed, highly elaborated, humorous portrait" was "not quite caricature but tending in that direction."[98] While Schildkraut focused on Gayev's battiness, he did not downplay the pathos; indeed, he had a stagehand spray menthol in his eyes before his Act III entrance, so that Gayev returned from the auction in floods of tears (Le Gallienne eventually talked him out of this trick by telling the hypochondriacal actor that permanent eye damage might result).[99] The final moments of the brother and sister leaving the house were deeply moving, though one critic detected "a touch of chin-up heroics."[100] The Ranevskys were the clear focus of the production; Stefan Schnabel's "large, lumbering" Lopakhin was barely mentioned by the critics.[101] The mixture of broad farce and "chin-up heroics" seemed to appeal to a wartime Broadway audience; *The Cherry Orchard* played for an unprecedented ninety-six performances, then went on a five-month national tour.[102] Burton Rascoe credited Le Gallienne and Webster with transforming *The Cherry Orchard*, in the American mind, from "a depressing, symbolical study in Russian futility and pessimism" to "a shrewdly constructed lively theatrical entertainment."[103]

Finally, in 1968, Le Gallienne directed the play for a non-profit company, the Association of Producing Artists, with Uta Hagen as Ranevskaya. Hagen had begun her career as Ophelia to Le Gallienne's Hamlet thirty years before. She was actually Le Gallienne's third choice for the role. Originally, Rosemary Harris was to have played Ranevskaya, and Le Gallienne Charlotta. Harris left the APA when she divorced its director, Ellis Rabb; when Geraldine Page also turned down the part, Le Gallienne turned to Hagen.[104] She had matured into a robust, Method-driven, emotionally powerful actress most famous for creating the role of Martha in *Who's Afraid of Virginia Woolf?* She was certainly odd casting for Ranevskaya; as Ellis Rabb put it, "She is a great actress, but you felt that at any moment she could chop down the cherry trees herself, saw up the lumber, and build condominiums."[105] The rehearsal period was fraught with tension, as Hagen tried to "be true to [herself]" and Le Gallienne rejected "this Method acting and Actor's Studio stuff." Le Gallienne found Hagen "so *heavy* – so *German* and she lacks style & grace . . . She won't listen to any suggestions of lightness or frivolity."[106] Le Gallienne also quarreled endlessly with Donald Moffat, who played Lopakhin. By the time of the opening she had suffered a heart attack.

The production was not a success. Clive Barnes, in the *New York Times*, called it "respectable, for the most part, but not vibrant," rather "an act of homage than an act of life."[107] Hagen received respectful notices, "but at times her acting seemed forced and it was not too easy to work up a strong sympathy for her and her misfortunes," according to Richard Cooke in the *Wall Street Journal* (21 March 1968). Hagen herself was so dismayed by the experience that she quit the stage for twelve years.[108]

The production was meant to have the same positive, comic tone as Le Gallienne's other versions of the play, and she used her own 1944 translation. The "happier and livelier moments" were carried off better than moments of "sadness and loss," and as usual there were complaints about intrusive comic business.[109] Le Gallienne had decided not to play Charlotta herself, and had cast instead the comedienne Nancy Walker. Her "not particularly Chekhovian" performance was much derided: "as appropriate as a Bronx taxi-driver in Mozart"; "beneath discussion . . . the New York dialect, the coarse humor, the sheer show-business of it is pure irritation."[110] No one else in the company attracted much notice, and the lack of ensemble was widely criticized. The production was a personal failure for Le Gallienne, and marked the end of her association with Chekhov.

Nonetheless, in his review, Clive Barnes acknowledged that Le Gallienne "has done more than anyone for Chekhov in America." Through her productions, she more or less single-handedly put *The Cherry Orchard* into the American theatrical repertory. As in Britain, by mid-century, the play had achieved the status of a classic, and was accordingly brought to life in a broader and richer range of productions.

CHAPTER 5

THE CHERRY ORCHARD AT MID-CENTURY: BARRAULT, SAINT-DENIS, STREHLER

In the first half of the twentieth century, the production history of *The Cherry Orchard* was dominated by the Moscow Art Theatre. The MAT itself had been seen across Europe and America, fixing its particular image of the play in the minds of audiences; and Stanislavsky and Knipper still held sway in Russia throughout the violent changes of the period. Abroad, Russian *émigrés* like Komisarjevsky, Nazimova, Germanova, Georges Pitoëff in France and Tatiana Pavlova in Italy heavily influenced the reception of Chekhov's plays. *The Cherry Orchard* was seen as quintessentially Russian, and was colored by evolving Western attitudes to Russia past and present. During the war years, the nostalgic and mournful attitude toward "the old life" that pervaded Russian productions of *The Cherry Orchard* was extended to Europe as a whole. Tyrone Guthrie's 1941 London revival, discussed in the previous chapter, suggested "a world resounding to the blow of the axe in a thousand cherry orchards."[1] In America, the Margaret Webster/Eva Le Gallienne version of 1944 was marked by a tone of heroic endurance, and prompted an open letter from Olga Knipper in which she spoke of Chekhov's belief in "the better future which will dawn for mankind no matter what sufferings some generations have to endure," and looked forward to "attending your productions when the alliance of great countries is crowned with victory over Hitlerite barbarity."[2] With the world ravaged by war, *The Cherry Orchard*, already shrouded in Russian gloom, became an emblem for suffering Europe.

All that began to change in the years following the war. The fiftieth anniversary of Chekhov's death, in 1954, brought about a revaluation of his work, challenging the MAT version. New productions throughout Europe and America began to cast Chekhov as a universal playwright of classic status, a staple of the repertoire comparable to the Greek tragedians, Shakespeare, Molière, and Ibsen. As the *émigrés* of the Revolution passed away and memories of the MAT waned, a number of major directors approached Chekhov in the context of the dramatic present. Chekhov's new status as a classic removed him from the theatrical trappings of turn-of-the-century realism, so he could be reconstituted in the vital world of mid-twentieth-century theatre: the theatre of Pirandello, Brecht, and Beckett. Productions by Jean-Louis Barrault (Paris, 1954), Michel Saint-Denis (London, 1961), and Giorgio Strehler (Milan, 1955, 1974) created a new vision of *The Cherry Orchard* as an international classic.

JEAN-LOUIS BARRAULT, PARIS, 1954

In France, Chekhov production was strongly influenced by the tours of the Moscow Art Theatre and the Prague Group in the 1920s and 30s. The beginnings of a French tradition of Chekhov performance came through the productions of Georges Pitoëff. Pitoëff was a Russian *émigré* who, encouraged by the French actor and director Jacques Copeau, translated and directed *The Seagull*, *Uncle Vanya*, and *Three Sisters* between 1921 and 1939. While Pitoëff's adaptations simplified Russian names and used cultural allusions that would be familiar to a French audience (substituting *eau-de-vie* for vodka and Pushkin for Nekrasov), the plays were still received as irresistibly Russian.[3] As Michel Achard wrote of *Uncle Vanya*, "The atmosphere is Russian, the characters Russian, the silence and the snow Russian, the décor Russian too."[4] Pitoëff often used *émigré* actors in leading roles, including himself, his wife, Ludmila, and Prague group veteran Maria

Germanova. Nonetheless, his staging broke with MAT traditions. Pitoëff was a disciple of Pavel Gaideburov, having acted in the Itinerant Theatre's *Cherry Orchard* before the Revolution. He emulated Gaideburov's use of simple settings, with draperies and sparse furniture in place of the detailed environments of Stanislavsky and Simov. Though he had admired Stanislavsky's *Cherry Orchard* in 1904 as "the epitome of realist production," when the same production played in Paris in 1922 he was "astounded by its futility."[5] His poetic and abstract stagings were in keeping with new trends in the French theatre, and drew praise from such luminaries as André Antoine and Aurélien Lugné-Poë.

However, Pitoëff's planned *Cherry Orchard*, to be produced by Copeau, fell through due to a dispute over the rights to the play, which were controlled by Olga Knipper. The French-language premiere of *The Cherry Orchard* (*La Cerisaie*) had to wait until 1944, after the end of the German Occupation, when the play was staged at the Odeon by Roger Bernard and H. Charpentier in a translation by Denis Roche. Suzanne Courtal played Ranevskaya, M. Chamarat Gayev, and Roual Marco Lopakhin. The play was performed *"sans grand éclat"* and was barely remembered ten years later, when the single most important French production of the play opened at the Théâtre Marigny under the direction of Jean-Louis Barrault.[6]

Barrault was one of the leading figures of twentieth-century French theatre. His career spanned a wide range of influences and venues: Artaud, the mime artist Etienne Ducroux, the Comédie-Française, the plays of Paul Claudel, the classical repertory, and the avant-garde political theatre of the sixties and seventies. Together with his wife, Madeleine Renaud, he produced, directed, and acted in *The Cherry Orchard* at the Théâtre Marigny, where their company performed a repertory of period and modern classics for a fashionable audience. The production was an immediate success, and made a considerable impression on audiences and critics. Paul Gordeaux declared it "simply a masterpiece," noting, "the play develops slowly, by small successive touches – silences, gestures, short phrases – through which little by little the characters reveal their state of soul and the action moves insensibly forward."[7] Barrault's understanding of the play as chiefly concerned with the process of time gave the production an unusual rhythm and a quality of universality. The chief theatrical exponent of the spiritual verse-dramas of Paul Claudel, Barrault found in *The Cherry Orchard* a poignant philosophy that transcended the historical contingencies of its composition.

Barrault, in a widely reprinted essay entitled "Why *The Cherry Orchard?*", laid out the view of the play that governed his production. He declared *The Cherry Orchard* Chekhov's masterpiece, because of all his plays, "this is the one which comes closest to universality and to generalizations which embrace all men."[8] He observed that "It is a play about the passing of time; therefore whether the characters are Russian or Japanese does not matter. Like some plays of Shakespeare and Molière it is a play which has universal value and which belongs to all mankind."[9]

Barrault found the structure of the play to be fundamentally musical, built around a single action conditioned by the process of time:

> Act I The cherry orchard runs the risk of being sold.
> Act II The cherry orchard is going to be sold.
> Act III The cherry orchard is being sold.
> Act IV The cherry orchard has been sold.[10]

Barrault's images for the play – "a nest of tables which stretch indefinitely one into another," and a Japanese paper flower unfolding in a bowl of water – are striking, and resonate in interesting ways with the "Chinese boxes" image of another important European director, Giorgio Strehler, to be discussed later in this chapter.

Barrault conceded that the play's silences, its fleeting themes, and the sorrowful unfolding of its action presented significant challenges to French actors. In the French theatrical tradition, according to Barrault, acting centered on the text, which contained the play's action. With Chekhov the actor had to move beyond the text to find a basis for the action; this meant adjusting the characteristically rapid tempo of French speech and performance:

> When the action is contained in the text, it unfolds at a quicker tempo than when it is outside the text. The French actor is therefore used to a quick tempo. *The Cherry Orchard* has a slow tempo, even for Russian actors, and besides that, Russian slowness is not the same as French slowness; therefore *The Cherry Orchard* must be produced according to French slowness and not Russian slowness, but this slowness constitutes for French actors an excellent discipline in the art of conveying the density of life.

Even played with "French slowness," Barrault's *Cherry Orchard* was lighter and quicker than it had been in the MAT tradition. One reason for this was Barrault's positive reading of the play. Given the inevitability of time's passage, humanity must be willing to part with the past:

> However attractive our past might be, however much we might cling to it, we must become worthy to receive the future, and in order to be so, we must have the courage to tear ourselves away from the past; it is the price we must pay for the right to live, it is the redemption and the ransom exacted by life.

This philosophical outlook on the play was reflected in the uncluttered staging, which was in a style Laurence Senelick has described as lyric realism. "Everything on stage had to be real but not naturalistic," according to Senelick. "One could dispense with ceilings, trees, distant views which did not intervene physically in the action."[11] The simplified staging used only a rough garden bench for Act II, a few arches and luxurious furniture for Act III. The lighting was crucial, not only at suggesting the different settings, but at defining a thematic atmosphere for each act, from the hopeful sunrise of Act I to the darkening orchard of Act II, the artificial brightness of the party and the desolation of the departure.

Madeleine Renaud as Ranevskaya was highly feminine, coquettish, and delicate, with huge eyes, fluttering hands, and alluring smile. One contemporary review described her as "a delicious widow, scatterbrained, weak, thoughtless, frivolous," but also "adorable."[12] Barrault characterized her as "a woman full of charm, generous and unconscious to the point of amorality," but at the same time a kind of universal human being: "her heart in her hand, a sinner full of love, distributing her money freely, Lyuba is the symbol of humanity."[13] Guy Demur noted that Renaud emphasized the French aspect of Ranevskaya; her return to Paris seemed inevitable and appropriate: "Nostalgic for Paris and the false love she has found, insouciant and melancholy, attached to a house, to an orchard, that she finally leaves without shedding many tears; attached to her family but ready to leave them for a scoundrel, this Russian tinged with *parisianisme* is marvelously suitable to Madeleine Renaud."[14] While Barrault intended to make the characters in the play universal – at least not specifically Russian – a sense of French national identity evidently contributed to the meaning of the production.

Barrault saw the three principal male characters who surround Ranevskaya as a triangle representing past, present, and future. For Barrault Gayev represented tradition and civilization, "an age which has lost its vitality . . . a good thing which has been lost and yet remains worthy of love."[15] One reviewer noted that Pierre Bertin "admirably conveys the dreamlike egotism of the man, who has come to look on reality as something not unlike an unpleasant medicine, to be taken in as small a dose as possible between games of billiards."[16] With his pince-nez, broad-brimmed hat, and elegant beard, he looked very much the Parisian dandy. Lopakhin, for Barrault, represented the present, "the hard-working business man, proud of his newly acquired strength, and also somewhat ashamed of the imperfections which he still drags about him."[17] Jean Desailly was "a magnificent figure in his white waistcoat and brown shoes" who "blunders about good naturedly," and who, the production suggested, would also be a victim of changing times.[18] Because of his reverence for Ranevskaya and the past she represented, his purchase of the cherry orchard was not a triumph, but a personal loss, and his final moments on stage were "steeped in pain and sorrow."[19]

Barrault himself played Trofimov as the herald of the future, "prophetic and dreamy." He was a gaunt and wiry figure in his heavy student's uniform, his pinched and bony face surmounted by black-rimmed, owlish spectacles. He illuminated the role "from within with such intensity, and so intellectually, that his scenes with Anya (Mlle. Nicole Bergier) are not in any sense romantic."[20] What Trofimov and Anya shared was a passionate belief in the future: "Soulmates, elective affinities, alien to their surroundings, they danced together at the ball with a gaiety that was the only one to seem genuine; even while waltzing with others, they stole glances at one another across a crowded room."[21] Throughout the play they shared this complicity, a clear-sighted awareness of the onslaught of time and a sincere belief that it was for the best.

This optimism, together with Barrault's poetic/philosophical reading and the Marigny troupe's expertise in high comedy, made the production one of the lightest and most buoyant *Cherry Orchard*s of the century; audiences left the theatre in a mood of joy. Perhaps the most important thing about the production was that it was thoroughly French. In the past, *émigrés* like the Prague Group and the Pitoëffs had given Parisians the impression that Chekhov had to be staged by Russians in a distinctly Russian manner.[22] With Barrault's production, the Russian gloom that had shrouded Chekhov – even if it was a misinterpretation – had been thoroughly dispelled. Not everyone felt that the play survived the transition. Gabriel Marcel argued that "The French language, French diction are at odds with such playwriting as Chekhov's," and Kenneth Tynan felt that Chekhov's genius "shrivels under the searchlight of the French language, which brusquely dispels his mists, sharpening his vague evocative outlines into razor-edged silhouettes."[23] For Tynan, only Desailly's Lopakhin was successful, because he was "the only character in the play whose approach to life is calculated, realistic, and thoroughly French." Yet French audiences responded warmly to the production, which remained in the Barrault/Renaud repertory even after the company left the Marigny Theatre in 1956.

With his time-based production, Barrault managed to transcend time. He loosened *The Cherry Orchard* from its MAT roots, and made it a work of the modern French theatre. He concluded his essay on the play with an observation from his favorite French playwright, Paul Claudel: "to know is to be born with, or at the same time as, the thing that one knows."[24] Through Barrault's production, *The Cherry Orchard* was reborn in 1954, and the French public came to know it for the first time.

MICHEL SAINT-DENIS, LONDON, 1961

A few years later, in England, another French director also undertook to present *The Cherry Orchard* as a contemporary play. Michel Saint-Denis directed it as part of the Royal Shakespeare Company's inaugural season at the Aldwych Theatre in London in 1961. The RSC, under Peter Hall, had been organized the previous year as a semi-permanent European-style ensemble that would present cutting-edge contemporary plays alongside the traditional Shakespearean repertoire. Inspired by the London visits of Bertolt Brecht's Berliner Ensemble, the Barrault–Renaud troupe and the Moscow Art Theatre itself, together with groundbreaking London productions like Beckett's *Waiting for Godot* (1955), John Osborne's *Look Back in Anger* (1956), and Harold Pinter's *The Birthday Party* (1958), Hall wanted to revitalize the British theatre by mixing the classical and the contemporary, the native and the continental. Saint-Denis, a director and teacher of international stature, was brought in to provide a new perspective on *The Cherry Orchard* for the young Aldwych audiences. Chekhov's play was part of an ambitious and diverse season that included John Whiting's controversial new play *The Devils*, Giraudoux's *Ondine*, and Anouilh's *Becket*, along with two Shakespeares and Webster's Jacobean tragedy *The Duchess of Malfi*. Saint-Denis's *Cherry Orchard* provoked strongly divided reactions, particularly for its lack of sentiment and its use of comedy, but it located Chekhov in a progressive and vital theatrical environment. "It is my belief and my hope that our interpretation has brought many people, particularly among the young, to a new understanding of this many-sided masterpiece," Saint-Denis wrote.[25]

While Saint-Denis had a strong interest in contemporary theatre, directing Brecht for the RSC and leading workshops on topics like Beckett, masque and mime for the RSC Studio, he also had roots in the theatre of the early twentieth century. A nephew of Jacques Copeau, he had grown up in the French theatre and had seen the MAT *Cherry Orchard* in Paris and discussed it with Stanislavsky. So while his production was ostensibly intended to break from the existing traditions of Russian and British Chekhov performance, Saint-Denis was significantly invested in both. The original MAT *Cherry Orchard* exerted a powerful nostalgic influence on Saint-Denis. Moreover, his one previous professional production of Chekhov had been a legendary success of the pre-war West End. His *Three Sisters* in 1938, with a cast including Gielgud, Peggy Ashcroft, Michael Redgrave, Alec Guinness, Gwen Ffrangcon-Davies, George Devine and Glen Byam Shaw, was held to be the epitome of British Chekhov. Laurence Olivier called it "the definitive production of this play in our profession," and even fifty years after its opening Irving Wardle declared it to be "the most legendary of all English Chekhov productions."[26] Saint-Denis's *Three Sisters* had all the romantic pathos of Komisarjevsky's productions, balanced by "a completely comedic view" of the play, according to Ashcroft; moreover, he rehearsed his star-studded cast for eight weeks to build a seamless ensemble.[27] The record-breaking box-office success of the production led Saint-Denis to prepare a *Cherry Orchard* the next year, again with a dream cast: Edith Evans as Ranevskaya, Ralph Richardson as Lopakhin, Ronald Squire as Gayev, Guinness as Trofimov, Ashcroft as Anya, Cyril Cusack as Firs. However, the outbreak of war cancelled the production after the first two weeks of rehearsals, and Saint-Denis returned to France for military service.

By the time Saint-Denis came back to the play in 1961, star-studded, elegiac productions of Chekhov had become a beloved staple of the British theatre. When the Moscow Art Theatre arrived in 1958 to play a season at Sadler's Wells, their boldly positive, socialist-realist retoolings of the plays provoked controversy and debate. Many critics questioned the apparently propagandistic alterations to the texts; in *Three Sisters* (Nemirovich-Danchenko's 1940 production), Chebutykin's nihilistic final mutterings were cut and Tuzenbach and Vershinin were made confident spokesmen for a better future. In Victor Stanitsyn's *Cherry Orchard*, a new production that year, Lopakhin and Trofimov were accorded similarly prophetic status, and Anya emphatically (and extra-textually) echoed the latter's welcome of the new life. The *Times* critic mourned the absence of the "poetic mingling of the tender and the eccentric" that provokes a "helpless warming of the heart" toward the characters in a British Chekhov production; the MAT characters had none of the "lovable absurdity" English audiences expected (30 May 1958). Citing Komisarjevsky to refute the charge that "this attitude to Chekhov springs from English sentimentality," the *Times* critic observed

> that a Madame Ranevsky who has no feckless airs and graces to excuse her inaction . . . is apt to appear a dull matron; that a Lopakhin who has quite squeezed the serf out of his blood is handicapped in the scene of his drunken triumph as the new owner of the orchard; and that a Trofimov cleaned up to give expression to the confident hopes of the younger generation is tripped up by difficulties put in his way by the dramatist whenever he tries to deliver his "message."

Another critic speculated that British audiences found Chekhov a little brash and vulgar "without Dame Edith, and Miss Seyler, and Sir

9. John Gielgud as Gayev, with Dorothy Tutin as Varya and Judi Dench as Anya, in Michel Saint-Denis's 1961 Royal Shakespeare Company production. (Photofest.)

John," and the atmosphere of genteel elegance with which those actors suffused the plays. On the other hand, Kenneth Tynan applauded the Russian company's ability to "blow . . . the cobwebs off" *The Cherry Orchard*, which the English had "remade in our image" as "a pathetic symphony, to be played in a mood of elegy." He found the production "straight Chekhov, not propagandistic distortion."[28] In any event, the interest sparked by the MAT visit served as the backdrop for Saint-Denis's new look at the play.

Hall had assembled a company of young actors, many drawn from dynamic new theatres like the Royal Court and Stratford East. *The Cherry Orchard* cast included Ian Holm as Trofimov, Judi Dench as Anya, Dorothy Tutin as Varya, and Roy Dotrice as Firs, alongside two veterans of the 1938 *Three Sisters*, Peggy Ashcroft as Ranevskaya and John Gielgud as Gayev. The youthful spirit of the company was actually at odds with Saint-Denis's severely autocratic directing style; the new RSC actors were used to the improvisational working methods of Hall and Peter Brook, and were surprised at the degree to which Saint-Denis arrived with his production already prepared. Moreover, much of the business derived directly from his memories of Stanislavsky's production. He had Ashcroft drop a cup when Firs poured tea on her hand, and like Stanislavsky he used real boiling water in rehearsal. He became obsessed with reproducing his memories of Anya's entrance in Act I. Writing about the moment in 1960, before he began rehearsals, he recalled how in 1922 Alla Tarasova had entered laughing with fatigue and strained nerves and jumped up on a sofa in the nursery, clapping her hands with excitement. "And on that piece of wordless acting the audience of two thousand five hundred people burst into applause," Saint-Denis recalled.[29] He worked on this moment endlessly with Judi Dench, driving her to tears of frustration as she failed to recapture the effect Tarasova had achieved.[30] Dench felt herself something of a "whipping boy" in the rehearsal process, unable to live up to the director's memories of the Stanislavsky production.[31] Saint-Denis's debt to Stanislavsky was not simply one of borrowed business, however. As he had with *Three Sisters*, he scheduled an eight-week rehearsal process so the actors could explore their characters in depth, looking for the hidden motivations on which the Stanislavsky system was built. At the first read-through, Saint-Denis told the actors that "the text is an important result of something else and their job was to find out what that something else was."[32]

In spite of the rehearsal problems, the production opened to a storm of interest and controversy. Many critics hailed it as definitive: J. C. Trewin called it "the finest British performance of *The Cherry Orchard* in our time."[33] Edmund Gardner, calling it "the definitive performance of our generation," noted that "each member of the company has at least one moment when the essential truth of their creations is flashed out at the audience in an unambiguous magnesium burst."[34] He cited, among many instances, the absurd moment at which Gielgud's Gayev, preparing to leave the house in Act IV, held up his inappropriate briefcase and proudly proclaimed, "I'm a financier. Pot the red." Eric Keown praised the "splendidly acted" production because it made clear "just why the Russian revolution had to be, while making us infinitely sorry for the old order – lost children who had no idea what was happening to them."[35]

Many critics, however, complained of the lack of pathos, while recognizing Saint-Denis's shift of emphasis. Anthony Cookman, linking Saint-Denis's production with the MAT's, observed that "a wind of change is blowing," and "English romantics will have to say good-bye for a while to the slightly sentimentalized Chekhov they have taken to their hearts, and make do with a more purposeful comic dramatist who will make them laugh more and sigh less."[36] However, Cookman was not prepared to concede that the new approach was better, and felt that Saint-Denis's production lost power in the later acts because of the "want of communion" between characters and audience. In the *Guardian*, Philip Hope-Wallace likewise noted that Saint-Denis followed the MAT in presenting a play "with far more of a comic thrust and tonic affirmation" than had been usual. "Yet admiring much in ensemble and detail, I felt cheated," Hope-Wallace wrote. "Of what? Of a communion with these people and their unspoken thoughts, of being drawn into their world and living with them."[37]

Saint-Denis's avowed intentions were to strip off the sentiment from the play:

> I wanted, on the one hand, to preserve the impressionistic character
> of the work and, on the other, to bring out its comedy, in accordance
> with Chekhov's expressed wish. To accomplish this, I toned down the
> romantic and charming qualities which tend to cling to the personalities
> of Gayev, of Madame Ranevsky, and of their household, in order to
> emphasize the frivolity, the ineffectualness, and indeed the immorality
> of these representatives of a disappearing society.[38]

While most critics recognized this intention, some actually found the
production too somber; W. A. Darlington (*Telegraph*, 15 December
1961) felt that "M. Saint-Denis hardly lets us laugh at all." Moreover,
despite the director's attempts to tone down their charm, Gayev and
Ranevskaya still dominated the production. This was partly due to the
star power and acting abilities of Gielgud and Ashcroft. Many critics
felt that Saint-Denis's approach to Ranevskaya kept Ashcroft reined
in: "Dame Peggy Ashcroft plays Madame Ranevsky with many charming strokes of comedy, but she seems forbidden to exhibit the warmth
of heart underlying her weakness," the *Times* observed (15 December
1961). "Dame Peggy Ashcroft has to be very careful to make sure
we shall not think too kindly of Madame Ranevsky," wrote Anthony
Cookman in the *Tatler*. "The general impression made is that, like
Gayev, she gets what she deserves and that warmth of heart which is
the lady's saving grace is scarcely felt." Nonetheless, many critics found
her both moving and appealing: 'The part suits her grace and her quick
comedy, and at the end, when the old house is shut up for the last
time, she wrings our hearts with her gentle sorrow."[39] Gielgud likewise
took Saint-Denis's narrowed conception of his character and made
it into a star turn. "Sir John Gielgud makes a brilliantly entertaining
figure of Gayev, but we laugh at, and hardly ever with, the feckless old
man," wrote Cookman. "The old fool deserves to lose his orchard."
Yet Harold Hobson, in the *Sunday Times* (17 December 1961), felt
Gielgud gained some sympathy for his childlike characterization: "He
makes Gayev a far richer character than we have suspected him to be
before ... There are great gifts in this Gayev, withered through the lack

of anything on which to exercise them, and smothered in kindliness and good nature." This essential goodness and essential foolishness were key elements for Gielgud's Gayev, who was most comfortable playing with his nieces. Dorothy Tutin, who played Varya, recalled that "Although he wasn't usually a physical actor, he *was* with us, he looked upon and treated us as children and it was easy to nestle up to him and put your head on his shoulder."[40] Gielgud's affectionate yet comic characterization was acknowledged to be one of his finest performances, and many critics considered it the best thing in the play; Tynan declared it "exactly right, elegant and gravely foolish, in John Gielgud's sympathetic reading" (*Observer*, 17 December 1961).

While Saint-Denis may have wanted to slant the production against the Ranevskys, his casting (as in the original MAT production) tipped the balance the other way. While Gielgud and Ashcroft gained all the attention, the production suffered because of the weak performance of George Murcell as Lopakhin. Tynan found him "sturdily dull," noting that "the dimension of self-torment is absent, and the climactic drunk scene in the third act goes for nothing." According to Jane Baldwin, it became clear early on that Murcell was not right for the part; Saint-Denis even went so far as to assign Gielgud to have private rehearsals with him to try to bring him along.[41] In the end, he made very little impression on the critics, and so the play once again came to be about the dispossessed gentry rather than the changing society that would replace them. However, Ian Holm, as a serious-minded Trofimov, did get more respect than had been traditional in the English theatre. Eric Keown noted (*Punch*, 27 December 1961) that "The key to M. Saint-Denis' production is the emphasis he puts on the prophetic visions of Trofimov . . . the sole realist of the play," played by Holm as a "burning fanatic" suggesting the revolutionaries of 1917. Cookson likewise observed that Holm "compels us to take his prophecies seriously."

The political dimension of the production was made clear in certain moments of stage business. In Act I, Roy Dotrice's ancient Firs, quaking with palsy, got down on the floor to massage Ranevskaya's feet. It was a vivid moment noted by many critics, especially Harold Hobson (*Sunday Times*, 17 December 1961):

> The physical weakness, the shrinkage of the muscles in the Firs of Mr. Dotrice are appalling. That so aged a skeleton should be called on to pour out tea for eupeptic, middle-aged employers is an affront. That he should have to sink to his knees to take off the shoes of Dame Peggy's swift-moving and radiant Madame Ranevsky is nothing less than a crime against humanity . . . It makes one hate Madame Ranevsky; it makes one hate Gayev.

For Hobson, this moment unbalanced the production, raising a laugh of "shocked incredulity against this woman who indulged in the selfish beauty of remembered happiness while she let this feeble old man grovel at her feet." Though Firs got his share of laughs, the Ranevskys' heartless treatment of him ran through the play as a motif, up through his final moments, when he lay "whimpering like a wrinkled old child, alone amid the dust, whining before his last, long sleep."[42]

Saint-Denis's willingness to challenge his audience directly was reflected in the scenic design. Inspired by the open-stage experiments of Tyrone Guthrie, Saint-Denis had a platform built out from the Aldwych proscenium into the audience. "On it were played the most important scenes," Saint-Denis explained, "while impressionistic lighting and the relationships between furniture and objects were achieving their effect in the background."[43] The contrapuntal effect Meyerhold had noted in the party scene, with Ranevskaya suffering in the foreground while the dancing went on behind her, was heightened by Saint-Denis's design choices. The sets, by Abd'elkader Farrah, emphasized the shaky economic position of the Ranevskys. The interiors created an atmosphere of shabbiness and seediness. Perhaps deliberately, they quoted the scenic overabundance of the previous century, so that one critic noted a "Victorian heaviness" in the overstuffed chairs and gloomy curtains (*Variety*, 27 December 1961). The Act II set marked a radical contrast. It consisted mainly of a bare cyclorama, with just a few suggestions of landscape and location, and was dominated by a huge telegraph pole center stage. Jane Baldwin describes it as "a landscape that has already undergone devastation"; it was closer to the world of Beckett, where aimless tramps wait on a barren plain under a single tree, than to the scenic plenitude of Simov and the landscapes of Levitan.[44]

The Cherry Orchard proved to be a very appropriate play for a company that mixed modern with classical in an attempt to keep the British theatre vital. The competing claims of the old and the new life were central to the production concept. In Saint-Denis's direction, the influence of Stanislavsky was still very much felt, but so were the concerns and techniques of the contemporary theatre. One critic noted that Charlotta's line, "Why I exist I have no idea," was the key to the play for an audience of the existential 1960s.[45] The breaking string sound effect was "terrifying, metallic and haunting," according to Edmund Gardner, and one of the company members spoke of it as "having the undertone of an atomic reverberation."[46] While the Ranevskys retained their hold on the audience's emotions, thanks to the performances of Gielgud and Ashcroft, the rest of the production was charged with the anxieties of post-war Europe. For a new generation of performers and theatre-goers, Chekhov's play had taken on meanings that he himself could not have foreseen.

GIORGIO STREHLER, MILAN, 1955 AND 1974

The director who did more than any other to break the MAT's hold on the play and redefine it for the late twentieth century was the Italian Giorgio Strehler. Strehler founded the Piccolo Theatre in Milan in 1947, the first permanent public theatre in Italy, and quickly became one of Europe's most influential directors. Though Strehler is associated especially with the works of Goldoni, Shakespeare, and Brecht, his productions of *The Cherry Orchard*, especially the second, had widespread influence and helped create a "universal" Chekhov. Building on what he had learned from the poetic drama of Shakespeare,

10. Giorgio Strehler's production of *Il Giardino dei Ciliegi* (Piccolo Theatre, Milan, 1974). Act II, with the train passing in the foreground and the veil billowing above. (Piccolo Theatre, photo by Luigi Ciminaghi.)

the Italian *commedia dell'arte*, and the modern experiments of Brecht and Pirandello, Strehler engineered a multi-layered approach to the play that created one of the definitive twentieth-century productions. Strehler declared that *The Cherry Orchard* was not limited by the time and place of its origin, but was, like *The Tempest* or *The Magic Flute*, a final masterpiece that surpassed the ordinary limits of theatre.[47]

In notes he wrote in conjunction with his 1974 production, he described *The Cherry Orchard* in terms of three Chinese boxes, one inside another. The innermost box, which Strehler calls Reality ("*vero*") deals with the narrative itself: the Ranevskys and what happens to them. The second, History ("*storia*"), contains the first, and deals with the characters from a greater distance, as class representatives in a Marxian dialectic of changing social relations. The third and outermost box Strehler calls Life ("*vita*"): "the big box of the human adventure; of man born, growing up, living, loving, not loving, winning, losing, understanding, misunderstanding, passing, and dying."[48] This poetic and universal level contains the other two. Focusing too strictly on any of the three levels distorts the play; too close an emphasis on reality results in an abundance of minute but pointless detail, such as critics found in Stanislavsky's original productions. Too much emphasis on history risks freezing the characters as mere symbols. Though he was an avowed disciple of the German playwright, director, and theorist Bertolt Brecht and his highly politicized "epic theatre," Strehler was conscious of the theatrical danger of a reductive Marxism. Finally, a production that focused too much on the level of life would be in danger of pure abstraction, "merely metaphysical," "outside time"; here Strehler placed the productions of the Czech scenographer Josef Svoboda, which did away with conventional scenery, and their antecedents in the abstract stagings of Pitoëff.[49] Strehler felt that to realize the play fully he needed to approach it on all three levels simultaneously.

Earlier Italian productions of the play had tended to focus on only one of these levels of meaning. When Nemirovich-Danchenko staged the production in Milan in 1933 with Tatiana Palowa, he was mainly concerned to correct Knipper's characterization by making Ranevskaya more comic and frivolous; he also made Trofimov's character more ideologically forceful, giving the whole production a somewhat Marxist slant.[50] Orazio Costa Giovangigli's production in 1946 focused on the level of abstraction, with a set after de Chirico, and with Firs and Charlotta played as symbolist specters, a ghost of the past and a quasi-diabolical medium.[51] Luchino Visconti's production of 1965, by contrast, was heavily realistic, full of cinematic detail, down to "a row of authentic – and therefore all the more fake and unconvincing cherry trees."[52] Strehler's own first production, in 1955, dissatisfied him. It had basically realistic designs by Tanya Moiseiwitsch, with box sets and a large cherry branch indicating the orchard. Strehler's focus was on the "history" level, with the characters as bourgeois representatives of a dying era, and on "the day-to-day lives of individuals tragically trapped in antagonistic social and historical circumstances."[53] The tone was harsh and weary; Strehler himself was exhausted by his work on Goldoni's monumental *Villegiatura* trilogy, one of his most celebrated productions. Though the production was warmly received, Strehler was unhappy with it and felt the need to return to the play in 1974.

In order to grasp the multiple levels of meaning he was striving for, it was important for Strehler to find the right design solution to what he considered the essential problem of the play: the orchard itself. The solution he eventually found was central to an oft-imitated design that set the visual pattern for the play in the second half of the twentieth century as surely as the Stanislavsky/Simov design had in the first. Strehler's overall visual concept came from Chekhov's letter of 5 February 1903 when, before the play was completed, he imagined (as Strehler expresses it) "a white summer garden, all white, totally white, with ladies dressed in white."[54] From this, together with his designer Luciano Damiani, Strehler devised an abstract, almost entirely white design, with a raked bare platform over which was suspended a gauzy and voluminous white veil filled with thousands of paper petals, which swayed and drifted and occasionally fluttered down onto actors and audience like snow, falling blossoms or autumn leaves, depending on the act and season. This part of the setting functioned at Strehler's level of life itself, poetic and abstract. The furniture, limited in scope but carefully chosen, as in Brecht's theatrical practice, to reflect period, place, and social class, provided the history level. The actors were allowed to choose their own costumes from several baskets of white and off-white costumes provided by the designer; thus each actor helped define his or her own character at Strehler's level of reality.

The production centered on Ranevskaya, played by Valentina Cortese, who became Strehler's leading actress in the midst of a distinguished film career (she appeared in both Hollywood and European movies and received an Oscar nomination for Truffaut's *Day for Night*). Cortese was a figure of glamour, pathos, and volatile emotion, "the beacon of Strehler's intent: mercurial, trembling, riffling her hair, incapable of standing still, registering sensations like the needle on an electrocardiograph."[55] She was constantly adjusting her appearance, donning and doffing hats, putting flowers in her hair, taking off her shoes and running around the stage in her stockinged feet. She carried a parasol in Act II that she toyed with incessantly, opening and closing it, inverting it and spinning it on the ground like a roulette wheel, into which she tossed the few coins remaining in her purse. She also threw into it the torn pieces of the telegram from her lover, which seconds later fell out over her head like carnival confetti. This moment exemplified her approach to the character, crying and laughing in quick succession, engaging the audience emotionally but also, in Pia Kleber's words, "displaying Brechtian contradiction in a precise *Gestus*."[56] Cortese identified emotionally with the role:

> She resembles me because she possesses my faults. She throws her money out the window, she is inconsistent, apparently superficial, careless, infinitely feminine, and she doesn't succeed in detaching herself from

her childhood. She resembles me because she is continually between despair and happiness, between frivolity and tears . . . she doesn't want to accept and doesn't want to believe, she always has the illusion that she will arrive somewhere, that a miracle will save her at the last moment.[57]

Despite this sometimes extravagantly emotional approach, Cortese strove for a degree of Brechtian detachment, or at least control, "because if one abandons oneself one can be sure that nothing of what one wants to express will be conveyed to the public."

The influence of Brecht was felt throughout the play in stage business that clearly revealed social relations; at the same time, Strehler was careful not to lose the multiple layers of meaning around which his production was conceived. He emphasized the nursery setting of Act I, with Gayev and Ranevskaya sitting at a miniature table, drinking from a diminutive tea set, and playing with their old toys; but the emphasis on childhood did not serve merely to mock the characters. The hundred-year-old bookcase was an enormous armoire, which Gayev at one point bumped into; it opened, and an array of dusty nursery paraphernalia tumbled out; from behind it came a baby carriage "that rolled across the stage like Grisha's coffin," bringing Ranevskaya to tears.[58] In Act II, the nursery motif returned in the form of a toy train, which passed across the back of the stage at one point (as Stanislavsky had once proposed), then drove directly in front of the characters just after Lopakhin's speech about giants. The characters remained frozen, suspended, for a long, eerie pause as the stage darkened and the train passed with a mournful whistle.

For Strehler, the train supplemented the moment with the breaking string. He described this famous sound effect as "a problem against which all stage directors have banged their heads," a literary trick intended to give extra impact to the end of the play, but unrealizable onstage. Strehler decided to make the breaking string something that the characters hear, but the audience doesn't: "the quavering of history cannot be made symbolic or objective by a sound."[59] Accordingly, the breaking string moment was visual rather than auditory: the veil above the stage suddenly trembled and billowed, while the characters looked about in shocked silence for the source of the disturbance. When the vagrant entered shortly after, he spoke in Russian, adding to the uncanny quality of the scene.

Act II ended in an upbeat manner with Anya and Trofimov. For this act, the up left corner of the stage platform had been hydraulically raised, creating a steep slope up which the young couple rushed, slipping and laughing, to look out at the orchard. Trofimov addressed his speech about how "all Russia is our orchard" directly to the audience with passionate fervor. At the end of the scene, Anya and Trofimov rolled down the hill like children, then made their way through the auditorium to evade Varya, thus bringing the audience into complicity with them; as Pia Kleber notes, "the proxemic and gestural signs of Anya and Trofimov create[d] a constant dialogue with the audience, as if demanding its support to reach their goal."[60] Thus the young couple, important figures in the production's political dimension, posited an optimistic future that would briefly return at the end of the play.

Act III marked a significant contrast in tone, bringing out the play's vaudeville qualities through the native Italian tradition of the *commedia dell'arte*. Pishchik's absurdity was heightened by having him dance with a chair; the moment of his falling asleep and then being unable to find his money was elaborated into a *commedia lazzo*, one of the self-contained comic routines for which Strehler's Goldoni productions were celebrated. Charlotta's performance drew on Italian circus traditions; she wore an oversized frock coat and enormous shoes suggesting a clown's costume. Her performance ended with Pishchik covered with the lap-rug, stumbling about and nearly falling into the audience. Yepikhodov's antics with the broken billiard cue further heightened the *commedia* atmosphere. The hapless clerk was played by Gianfranco Mauri, who played Brighella in Strehler's famous production of Goldoni's *The Servant of Two Masters*. The physical slapstick written into the character gave him opportunities for repeated *lazzi*, so that Yepikhodov came across as a character from Italian comedy: he even played *O Sole Mio* on his guitar in Act II.[61]

Strehler's *commedia* techniques sometimes crossed over into the theatre of the absurd. The primary scenic element of Act III was a large number of chairs, arranged in rows facing up left for Charlotta's performance. As in many Strehler productions, the chairs were carefully chosen to highlight the historical circumstances of the play, following Brecht's epic theatre; in this instance, however, they took on a life of their own suggesting Ionesco's absurdist masterpiece *The Chairs*. Characters bumped into them, danced with them, leapt up on them, rearranged them. During Varya's quarrel with Yepikhodov, she obsessively and frantically arranged the chairs into different patterns, making them a physical expression for her anxiety and frustration. For Strehler, these chairs functioned on all of his levels of meaning:

> Where does the plastic/symbolic/realistic element reside for the characters in this room? In the chairs. These represent the crucial element that gives the action meaning. They speak volumes: they represent the idea of property that has been squandered; an empty chair has a hidden, deeper meaning: it is a pointer to the present and the past. A chair onstage represents the most powerful alienation device – there's far more to it than just sitting down. A lot of empty chairs signifies tension, uncertainty, mystery. Who will sit there? Will anyone, ever? What are these chairs waiting for? and for whom?[62]

The chairs were used for many metaphorical purposes. When Lopakhin was explaining his plan to clear the land in Act I, he pushed a chair like a bulldozer, inadvertently bumping the miniature table and knocking Ranevskaya's tea set to the floor. When he gave his speech of triumph in Act III, he leapt up onto two of the chairs to dominate the stage; as he left the scene, inviting the audience to watch him take an axe to the orchard, he knocked the chairs over menacingly, one by one, as though they were the cherry trees.

The element of metaphysical absurdity was developed further in the final act, which quoted one of Strehler's most famous productions,

Luigi Pirandello's final unfinished play, *The Mountain Giants*. For this act the furniture, including the enormous armoire, was piled at the back of the stage, and the white floorcloth was pulled over it to create a snowy "mountain," an image that for Strehler always evoked the Pirandello play.[63] In Pirandello the mountain giants are unseen figures of power, greed and brutality who serve as a harsh audience for an idealistic troupe of players. The leading actress, Ilse, in some ways a parallel character to Ranevskaya, is finally murdered by the giants; in Strehler's staging the play ended with the heavy metal safety curtain coming down and crushing the actors' cart. The contrast of Ranevskaya's poetic and emotional worldview and the practicality of Lopakhin (whose evocation of "giants" in Act II took on special meaning in this context) corresponded, in Strehler's *Cherry Orchard*, to a similar division in Pirandello. *The Mountain Giants* contrasts "the world of the actors, . . . for whom the poet's words are not merely the highest expression of life, but actually the only certain reality in which and on which one can live, and the world of the people . . . under the rule of the giants, who were bent upon grandiose projects aimed at owning the strength and wealth of the earth."[64] Though Strehler's Lopakhin was associated with Pirandello's giants, he was not a brute; Franco Graziosi was a handsome and elegant figure, passionately in love with Ranevskaya, with a great enthusiasm and appetite for life. Anya and Trofimov, similarly, established some hope for the future in the final scene, waving their hats high in the air as they greeted the new life. But the production's finale echoed the crushing despair of Pirandello's vision. All of the characters, at the same moment, swept dark cloaks and overcoats over their white costumes, "as if angels of death had flung their black wings over the living," and then moved slowly off the stage.[65] There followed a chilling tableau in which Ranevskaya threw out her arms and fell back against Gayev, who "upheld her as if they were facing a firing squad."[66] She was the last to leave the stage, alone, first picking up a handful of earth and clutching it to her bosom. Firs entered to give his final speech with painful slowness, as the axes rang in the orchard. While at the level of history Strehler acknowledged the necessary passing of the Ranevskys' world, at the level of life he mourned the inevitable vanquishing of beauty by time. The falling of the veil, the settling of the paper petals like dead leaves over Firs, the stage and the audience, marked the end of this most rich, complex, and poignant evocation of Chekhov's play.

With the productions of Barrault, Saint-Denis, and Strehler, *The Cherry Orchard* entered a new era. The passing of the Moscow Art Theatre tradition, the advent of theatrical modernism, and the recognition of the play as a European masterpiece all opened the work to a wider range of artistic possibility. The political and artistic ferment of the 1960s and 70s, however, would soon redefine the work once more: not as a universal classic, but as a piece of political theatre thoroughly implicated in the radical struggles of the age.

CHAPTER 6

RADICAL REVISIONS, 1975–1977

By the early 1960s, Chekhov's new status as a classic made his works susceptible to one of the most frequent forms of avant-garde production. Aggressively remaking classics to comment on contemporary issues became an important form of theatrical innovation in the 1960s and 70s. This approach was very popular in the Soviet bloc, where it allowed directors to evade official censorship, but also in Western Europe and the USA. Russian directors used the works of Chekhov alongside those of Shakespeare, Molière, and the Greeks to address issues of life in a totalitarian state. In Britain, the Royal Shakespeare Company regularly created politically inflected, "relevant" productions like Peter Brook's *King Lear* and Peter Hall's *Wars of the Roses*. In the USA, Joseph Papp's New York Shakespeare Festival staged populist, aggressively contemporary Shakespeare in Central Park, notably a Vietnam-era anti-establishment *Hamlet* and a hippie musical version of *The Two Gentlemen of Verona*. Chekhov's canonical status as a classic of world drama, together with *The Cherry Orchard*'s potent mixture of class conflict and historical change, led to several confrontational productions that foregrounded the play's political dimensions while remaking it in a contemporary theatrical vernacular.

ANATOLY EFROS, MOSCOW, 1975

In the Soviet Union, the production of *The Cherry Orchard* that used this approach most visibly was that of Anatoly Efros at the Taganka Theatre in 1975. The political background of the production, the theatre, and the director are worth detailing. Soviet life changed dramatically after the death of Stalin in 1953. Party Secretary and future Soviet premier Nikita Krushchev denounced Stalin's crimes at the 20th Party Congress in 1956, ushering in the period known as the Thaw. In the theatre, the Thaw was a period of freedom and experimentation in which a new generation of writers and directors rejected the false optimism and moribund stagecraft of Socialist Realism. The vibrant theatre led by new directors like Efros, Yuri Lyubimov, and Oleg Yefremov flourished for a few years, but by the mid-sixties again found itself in changing times. The crushing of the "Prague Spring" by Soviet tanks dispelled the hopes for "communism with a human face," and the period of stagnation under Leonid Brezhnev brought social and political malaise. With the economy deteriorating, the government mired in an inefficient bureaucracy presided over by geriatric Party leaders, and a reversal of many new freedoms, the Russian theatre began to develop subtle strategies of defiance. While the theatre continued to incorporate elements of popular culture and anti-realistic staging techniques, it often turned to the classics as a means of avoiding censorship. The Taganka Theatre, under Lyubimov, gained a following for Brechtian revisions of classics with an aggressively anti-authoritarian edge. Lyubimov's 1971 *Hamlet*, for instance, featured radical poet and singer Vladimir Vysotsky as a counterculture hero in black sweater and jeans.

Since Chekhov had been enshrined as a Russian classic by the Moscow Art Theatre, his plays became vehicles through which radical directors could express their frustrations with the limits of Soviet life. Anatoly Efros, though not as topically political a director as Lyubimov, nonetheless used Chekhov and other classic writers to explore themes that were closed off to the contemporary theatre. "He confronted the spiritual experience captured by Chekhov, Shakespeare, Dostoevsky and Molière, with the experience of Soviet life – his personal experience," according to Anatoly Smeliansky.[1] His 1966 *Seagull* focused on the role of the artist in an oppressive society, with Treplev martyred through his desire for "new forms." At a stroke, Efros overturned the tradition of earnest naturalism and sober piety that had dominated

Chekhov performance in Russia since the early Moscow Art Theatre, replacing it with a frenzied, young, and angry Chekhov.[2] Efros' *Three Sisters* of 1967 was equally radical, a corrosive jeering against the stasis of Soviet life. The stage was dominated by a tree with metal leaves, the sisters were driven by sexual neuroses, the bowler-hatted Baron went to his death like a tragic version of Chaplin's tramp, and the nihilistic spirit of the drunken doctor Chebutykin presided over the play. "The production was compellingly expressive of painful foreboding, of anguish, young hopes and bitter disappointments," according to Tatiana Shakh-Azizova.[3] Efros so thoroughly derided the hopeful speeches of Vershinin and Tuzenbach, about the glorious future when everyone will work, that in the end the authorities banned the production.[4]

Efros' *Cherry Orchard*, at the Taganka in 1975, was the most radical production of this play in a Soviet theatre since before the days of Socialist Realism. Stanislavsky's Moscow Art Theatre production had survived into the 1950s, to be replaced with one by Victor Stanitsyn that was essentially the same. Stanitsyn said during rehearsals that "There is no need for a re-staging of the Chekhov plays. The present production is still in an unbroken tradition of original business and interpretations."[5] Stanitsyn's production was touched up here and there with added Soviet optimism, but retained much of Stanislavsky's original, including some members of his company. Alla Tarasova, once a buoyant Anya, was now a leaden Ranevskaya and was evidently the dullest feature of the production. A more innovative approach to the play came a few years later, in Maria Knebel's staging for the Soviet Army Theatre. Knebel and her designer, Yury Pimenov, broke with tradition by not physically representing the cherry orchard itself; instead they used projections to create a montage of Chekhovian associations along with suggestive locales for each act. Nevertheless, her approach to the play more or less accepted the optimistic socialist party line. While she wanted to avoid the tired historical realism of the MAT and remake the play for a contemporary audience, her declared approach was basically positive: "Each of us has lost and will lose our own 'cherry orchard.' Each of us is trying to hold on to it. The moment when you lose 'the cherry orchard' you think you lose everything. But ahead lies life, a thousand times richer than any loss."[6] Knebel's Ranevskaya, Lyubov Dobrzhanskaya, "evoked admiration rather than pity" for her courage in accepting loss and facing the future.[7] Knebel's sympathy and hope extended to all of the characters in the play. Andrey Popov's gentle Yepikhodov, for instance, took a moment to comfort Dunyasha in Act III, even after she had rejected him. According to Emma Polotskaya, he knelt next to her and patted her hands "with the soft graceful gesture of a cat. He was talking to her as if she were a child, and all of a sudden in this ridiculous looking character one could see a beautiful soul."[8] Knebel's universal sympathy for her characters helped the production transcend the crude categories of Socialist Realism: according to Tatiana Shakh-Azizova, "the characters aroused interest not because of their social status, or class as merchants or aristocrats, but by their human characteristics; they were quite simply fascinating people."[9]

Efros' production was much more extreme in rejecting the MAT tradition. He had been invited to direct at the Taganka by his friend and rival Lyubimov; the production was an occasion of tension between the two men, and an ominous foreshadowing of the theatrical crisis of 1984, when the Soviet authorities cashiered Lyubimov and put Efros in charge of the Taganka. For *The Cherry Orchard*, Efros worked with Lyubimov's leading actors and adopted something of his Brechtian style. In an essay on directing Chekhov, Efros identified two possible approaches, calm and aggressive. While in later years he favored the calm style, *The Cherry Orchard* was directed aggressively, "not as a museum piece, or an anthology piece, but so as to knock the corners off it and shove your face in it. Aggressively means to splatter it with your own up-to-date feelings."[10] Accordingly, Efros made the play a bleak, even grotesque parable about refusing to face brutal realities. While the production did not have a single, clearly defined political message, it was openly confrontational on many fronts, challenging both the malaise of stagnating Soviet life and the

moribund MAT vision of Chekhov. "Everything about this production seems to be aimed at a sacred cow," Spencer Golub observed,
defining it as "exceptionally cruel" and "single-mindedly bleak."[11]
The play opened and closed with a dirge-like rendition, sung by the
entire cast, of Yepikhodov's ballad, "What should I care for life's clam-
our, / What for my friend or my foe?" This musical motif recurred
throughout the play; Yepikhodov crooned the song into the barrel of
his revolver as though it were a microphone. The set was dominated
by a large central mound covered with gravestones; one observer wryly
commented that "The Moscow Art Theatre lies buried there."[12]

This set, by Bolshoi designer Valery Levental, was one of the production's most distinctive features. Along with the graves, the central
mound contained pieces of furniture and cherry trees; on the back
wall hung faded family portraits; white curtains blew at the sides of the
stage; and a single cherry branch hung out over the audience. It was
an image of nostalgia and decay. The central grave-mound encouraged circular patterns of movement that one commentator described
as "a carousel of lost souls"; uprooted from their past and unable to
face the future, the characters lurched and skittered around the stage
in a desperate flight.[13] Efros, in rehearsals, compared them to the
grotesque clowns of Fellini, or to children playing in the middle of a
minefield.[14] Yet his sympathies were with them, and he viewed the
loss of the orchard as catastrophic.[15]

The style of the production was variously described by Efros as
grotesque tragedy and psychological farce. He mixed the approaches
of Stanislavsky on the one hand and Brecht and Meyerhold on the
other, encouraging his actors to combine moments of deep immer-
sion in their roles with moments of sharp separation.[16] The actors
moved in precise, sometimes mechanical ways, sometimes restrained
and stylized, sometimes exaggeratedly emotional, by turns ridiculous and pathetic. However, Efros treated most of the dramatis personae as background figures to the two characters who dominated
the production: Alla Demidova's Ranevskaya and Vladimir Vysotsky's
Lopakhin.

Demidova, a leading actress at the Taganka who had played Gertrude in Lyubimov's *Hamlet*, developed a dynamic, volatile, and highly-strung performance of Ranevskaya that provided the emotional core of the production. From the first moments of the play, she separated herself from the traditional Russian characterization of Ranevskaya as "a grande dame exuding old world charm and given to melodramatic handkerchief clenches."[17] Demidova ran onto the stage as lightly and happily as Anya, so that it took a moment for the audience even to identify her character.[18] Vital, sensual, possessed of a feverish intensity, Demidova came across as a contemporary woman of fashion "who stalks about the stage with the grace and beauty of a thoroughbred," according to Spencer Golub: "Slouching one moment, a cigarette dangling carelessly from her hand, she is seized in the next by a blast of neurotic energy that leaves her breathless."[19] Efros and Demidova found the expression of Ranevskaya's suffering "not in [her] traditional sighs and tears, but in her perpetual motion."[20]

In the first act, Demidova was a kind of emotional tuning fork for the other characters; their varied attitudes to the family's predicament were revealed largely through her receptive response to them, according to Maria Szewcow: "Varya's insecurity, Anya's wide-eyed delight at surroundings that have become unfamiliar, Gayev's fondness or peevishness, Yepikhodov's nonchalance, and Charlotta's whimsy are caught and temporarily transformed by how she receives, connects, and bounces back whichever cue she is given."[21] Demidova's approach to the character was particularly evident in her various encounters with Lopakhin, which were central to the production. Vysotsky, for most of the play, was restrained, practical, and gentlemanly, far from stereotypical images of the vulgar peasant or aggressive businessman. He was also quite far from Vysotsky's own image as the rebellious poet-singer. A trace of the gritty defiance and counterculture sex appeal that marked his Hamlet remained in his gravelly voice and shoulder-length hair, but for the most part he was a slight, dignified figure in a neat white suit, calmly and patiently explaining to Ranevskaya the danger to her estate. In these scenes her personal resources were taxed to the fullest:

> nowhere else does she make so great an effort to counteract reason with playfulness, love, exaltation – with anything else but sense. She laughs, grimaces, slips momentarily into silence only to jerk back into her own flow or interrupt somebody else's. She jokes or flirts with Lopakhin, feigns indignation, stops short suddenly, and just as suddenly launches back into signals that appear to say the opposite of what they mean. The meaning is, in fact, clear: Demidova's effervescence spells out distress. Chekhov's last stage direction is more than an epilogue: Demidova *is* that tight string, which breaks only after Lyubov Andreyevna walks off the stage in Act IV.[22]

The crucial confrontation between the two characters, at the end of Act III, was the most celebrated moment of Efros' production. Demidova compared the act to waiting for the results of a surgical operation: "Here the discrepancy between the situation and the behavior of the characters reaches its peak: they want to cover the deadly fear with music, dancing and magic tricks. Finally they learn the result of the surgery – death."[23] When Lopakhin arrived, the previously dignified Vysotsky appeared dangerously drunk; when he spoke of how long they had had to wait for the train, he tapped the side of his throat with the back of his hand to indicate, in the gestural language of the Soviet worker, how much he had consumed during the wait.[24] Ranevskaya's nerves were strained to the breaking point when the news of the sale arrived. When she asked "Who bought it?", Demidova smiled, as though asking about something trivial; Anatoly Smeliansky found this "sheepish smile before being slaughtered . . . the most moving 'Efrosian' moment in the play."[25] In the speech that followed, Vysotsky's Lopakhin exploded with triumph and resentment fuelled by his thwarted love for Ranevskaya. Demidova recalled that Vysotsky played the speech as though it were one of his tragic songs, stretching his words and then snapping them off abruptly, dancing, singing, climbing on chairs, leaping up to try to reach the cherry branch suspended over the audience. In a hysterical high-stepping victory dance, Lopakhin repeatedly fell to the ground, only to leap up again until totally spent.[26] Demidova's reaction was equally violent; rather than crying quietly, as Chekhov specifies, Ranevskaya emitted short, terrifying shouts, bending over as though wounded in the belly. Lopakhin's triumph was also a defeat, a recognition of loss and failure, expressed through "uncontrolled fury for himself and his destiny," which, according to Shakh-Azizova "conveyed the tension of a Shakespearean tragedy."[27] In the end, he had to be helped from the stage, while Ranevskaya continued to wail and Anya helplessly spoke of a new and beautiful life. Vysotsky's "bacchanalia of loutish freedom," as Smeliansky characterized it, became the central image of the production, and a "metaphor for Russia's future."[28]

Other Eastern bloc directors in this period expressed a similarly disillusioned and caustic view of the play. The Czech director Otomar Krejca, after having his previous Chekhov productions banned in Prague, directed *The Cherry Orchard* at the Düsseldorfer Schauspielhaus in 1976. All of Krejca's productions rejected both the sentimental elegiac interpretation and the optimistic socialist one, favoring instead a cruel and sardonic Chekhov played in non-realistic, metaphorical settings (many of them designed by master Czech scenographer Josef Svoboda). Krejca's approach to Chekhov was "more violent than anything since Vakhtangov," according to Laurence Senelick: "Instead of muted pastels, hysteria; instead of elegance, vulgarity and aggression; instead of sadness, desperation."[29] Krejca found in Chekhov's plays a dangerous volatility: "Outwardly, nothing happens – and suddenly there is a violent explosion," he wrote, "as if each element might explode if it were touched in a certain way – that's how unstable, how easily combustible Chekhov's milieu is. We are alarmed by it – we weren't prepared for it."[30]

In Düsseldorf the scenery was devised by Krejca himself together with Theodor Richter-Forgach. A huge stage, over 100 feet deep, was surmounted by a white veil, on the order of Strehler's but designed in deliberately bad taste, suggesting the frilly drapery of operetta. The stage was cluttered by ugly furniture, sofas, and beds, from which the characters rarely had the will to rise. For Act II, the veil covered the furniture, suggesting a landscape of whited sepulchers that recalled Efros' burial mound. In the final act the furniture was all pushed into a heap over which Firs clambered like a wretched insect.

As he had in other productions, Krejca took liberties with the text, intercutting thematically related bits of dialogue throughout the play. In Act II, the duet of Anya and Trofimov, rather than providing a romantic or revolutionary coda, was ironically juxtaposed with the Ranevskaya/Lopakhin/Gayev conversation about the fate of the orchard. Krejca often linked the sexual and the political in *The Cherry Orchard*. Ranevskaya (Ingeborg Engelmann) negotiated her relationships with men through sex and class: she allowed Yasha to massage her thighs, sensually embraced Trofimov, and repeatedly tempted Lopakhin. Their barely sublimated relationship led to an Act II kiss, from which both quickly recoiled in alarm. Like Vakhtangov, Krejca explored what Senelick calls the "comic grotesquerie of the Chekhovian world: his guests danced with chairs on their heads, Epikhodov climbed the bookcase to escape muscular Varya, a diminutive Gayev sat on an ashtray."[31] Krejca's grotesque vision of *The Cherry Orchard*, together with Efros' despairing one, was part of a radical reappraisal of the play that began in the disenchanted Soviet bloc and quickly made its way to the theatres of the West. A chief agent of that move westward was the young Romanian director Andrei Serban, whose *Cherry Orchard*, performed in New York in 1977 and subsequently around the world, gave the play a boisterous contemporary tone and a stunning new look.

ANDREI SERBAN, NEW YORK, 1977

Serban's *Cherry Orchard* challenged and invigorated the unadventurous tradition of American Chekhov. Following the genteel and civilized productions of Eva Le Gallienne, there developed a perception in the American theatre that Chekhov was polite, worthy, but rather boring; the sort of thing the British generally did better. The only major challenge to this view before Serban was at the Williamstown Theatre Festival in Massachusetts under Nikos Psacharopoulos. At Williamstown there were twelve Chekhov productions between 1963 and 1980, including three of *The Cherry Orchard*, all directed by Psacharopoulos. The Greek-born director developed a passionate, wide-open style of Chekhov playing. Psacharopoulos, contrary to Method traditions, had his actors play as if there were no subtext: "what they say is exactly what they mean and this is a direct expression of the passionate feelings that the characters have."[32] Correspondingly, though the productions were conventional in appearance, they were passionate in the extreme, with characters continually leaping up on chairs and benches or throwing themselves to the floor. In *The Cherry Orchard*, Psacharopoulos conceived of Ranevskaya as a character who was "hurling herself at life," rather than as an ineffectual idler: "she wants the orchard but she wants Paris and she wants them both absolutely passionately."[33] Olympia Dukakis, in 1969, embraced this vision of the character – "Lyuba's name means 'love'! That's it! The woman is that" – whereas Colleen Dewhurst later tried to play a more reserved "Chekhovian" heroine, and the production foundered as a result.[34] Generally, however, the Williamstown productions were full of vitality, and favorites with the summer audiences. They expressed a Chekhov that was not historically situated, but universally human; a Chekhov of raw emotions suited to vigorous American acting, intelligible not in terms of the social and historical conditions of the characters, but their hearts and guts and sex drives. Williamstown Chekhov productions invariably foregrounded the sexuality of the characters; Austin Pendleton, who twice played Trofimov for Psacharopoulos, observed that "Everyone was the romantic lead" in Williamstown productions of Chekhov: "Everyone's passion was utterly acknowledged."[35]

A different kind of Chekhov emerged when this type of full-hearted and energetic American acting met the experimental and eclectic approach of an East European director, Andrei Serban. Serban, born in Romania in 1943 but working in New York by 1970, made a name for himself by directing highly ritualized, controversial productions of classic plays. *Time* magazine, declaring that "Revisionist drama has become the bane of the theater," attacked Serban and his mentor Peter Brook for believing that "the text is simply a mask that must be ripped off to reveal the unconscious, irrational blood flow of the play" (T. E. Kalem, *Time*, 30 May 1977). Serban's primal-scream-laden productions of Greek tragedies at La Mama in the early seventies earned him the chance to direct *The Cherry Orchard* for Joseph Papp's New York Shakespeare Festival at the Vivian Beaumont Theatre in Lincoln Center in 1977. The production provoked intense critical debate, but was a great public success, and redefined *The Cherry Orchard* for American audiences for decades. Serban went on to remount the production in Japan, Bucharest, and Moscow, making a significant mark on its international interpretation.

Serban's approach to the play was influenced in part by his experiences working with Peter Brook, but also by the production of another Romanian director, Lucian Pintilie. Pintilie's *Cherry Orchard* played in 1965 in Bucharest while Serban was a young directing student there. Pintilie found the play "a very strange, special, magical comedy" about "our unconsciousness and all its consequences."[36] Making an explicit connection between Chekhov and Beckett, he imagined Ranevskaya as like Winnie in *Happy Days*, "engulfed in sand, smiling, her eyes aglow with morphine, as we hear the music of the spheres." Pintilie treated all the play's characters as lost in delusions, living only in the past or future; he rejected Trofimov's vision as fanaticism. But perhaps the aspect of Pintilie's production that most influenced Serban was his approach to the setting, "breaking away from the walls and windows of naturalism and flooding the open space with light."[37] Inspired by this non-illusionistic approach, Serban and his designer Santo Loquasto created an image for the play that, while related to Strehler's, has perhaps exceeded even its influence worldwide.

Serban's *Cherry Orchard* took place in an all-white world, as Strehler's had done. Loquasto took advantage of the great size and

11. Santo Loquasto's design for Andrei Serban's 1977 Lincoln Center production, New York City, with Irene Worth as Ranevskaya and Michael Cristofer as Trofimov. (New York Public

depth of the Vivian Beaumont stage to create a vast indoor–outdoor space, with furniture in the foreground and cherry trees in back, all silhouetted in front of a luminous white cyclorama. Jennifer Tipton, one of the leading lighting designers in the USA, contributed a highly expressive and stylized design that transformed the look of the space from scene to scene. "Suddenly, *The Cherry Orchard* becomes a big play and a dreamy one," wrote Martin Gottfried. "The enormous height and depth of the Beaumont stage breathe with presence" (*New York Post*, 26 February 1977). For the party in Act III, Serban added a gazebo through which the dancers whirled, occasionally freezing while the actors downstage broke through the fourth wall to address lines directly to the audience. Serban used the depth of the space to add non-textual moments of action that commented on the play. At the beginning of Act II, a group of workmen dragged a heavy plow along the back of the stage "like a lost prop out of *Mother Courage*"; at the end of the act, an industrial landscape glowed on the backdrop as the sun set.[38] These bold visual metaphors caught the attention of many critics, though they did not add up to a consistent political interpretation. While Trofimov's speeches were played straight, apparently endorsed by the production, the central presence of *grande dame* Irene Worth as Ranevskaya demanded audience sympathy and precluded a socialist reading of the play. It seemed that the production was trying not so much to advance a particular thesis with the play, but to express its theatrical values through a range of bold and not necessarily cohesive strategies.

The most striking of these strategies was comedy, or more specifically farce. Serban's production went farther than any previous major production in the West in subjecting the characters to slapstick indignities and exuberant pratfalls. In this regard, the standout performance was a star-making turn by the young Meryl Streep as Dunyasha. She mugged, wailed, giggled, and took every gesture to exaggerated extremes; when complaining of her nerves, she fell on the floor in a dead faint. Her attempted seduction of Yasha was a vaudeville *tour de force* that incurred the ire of many traditionalist critics:

To our dismay, we see Dunyasha, the amorous, "sensitive" maid, somersaulting voluptuously over the valet she is in pursuit of, doing a partial striptease, tripping over her discarded undergarments, and finally tackling the valet and hurling him full on the ground as if they were on a football field and it were fourth down and goal to go. That, shall we say, is not Chekhov.[39]

Some of the slapstick had interpretive implications that went beyond mere comedy. Jack Kroll considered that the way Streep "ape[d] the manners of her superiors with extravagant flutterings and faintings" suggested she was enacting "her own little behavioral revolution, prefiguring other revolutions."[40] Looked at in this light, even Yasha's caddish desertion of Dunyasha took on a political significance. As Martin Gottfried observed, Ben Masters' Yasha was no longer prepared to settle for a maid/valet marriage: "Dunyasha is crushed when he walks out on her, but he is more interested in what he is walking into: a future with other possibilities."[41] While Serban's use of abrasive comedy provided occasional insights, it also created emotional alienation. Even critics who liked the production acknowledged that this was one of the least moving *Cherry Orchards* they could remember. One critic, exhausted by the amplified farcical business, spoke of the "tragic relief" provided by Worth's Ranevskaya.[42]

Irene Worth was a leading classical actress who had established herself at the Stratford Festival in Canada and developed a reputation for austerely regal lead roles. Some felt she was not ideally cast: "Madame Ranevskaya is sensual, weak-willed and vague; Miss Worth is intelligent, forceful and queenly."[43] Worth's Ranevskaya had some moments of vulnerability. After she saw Trofimov in Act I, she mimed reaching her hand into the river, as though trying to touch her drowned son. Likewise, her response to her lover's telegram was a protracted, anguished moment noted by many critics: "she tears a telegram slowly, painfully in two, pulling apart each inch of paper as if it were her heart she were tearing."[44] Before her last exit, she darted several times about the stage, as though unable to leave the room of her childhood: Jack Kroll felt that "her final, panting run around the nursery as she leaves the house forever has the forlorn desperation of a queen bee in her last majestic throes" (*Newsweek*, 28 February 1977). Michael Feingold (*Village Voice*, 14 March 1977) also found this a "bold and astonishing" moment suggesting "that some spirit in the play, in the character, has at last been set free." On the other hand, some audiences found the repeated movement confusing or even comical, so that its pathos was broken by laughter.[45] In general, however, Worth's dominant presence helped anchor the production, and received praise even from those critics who decried Serban's directorial excesses.

Lopakhin, played by Raul Julia, was young, vigorous, and aggressive. He was openly in love with Ranevskaya, so that the non-proposal to Varya was neither surprising nor particularly moving. His most striking moment came after his triumphal speech in Act III, when, instead of merely bumping a table and nearly knocking over a candelabrum, as Chekhov suggests, he began to trash the place like a drunken rock star. Julius Novick found this a moment of great power: "Madame Ranevskaya lies full-length on the floor in her black beaded ball-gown, weeping, while behind her Lopakhin rampages drunkenly around the little circular pavilion where the ball has been taking place, yelling that he is now master, throwing chairs around and shouting that he can pay for them. Stunning." Many other critics, however, felt that Julia's "violent, vulgar" Lopakhin was too much on one note, "a maniacal, melodramatic villain."[46]

On the large Beaumont stage, subtlety of characterization was difficult and the production often relied on large visual gestures to achieve its effects. The past of the family was made palpable, not only through the Strehlerian toy train and rocking horse of the Act I nursery, but by the visible presence of ghosts in the orchard: Ranevskaya's mother and the boy Grisha. At the end of Act III, the ballroom pavilion receded into the darkness, the candles being put out one by one as Ranevskaya came to terms with the loss of her home. The play ended with a striking piece of symbolic action. As Firs completed his final speech, the silhouette of an industrial city that had appeared in Act II again loured upon the cyclorama, but this grim image was offset by a little girl who walked hesitantly downstage carrying a flowering cherry branch and knelt by the dying Firs. This action puzzled some critics and annoyed others, but most agreed that it was a moment of strange beauty; not Chekhov's ending but nonetheless one that captured the play's poignant mixture of sorrow and hope.

When Serban restaged the play in Romania in 1992, he took a more cynical view of the Soviet future. Whereas at Lincoln Center Michael Cristofer had played Trofimov with earnest intensity, Serban's Romanian Trofimov, Klaudiu Bleonc, mocked the character. He played him as a parody of an ideologue, a lisping, fist-waving fanatic who suggested the late Romanian dictator Ceausescu. In this context, the farcical elements that had puzzled New York critics had a clear political force. According to Laurence Senelick, "In the wake of political events in Romania, the pratfalls, belly laughs and breakneck speed took on a new meaning, as if this Chekhov were burning to ashes in a wild Moldavian dance of despair."[47] After the collapse of communism, those elements of the play, and of Serban's production, that held out hope for a new life were subjected to withering scorn. In the years preceding that collapse, however, some Western productions, particularly in Britain, chose to take the socialist view of the play very seriously indeed.

TREVOR GRIFFITHS AND RICHARD EYRE, NOTTINGHAM, 1977

In Britain in the 1960s and 70s, *The Cherry Orchard* was presented as politically radical. The freedoms of the 1960s, and the crisis years of the decade that followed, pushed many theatre artists toward aggressive experimentation, outright declarations of war on the establishment, and calls for socialist revolution. *The Cherry Orchard* was pressed into service in this fight in a radical new adaptation by the socialist playwright Trevor Griffiths. Griffiths, the author of *Comedians*, one of the leading left-wing plays of the 1970s, conceived of *The Cherry Orchard* as a play that dealt, not with the "subjective pain" of the Ranevskys' dispossession, but with its "objective necessity."[48]

The way for Griffiths' radical version of the play was paved by a production by Lindsay Anderson at Chichester in 1966. Anderson, a leftist Royal Court director and filmmaker, gave a harshly socialist reading that resonated strongly in the midst of an economic crisis. While Prime Minister Harold Macmillan struggled with debt and deflation, the problems of the Ranevskys looked to be very much their own fault, as Harold Hobson observed:

> It might easily be argued that this is, for the first time in England, the sort of production that Chekhov desired for his plays. [Anderson] sees Madame Ranevksy, not through a mist of water, but in the harsh clear light of understanding . . . There is no sympathy here for the sad twilight of a gentle and cultured ruling class; all is hard and relentless.[49]

Celia Johnson played Ranevskaya as giggly and shallow; she later gave a more dignified version of the character in a BBC-TV version directed by Cedric Messina in 1971. Ray McAnally was an aggressive Irish Lopakhin. The standout performance was Tom Courtenay's Trofimov, a more sympathetic but equally implacable version of the bloodthirsty revolutionary he had played a year before in the film *Doctor Zhivago*.

The radical tendencies of the Chichester *Orchard* bloomed again a decade later in Richard Eyre's production, at Nottingham, of Griffiths' Marxist version. Eyre commissioned Griffiths based on the playwright's ability to give voice to conflicting ideological positions.

> [*The Cherry Orchard*] presents an entire spectrum of society, in which every social gradation, every class interest, is represented . . . I felt that Trevor's methodology as a writer made him the ideal choice as translator; in *Comedians*, for example, he attempts a similar spectrum of positions. The brief, then, was not to politicize the play, but to strip away the varnish; to enable us to see the picture more clearly.[50]

Nonetheless, when Griffiths tackled the play, he had an ideological purpose. He felt that fifty years of translation and production had made British Chekhov thoroughly conservative, and he set out to redress what he saw as a prevailing distortion:

> For half a century now, in England as elsewhere, Chekhov has been the almost exclusive property of theatrical class sectaries for whom the plays have been plangent and sorrowing evocations of an "ordered" past no longer with "us", its passing greatly to be mourned. For theatregoers . . . Chekhov's tough, bright-eyed complexity was dulced into swallowable sacs of sentimental morality . . . Translation followed translation, that idiom became "our" idiom, that class "our" class, until the play's specific historicity and precise sociological imagination had been bleached of all meanings beyond those required to convey the necessary "natural" sense that the fine will always be undermined by the crude and that the "human condition" can for all essential purposes be equated with "the plight of the middle classes".[51]

Griffiths' adaptation of the play, which was billed as "a new English version," was based on a literal translation by Helen Rappoport; Griffiths did not himself read Russian. In defending his text, Griffiths pointed out that he cut only a few lines and added only fifty words to a 21,000-word play.[52] The main political force of his version came in slight changes of emphasis and in the kind of language he chose to give his characters. He diminished the centrality and emotional impact of Ranevskaya while increasing the importance of Trofimov and Lopakhin. He also altered the register of many characters' speech in order to change their effect on the audience.

The language of Trofimov provides the clearest examples. Noting Chekhov's concern over how to express Trofimov's political activities, Griffith made the line about being a perpetual student into "I'm still a student. If the authorities have their way, I suspect I'll always be one."[53] His speeches complaining of the conditions of the workers, which Chekhov had to censor, were given vivid expression by

Griffiths. Where Chekhov had the workers eat disgusting food and sleep without pillows in stench and dampness, Griffiths had them "eat scraps of rancid meat and sleep on bare boards" amid "shit" and "leaking roofs."[54] Where Chekhov spoke of the need to "work" (*rabotat*), Griffiths used "struggle," deliberately invoking the language of Lenin. As Griffiths explained, by 1902 Lenin's *What is to Be Done?* would have been circulating in Russia: "A new language was in the air: a new way of perceiving and accounting for the conditions of social reality and the possibilities of change ... It seemed to me improper not to give Trofimov a *hint*, at least, of a different kind of language from the traditional nineteenth-century bourgeois-liberal language that student intellectuals would have deployed" – and that Chekhov's Trofimov, in fact, did deploy.[55] In his Act II monologue, Griffiths' Trofimov was clearly talking in political and not philosophical terms about humanity's advances. Chekhov's Trofimov says merely that humanity is moving forward, perfecting its powers, and that the things that are beyond it now will one day fall within reach, but that it is necessary to work to help those who are seeking the truth. In Griffiths' version, the speech was plainly a political statement: "Man *can* make progress, struggle for perfection. There *is* a discernible future in which we'll find solutions to the problems that confront us now; but we'll only achieve it through unremitting struggle, by working with all our strength to help those who are even now seeking the answers."

Griffiths went even further in Trofimov's speech to Anya at the end of the act, turning an image of spectral haunting into one of appalling violence. In Chekhov's text, Trofimov asks Anya whether she sees the human beings looking out at her from every leaf and trunk of the orchard, whether she can hear their voices. In Griffiths' version, the image was much more brutal: "from every tree in the orchard there are people hanging, they peer at you through the branches, you can hear their voices moaning in the leaves."[56] This image, with its suggestion of lynchings and pogroms, made Trofimov's line even more accusatory and confrontational than it is in Chekhov's text.

Griffiths' linguistic choices were part of a conscious overall pattern of foregrounding Trofimov and Lopakhin at the expense of Ranevskaya:

> Ranevsky is usually seen as the centre of the action; the other characters revolve around her . . . As I read the play, however, it seemed to me that its structure had in the past been misrepresented. Trofimov and Lopakhin represent two possibilities for the future: bourgeoisification and commoditization, or revolutionary change. These are the only futures available to these people. The ground of the present is like a building, and the pillars of the building are Trofimov and Lopakhin. Together, they form an arch over the other characters.[57]

Ranevskaya was diminished in part, in Griffiths' text, by reducing the emotional scope of the character. He explained that his goal was "to tighten the language, to negotiate the shifts of feeling – to make the emotional life of the character *coherent*, rather than beyond the range of the English sensibility."[58] Nonetheless, many of the textual changes make the character less expressive, and arguably less sympathetic. Ranevskaya's initial response to Trofimov, and the memories of Grisha he brings with him, is contained. Griffiths' added stage directions specify that she speaks "in a very plain, normal voice," when she mentions Grisha, and that she is "controlled, steady," as she greets Trofimov.[59] Her apostrophe to the orchard is similarly denatured. And at the end, where Ranevskaya and Gayev say farewell to their house – a passage of extravagant emotion in the Knipper/Stanislavsky version – the brother and sister stand silently holding hands, without the embrace, the sobbing, or even the lines Chekhov specifies. Ranevskaya does not speak her farewell to her life, youth, and happiness, she does not look for a last time at the walls and windows or recall her mother walking down the room. As David Allen has noted, Ranevskaya's silence is filled by the optimistic voices of Anya and Trofimov: theirs is the dominant note in the ending.[60] While Griffiths has denied specifically trying to undermine the emotion in the Ranevskys' departure, there is no doubt that the tone of his ending is very different from that of most productions of the play.

Richard Eyre's staging of Griffiths' text at Nottingham in 1977 emphasized the revisionist tendencies of the translation. Mick Ford, a charismatic actor with a line in proletarian heroes, dominated the play as Trofimov. "Almost at the centre of this production, we have a superb student," reported Michael Coveney in the *Financial Times* (14 March 1977). "He says unpopular things, loudly and passionately. At the end of Act II, he stands on a bench, almost mocking his own powers of oratory, as he indoctrinates Anya with his strident optimism. Mick Ford's performance is superb; and its internal effect on the production is underlined by Lynsey Baxter's clever transformation from lisping child to sensible, severe young woman." Irving Wardle noted that Griffiths' version had clarified the characters' individual economic stakes in the estate:

> All attention is focused on anatomizing the characters' desires and their class inheritance. You see the pattern at its clearest in the ambiguous duel between Dave Hill's Lopakhin and Bridget Turner's Madame Ranevsky. "This," she snaps, "is *my* cherry orchard." And she can instantly subdue him to an awkward hand-flapping inferior. But towards Ranevsky's class he is a formidable, snarling antagonist.[61]

Master–servant relationships were highlighted throughout the production, in which Annie Hayes' Varya, for instance, was more than usually abusive with the domestic staff. The rest of the family were similarly snobbish: Anya spoke disdainfully of Charlotta, Yasha, and the "French people" in her mother's Paris flat, and Gayev, rather than being dependent on Firs, was curt and rude to the old man, snapping at him to "Shut up!" However, as Irving Wardle noted, "Neither in Firs nor in anyone else is there any invitation to poetic sympathy: in their own way they are all tough and less important than the historical forces moving around them: a point brought out clearly in the puppet-like tableaux at the opening of each act" (*Times*, 15 March 1977). To add an element of Brechtian *Verfremdung*, or alienation, each act opened with the first few lines read in amplified Russian over the theatre's public address system. The stage pictures themselves often had a political force: in Act II, Gayev and Ranevskaya were posed on a bench like the snobbish landowners in Gainsborough's painting *Mr. and Mrs. Andrews*, an iconic image of genteel smugness.

One of the most telling moments of the production involved the entrance of the tramp at the end of Act II. His appearance clearly connected him to Trofimov's speech about the suffering workers, which had just preceded it. He was dressed in "a battered military hat and overcoat: a deserter perhaps, or a political refugee."[62] He was neither an eerie specter nor a comic drunk, but "what he claims to be, a starving Russian citizen, a sickly, skeletal figure with a tubercular cough."[63] The fragment of Nekrasov's poetry that he recites in Chekhov's original was taken by Griffiths as a revolutionary appeal to other desperate Russians: "Brothers, starving and suffering comrades, unite now by the river, let them *hear* your misery."[64]

Benedict Nightingale, in an enthusiastic review in the *New Statesman* (18 March 1977), found that Eyre and Griffiths had made *The Cherry Orchard* into "a play that looks forward with excitement rather than back with regret." Summing up the production, he found that it had opened up a new angle of interpretation on the play:

> What performances like this do . . . is concentrate our minds on property, class, social discord, political crisis, the fading away of an old order and the absence of a satisfactory substitute for it, matters which, God knows, still preoccupy us today. The effect is not, I think, to diminish the play, still less shrink it into a Marxist tract: it is rather to remind us how large it is, how sweeping its interests and sympathies, how adventurous the interpretations it can safely contain, and how much of it we commonly miss. I, for one, will never be able to look at it in quite the same way again.

Eyre's production, and Griffiths' text, attracted national attention, and led to a 1981 television production, with Anton Lesser as a fervent Trofimov, Bill Paterson as a sensitive Scottish Lopakhin, Harriet

Walter as a hysterical Varya, and Judi Dench as a manipulative but sympathetic Ranevskaya. However, Griffiths' reading of the play never fully took hold, and his translation of the play remained unproduced in London. As critics like Vera Gottlieb and John Tulloch have noted, the tradition of British Chekhov production remains basically conservative and elegiac; the Eyre/Griffiths version remains exceptional in its overt political stance.[65]

In 1978, within a year of the Nottingham production, the pendulum swung back the other way with two highly visible London *Cherry Orchards*. Peter Gill and Peter Hall both took fairly traditional approaches to the play, at the Riverside Studios and the National Theatre respectively. Gill's version, played on an almost bare stage of narrow wooden planks, was serious and internal, with an ensemble cast exploring subtle nuances of character psychology. Hall's, in the cavernous Olivier auditorium, was both more historically specific and more broadly played. Frank Marcus found the two approaches complementary: "Where Gill pared the play to the bone, giving us as it were the subtext, Hall concentrates on surface behavior, while allowing us to glimpse the sad reality underneath."[66] The more comic approach of Hall's version was supported by the sparkling translation of farceur Michael Frayn, and the vaudeville turn of Nicky Henson as Yepikhodov. Hall followed the English tradition of star-studded Chekhov: Albert Finney as Lopakhin, Dorothy Tutin as Ranevskaya, Ben Kingsley as Trofimov, and Ralph Richardson as Firs all made strong impressions, without ever quite establishing clear relations with each other. The lack of ensemble tied in with Hall's central contention that Chekhov's characters are all "monumentally selfish."[67] Gill's cast was more tightly knit; none of the performances dominated, the big climaxes were underplayed, and all of the characters fit into a proportionate whole. Bernard Levin found Gill's cast "so astonishingly suitable in every role that I began hallucinatorily to believe they had been assembled first, and that Chekhov had then written the play round them."[68] The production was marked by concentration and intensity of focus; subtle shifts in the relationships were revealed through precise alterations in the stage compositions or changes of vocal tone. But neither Gill's precise and chilly production nor Hall's sprawling, boisterous one took much of a stand with regard to the play's politics. In his review of Hall's version, Sheridan Morley noted that it was "as remarkable for what it avoids as for what it achieves"; Hall advanced "no guiding thesis, no theory, no historical or social or political comment . . . Frayn's translation is also a model of non-commitment."[69] These two productions returned *The Cherry Orchard*, in England at least, mostly to the questions of tone and style that had dominated the early history of the play. But with productions like Richard Eyre's, together with those of Efros, Serban, and Krejca, the precedent had been set for boldly experimental productions of *The Cherry Orchard* that did not shy away from its radical political implications.

CHAPTER 7

BROOK AND STEIN, 1981–1997

In the final decades of the twentieth century, two of the world's leading directors staged versions of *The Cherry Orchard* that achieved international fame and influence. Each of these productions redefined the play, rejecting narrowly political readings to give expression to richly nuanced and layered explorations of Chekhov's text. The legendary English director Peter Brook stripped away the trappings of realism to create a spare, balanced, rapidly paced production. The German director Peter Stein, by contrast, reinvented Stanislavsky-style naturalism to create a lovingly detailed evocation of Chekhov's world. Brook's *La Cerisaie* played in Paris, New York City, and Moscow between 1981 and 1989; Stein's *Der Kirschgarten* in Berlin, Moscow, Salzburg, and Edinburgh between 1989 and 1997. In a way, the two productions symbolized the basic divisions that had beset the play since its origin at the Moscow Art Theatre. Brook, following Meyerhold, made the play stylized and swift, with touches of farce; Stein's production, nearly twice as long, was swathed in realistic detail and deep emotion. Yet both productions became international successes and touchstones for the play.

PETER BROOK, *LA CERISAIE*

Peter Brook's *Cherry Orchard* was the product of a long process of theatrical experimentation that had led him around the world and into contact with most of the revolutionary figures of the twentieth-century theatre. In its style and aims, the production recalled Brook's 1968 theatrical manifesto *The Empty Space*. Brook had demanded an end to museum-style "deadly theatre," specifically attacking the embalmed Chekhov productions of the Moscow Art Theatre. He noted that "it is an easy mistake to consider Chekhov as a naturalistic writer," and pointed instead to the "exquisitely cunning, completely artificial and meaningful order" of Chekhov's plays, to their craft and precision.[1] To reveal this craft, Brook felt a different approach to Chekhov was necessary, one that rejected the superficialities of slice-of-life naturalism. "I can take any empty space and call it a bare stage," Brook wrote in the opening sentence of his manifesto: with *La Cerisaie*, he did just that.[2]

Brook's production first appeared in 1981 in the empty space of the Bouffes du Nord, a derelict theatre in a working-class district of Paris that was the home of his International Centre of Theatre Research. Brook, a pioneering Shakespeare director at Stratford-upon-Avon and a leading British exponent of the ideas of Artaud, Brecht, and Grotowski, moved to Paris in 1970 to try to create a truly universal style of theatre. Working with actors, dancers, musicians, and mimes from many countries, he explored performances that would transcend cultural boundaries. He tested his process by taking his actors to Iran and Saharan Africa, where they improvised performances, using a simple carpet for a stage, for audiences with no experience of theatre. Brook's experiments included the Persian fable *The Conference of the Birds*, Jarry's grotesque parable *Ubu Roi*, a contemporary political *Timon of Athens*, and a documentary evocation of the lives of starving African villagers, *The Ik*. With *The Cherry Orchard*, however, he made his first attempt to stage one of the great works of modern naturalism. Using a French text prepared by his long-time collaborator Jean-Claude Carrière, Brook undertook what he described as "a poem about life and death and transition and change," with the theme that "something loved has to be relinquished; disappointment has to be accepted."[3] In the end, the production was remarkably life-affirming, played with great theatrical energy and rapid changes of mood by a tight-knit and balanced ensemble; it became recognized as "the best Chekhov most Parisians have ever seen."[4]

Brook's approach to the play represented a somewhat modified version of his internationalist experiments. He used only two of the Centre's actors, his wife Natasha Parry, who played Ranevskaya, and Maurice Bénichou, who played Yasha. Otherwise he assembled a seasoned pan-European cast, rather than his usual multicultural ensemble. He explained:

> The very basis of an international group is that anyone can play anything. Blacks play whites and young play old. But there are degrees of obligation, correspondence and physique in Chekhov. Every actor has a different background, but they have several things in common: a degree of aptness physically and a level of competence with Chekhov. They are experienced professionals who have not lost their innocence, their knowledge of what first brought them in to the theatre.[5]

The French film actor Michel Piccoli played Gayev; Niels Arestrup, a French actor of Danish descent, played Lopakhin. When Brook recast the production for New York City, he tried to retain something of the original production's international flavor: the English Parry again played Ranevskaya, the Swedish actor Erland Josephson Gayev, and the American Brian Dennehy Lopakhin; Trofimov was the Yugoslav-born Zeljko Ivanek, Yasha the Czech Jan Triska, and Charlotta the Asian-American Linda Hunt.

Brook's rehearsals employed his signature methods of exploration and improvisation. The first rehearsal was simply a Russian feast for the entire company, prepared in consultation with Brook's Russian-born mother-in-law. "When in the afternoon we settled at a large round table with a green baize cloth, we were already like friends and relatives in a country dacha," Brook recalled. "For the rest of the day, we enjoyed the simple pleasure of reading Chekhov's short stories to one another and chatting freely about them, as though we had no other purpose than to pass the time."[6] However the details of place, period, and nationality soon ceased to be important features of the production. During the rehearsal and production process, Brook pared away the external trappings of naturalism, so that in the end there was very little in the way of a historically or culturally specific physical environment for the characters – indeed, hardly any set or props at all. Instead, the production was set in the theatre itself.

The Bouffes du Nord was a dilapidated vaudeville house that retained touches of turn-of-the-century glamour, and as such was an appropriate environment for the decayed gentility of the Ranevskys. Natasha Parry recalled the process by which the play began to merge with its environment:

> During rehearsals we started using the whole theatre for improvisations – all of the balconies, the windows, the stairs. The whole building became a living thing for us, and I think this familiarity helped to communicate a certain domestic spirit during the performances. We had been working with some elements of scenery, but during a read-through on the day of the first public preview Peter decided to have us all sit on the carpet and just get up when we were in a scene. It worked quite well, and he announced that we would put aside all the scenery that night and use only the carpet. . . . I thought at first it was rather strange to play Chekhov sitting on the floor.[7]

In the end, Brook allowed some furniture into the production, including the famous Act I bookcase and two screens to demarcate the ballroom in Act III, but the production remained very spare, with the bare, peeling back wall of the theatre visible to the audience. The stage space was covered with Persian carpets, which provided a rich range of associations: they suggested the threadbare elegance of the Ranevskys, they hinted at the Orientalist exoticism of Brook's International Centre, and they recalled the improvised "carpet shows" Brook's actors used to give in villages in the Sahara. The carpets were a favorite device of designer Chloe Obolensky, who went on to create Brook's celebrated Indian epic, *The Mahabharata*. Obolensky, an expert on Imperial Russian culture, provided very detailed and specific costumes for the characters, but exercised extraordinary restraint in creating the physical environment for the play. Mel Gussow, who reviewed both the Paris and New York productions, noted the absence of characteristic Chekhovian business: "think how many minutes are spent in other productions, preparing and sipping tea from the samovar – or eating herring and drinking vodka . . . The menu in [Brook's] *Cherry Orchard* is reduced to a bottle of champagne, a cup of coffee and a single cucumber. In so doing, he must save at least half an hour of running time" (*New York Times*, 30 January 1988).

What the production lost in period detail, it made up for through the intimacy and simplicity of the staging, and the degree to which the play inhabited the theatre space of the Bouffes du Nord. During the play, Varya bustled about through the audience, and flung Trofimov's galoshes from the circle to the stage; at one point Yasha, fetching down luggage, climbed a ladder from the third gallery into the theatre's actual attic. Without furniture, the actors sat or lounged on the floor, or on the rolled-up carpet that suggested a fallen log in the outdoor setting of Act II. The "empty space" set gave the acting an athletic, even balletic quality, as Barbara Bray noted in her review of the Paris production: "Bodily movement, instead of being tamed and conventionalized by furniture, reflects mood and emotion."[8] The carpets covering the stage extended to the feet of the front-row spectators, who sat on the same level as the acting area. The actors entered through the audience, and often faced them or addressed them directly. According to Natasha Parry, "There was an extraordinary moment just after the play began, when we would stand in the corridor of the theatre behind the audience, improvising the excitement of the family's arrival at the house. We would build this up more and more, until suddenly we all burst into the acting space."[9] The orchard was placed in front of the stage, rather than behind it as in a box-set production; so when Ranevskaya apostrophized it in Act I, she stood just a few feet from the audience and looked out among them, giving great intimacy and immediacy to her childhood memories and her sudden vision of her mother. At the end of the play, about to leave the house for the last time, Parry looked round at the space of the Bouffes du Nord; when she said, "It seems to me I've never seen what the walls of this house are like, nor the ceiling; I look at them now avidly, with such tender love," there was no doubt about which walls and ceiling she referred to.[10]

Parry's Ranevskaya was not the dominant presence, the hub of the play's world, that many other actresses have been in the role, but her performance served the ensemble nature of the play: "its world is a world without a hub, without a cherry orchard or a heroine to weight it or claim it," wrote Jane Kramer. "The brilliance of the 'Cherry Orchard' that Brook and Carrière put together is that it returns the play to its twelve players."[11] Richard Eder noted that "one could almost imagine the production done without Mme. Ranevsky," given the strength of the ensemble, and that "Mr. Brook's only star is the play."[12] Brook himself believed the key to Chekhov's achievement was his ability to diffuse the narrative interest of the play among all the characters, not merely a single protagonist:

> He understood that essential aspect of the theater (which only Shakespeare and a few others have also understood): that theater exists only when the necessarily personal viewpoint of the narrator is effaced by multiple viewpoints. That might seem impossible – it's like someone in India looking at the statues and thinking, Oh! Wouldn't it be wonderful to have twelve arms? It's one thing to make the statement, but another thing to achieve it.[13]

In order to achieve his twelve-armed statue – a production equally balanced among the twelve characters – Brook prevented Ranevskaya from being the center of the production. Parry played not a *grande dame* nor a tragic figure, but a "charming and bewildered woman" caught up in a web of relationships and events that she responds to moment by moment. Brook worked against emotional indulgence, for Parry as for all the actors, and maintained a forward-moving rhythm throughout the play. The references to the dead Grisha, for instance, were never allowed to become sentimental. Maurice Bénichou, who served as Brook's assistant director as well as playing Yasha, discussed the emotional rhythms of Trofimov's first appearance:

Everyone is happy, congratulating themselves, talking, joking, laughing. Then the tutor of the dead child appears. A leaden silence embraces all: suddenly emotion and tears replace the carefree frivolity of a few moments before. Then all of a sudden Ranevskaya looks at Trofimov, and asks him why he has become so old and ugly. It's over, the pain is dissipated. It's ridiculous for her to continue crying in front of everyone else . . . A trace lingers in her heart, and in the spectator's imagination: we now know she retains a deep scar inside her.[14]

Parry was able to tap into this pathos again at the mention of Grisha in Act II, but to move away from it as quickly and lightly. According to Albert Hunt, "the memory of her son's drowning years before was deeply touching, yet it was immediately dispelled by the brash strains of the distant band, and she rapidly recovered her equilibrium."[15]

Parry saved the emotional weight of her performance for the sale of the estate in Act III, but this scene was as much about Lopakhin as it was about her. When she learned of his purchase of the orchard, she grasped the back of a chair and bent sideways as if in sudden physical pain; then she sat and cried quietly while Lopakhin launched into his speech of triumph. At the height of the speech Lopakhin stumbled into one of the screens, knocking it over and revealing, behind it, the mortified Gayev and Firs, who stood back to back, eavesdropping on the disaster. At the end of the speech Lopakhin sank to the floor behind Ranevskaya, ineffectually clutching her hem, perhaps recalling the girl who once bathed his bleeding nose and overcome with despair at having failed her.[16] In the New York production, Brian Dennehy took the scene to extremes of emotional and physical violence, entering with a whooping laugh, dancing a jig of triumph, hurling himself about the stage touching the walls to prove that they were his.[17] His Lopakhin was a great bear of a man, variously compared to "a hand-slapping football coach" and "a Wyoming rancher"; by contrast, Niels Arestrup in Paris had been "a man of considerable sensitivity . . . lacking in table manners but not in taste or sympathy."[18] Nonetheless, both actors managed to convey Lopakhin's essential decency and something of his poetic soul. Critics in both Paris and New York noted that

Trofimov's tribute, that Lopakhin has the hands and soul of an artist, was sincere and appropriate.[19]

Gayev, in Brook's conception, was neither a dissipated aristocrat nor an absurd fool but a grown-up child, with a child's capacity for wonder, sensitivity, and sorrow. Both Michel Piccoli and Erland Josephson captured this quality of sweetness and vulnerability. Piccoli, in "a performance of remarkable tenderness," was an "ageing innocent and seraphic wastrel," acutely aware of his sister's anguish but constitutionally unable to offer any help other than consolation and love.[20] Richard Eder commented on "the long, tired face, full of foreknowledge . . . fallen into a childlike innocence: thoughts flutter across it, briefly and one by one."[21] Piccoli later achieved international acclaim as the hero of Louis Malle's Chekhovian film *Milou in May*; Piccoli and Natasha Parry also performed a program of the letters of Chekhov and Olga Knipper. In New York, Erland Josephson, an actor best known from the films of Ingmar Bergman, won praise for his "touchingly ineffectual Gayev," variously described as "a rosy cherub in grownup clothing" and "a white-haired, bearded baby, scarf askew, fingers quizzically dabbing at his chin as if in half-hearted readiness to shut himself up."[22] His speech to the bookcase was a comic high point of the production, but his most memorable moment was his Act III entrance, "in which his exhausted posture and sad, dangling bundle of anchovy and herring tins announce the estate's sale to his sister well before Lopakhin does."[23]

Pace and rhythm were among the keys to Brook's conception. In discussing the play, he invoked Meyerhold rather than Stanislavsky: "The greatest reproach Meyerhold made to Stanislavsky after *The Cherry Orchard* was to say that Stanislavsky did not know the fundamental rhythm of the play, and that, by acting it too slowly, he missed the essential movement."[24] In both its New York and Paris incarnations, Brook's *Cherry Orchard* was played rapidly, straight through, without an interval. As Gordon Rogoff observed, this approach showcased "Chekhov's architectural integrity, the astounding way in which his echoes, counterpoints, and symmetries are constructed," as well as Brook's "clean sense of line and rhythm."[25] The pace was generally quick, the tone generally light, with bright white lighting, rapid and overlapping entrances and exits, and a farcical approach to the supporting characterizations. Brook approached *The Cherry Orchard* as "a theatrical movement purely played . . . From the start, I wanted to avoid sentimentality, a false Chekhovian manner that is not in the text. This is not gloomy, romantic, long and slow. It's a comic play about real life."[26] In Paris, at least, Brook's approach did not forestall emotional involvement on behalf of the audiences. Traditionally unsentimental Parisian spectators wept at the production, and Paris critics were lavish in their praise; *Le Monde* noted that Brook's "superb intelligence" turned Chekhov's characters into "points of reference for our own disarray; and we love them," while *Figaro* called *Le Cerisaie* "the most beautiful and honest work to be seen in Paris."[27] Brook's rapid pace and economy of style heightened the emotional impact of Act IV, when the carpets were finally stripped away, leaving a desolate space for the ancient Firs of Robert Murzeau, who delivered his last lines "in a whisper, a quiet verbalization of the offstage cry of the falling trees."[28]

The production's success in Paris – it ran for two seasons, was filmed for French television, and was attended by Prime Minister François Mitterrand – led to its transfer to the Brooklyn Academy of Music in New York City. While the New York production had great impact, it was not immune from criticism. The venue itself presented some major problems. The Majestic Theatre, which had hosted Brook's epic production of *The Mahabharata*, had been a decayed Vaudeville House like the Bouffes du Nord, before it was reclaimed by BAM. In the interim, however, it had been converted to a cinema, so that it required a somewhat artificial transformation to create the desired effect of crumbling Edwardian grandeur. Scenic artists painted the passageways to resemble decaying arches, and deliberately chipped and mottled the plaster; there was atmosphere, but no authenticity. Furthermore, the Majestic was much larger than the Bouffes du Nord, preventing the intimacy between actor and audience that the Paris production enjoyed, and forcing long running entrances across the sixty-two-foot-deep stage. Moreover, Brook's New York company was much less of an ensemble than his Paris cast, and included actors of very uneven abilities. Rebecca Miller (Anya) and Kate Mailer (Dunyasha) received a critical shellacking, dismissed as inept beginners trading on the fame of their fathers, writers Arthur Miller and Norman Mailer. The unity of the Paris company seemed to have been lost, as Geoffrey Reeves observed: "everyone seemed to be acting in a different style: noisy Americans jostled with refined Europeans, here the English classical actor, there someone from the Actors' Studio, first a soap cameo, then a vaudeville turn." Reeves noted that while the productions were essentially identical, much of the effect was lost in New York: "One was looking at a production which looked almost exactly the same as that in Paris, with the same shape and rhythm to it, the same grouping, the same timbre," but "it had almost none of the quality of the ebb and flow of life, the light and shade of emotion, the joy of watching actors work together that had made *La Cerisaie* so memorable."[29]

Nonetheless, many New York critics lauded the production, and it was a major event of the theatrical season. Frank Rich, citing Brook's combination of Beckett-like bleakness and spirited theatricality, noted, "This is a 'Cherry Orchard' that pauses for breath only when life does, for people to recoup after dying a little. I think Mr. Brook has given us the Chekhov production that every theatergoer fantasizes about but, in my experience, almost never finds." Parry, Josephson, and Dennehy were widely praised. Dennehy's performance was especially memorable, combining bull-in-a-china-shop explosiveness with moments of deeply felt emotion. One scene in particular came close to achieving the intimacy and emotional intensity for which the Paris production was celebrated. The Act IV proposal scene with Varya was played downstage center, very close to the audience, with Dennehy and Stephanie Roth standing side-by-side, looking out through invisible French doors toward the imaginary orchard in the auditorium. For this scene Brook slowed the pace, so that the nervous banalities the couple exchanged were painfully protracted. Finally a voice called "Yermolay Alexeyevich!" from one of the downstage exits. Dennehy responded "Coming!" in an abrupt and impatient tone, as though angered at being interrupted in this intimate moment. There followed ten or fifteen seconds of excruciating tension, during which Lopakhin struggled with, and then made, his decision. With a muttered "Right away," Dennehy strode straight forward through the exit, while Roth collapsed to the stage floor like a slaughtered animal. It was a moment of great theatrical power, true to the spirit if not the letter of Chekhov, and it revealed Brook's genius as a director of actors and an architect of theatrical effect.

After the New York run, Brook's *Cherry Orchard* toured to Moscow, with Tom Wilkinson replacing Dennehy, who was making a film, but with the rest of the American cast intact. In the new atmosphere of *perestroika*, the production, at the Taganka Theatre, was rapturously received. Lev Dodin, a bold and iconoclastic director from Leningrad, called it the most Chekhovian *Cherry Orchard* he'd ever seen: "It comes closer to the spirit of Chekhov, and of the people of Russia, than anything I've seen by our own companies. And it is all done with such simplicity, such directness, that the real art comes through."[30] In the intimacy of the Taganka, and in the atmosphere of political transition, anxiety, and hope of that moment in Russian history, Brook's production had perhaps found its ideal venue. After eight years of evolution, Brook's *Cherry Orchard* – spare yet poetic, brisk yet humane – had achieved Brook's goal of using theatre to transcend borders. "This is a play that has a complete world within it," he said in Russia. "What's more, it's a play about a society in the process of change. . . . If what we do is any good, it can convey the message that political, geographic and cultural barriers are not what they seem to be at all. I hope what we do here can help stir a little of that hope."[31]

PETER STEIN, *DER KIRSCHGARTEN*

While Brook's production eschewed naturalism to explore the play in an avant-garde empty space, Peter Stein's landmark version at the

Berlin Schaubühne attempted to rediscover Stanislavsky's approach to creating reality on the stage. Stein declared that "It is impossible to understand Chekhov's plays without taking into account his personal relationship with the Art Theatre," which Stein saw as primarily one of fruitful collaboration rather than conflict and misunderstanding.[32] Stein went back to Stanislavsky's original production notes, created an elaborately detailed soundscape, and used all the resources of scenery, lighting, and theatrical technology, together with exhaustively rehearsed, beautifully detailed acting, to create an homage to the original *Cherry Orchard* production that nonetheless gave the play a powerful resonance at the end of the twentieth century. When Stein's *Kirschgarten* played in Moscow in 1992, according to John Freedman of the *Moscow Times*, it "prompted many Russian observers to gush – and lament – that the great, lost Russian theatrical tradition had been preserved in the heart of a German."[33]

Stein, a German director of international acclaim, made his reputation at the Schaubühne in the 1970s and 80s, directing large-scale, historically and socially contextualized productions of Aeschylus, Shakespeare, and Chekhov. His 1984 *Three Sisters* was hailed as a masterpiece of naturalism, conceived on a grand scale. Stein used the remarkable technological resources of the new Schaubühne am Lehninerplatz to stunning effect. In the first three acts, Karl-Ernst Hermann's carefully crafted period interiors increasingly hemmed in the Prozorov sisters as Natasha steadily reduced their power within the house. The fourth act provided a breathtaking *coup de théâtre* as the sisters were finally dispossessed, driven out of the house into an enormous, 150-foot-deep space (incorporating the back-to-back stages of two Schaubühne theatres) that left them dwarfed and stranded like Beckettian wayfarers on the barren steppe.

Der Kirschgarten, which opened in 1989, was not designed on as large a scale, but it incorporated the same sense of the power of stage space and the imaginative possibilities of scenography. Stein again went back to Stanislavsky's own production notes and Chekhov's letters, though he seemed to follow the former rather than the latter. His

Cherry Orchard, like Stanislavsky's original, was slow, long, mournful, and grounded in a mass of specific scenic and sonic detail. Stein insisted on the importance of apparently trivial minutiae of social existence as depicted in the play. He conceived his production of *The Cherry Orchard* in deliberate opposition to Brook's:

> When you stage *The Cherry Orchard* as Peter Brook did, having it played on a carpet, then I have difficulty imaging how the charm of the concrete in the actor's performance – which the play requires – can take effect . . . [Chekhov] did not want the spectators to rely on their imagination to give shape to what the characters are saying, but instead he wanted them to show in a clear, distinct manner the absurdity in this object they speak of so passionately, which, a few moments earlier, others were considering the worst of white elephants. They make fun of the samovar, and then they repeat endlessly that they absolutely need samovars. At bottom, this quotidian incoherence, both concrete and funny as well, constitutes the true frontlines of human combat, to wit, the combat for control of everyday life, and not control of great crisis situations.[34]

Stein took great care to reproduce the details of daily social existence, noting the way they connect to form a complex mosaic within Chekhov's play. For Stein, the cucumber that Dunyasha is compared to in Act I is linked to the bucket of cucumbers that Pishchik consumed in Holy Week and the actual cucumber Charlotta eats in Act II.[35] These mundane details, scrupulously observed and poetically linked, make up what Stein called Chekhov's innovative "drama of daily life."[36]

Stein was concerned not only with the social, but with the natural world as it impinges on the characters:

> It is . . . regrettable that some directors fail to introduce into their production the representation of certain essential natural phenomena. One finds them in all of Chekhov's plays, where they constitute a frame, a receptacle for the banal and everyday elements with which one then acts onstage . . . I consider it necessary to supply this frame to the actors,

to insist on heat and cold, summer and winter, springtime and autumn, morning and evening, on certain hours of the day as the different seasons color them.[37]

Accordingly, Stein's cherry trees became characters themselves, heavy with bloom in Act I, barren and doomed in Act IV. The lighting of Wolfgang Goebbel evocatively created different times of day, notably the dawn of Act I and the sunset of Act II. Stein used the full resources of his theatre to create an entire Chekhovian world, where the environment is as important as the characters within it:

> The play is not centered on the story of an individual or a group of people, but instead on a part of nature, an orchard, which the hands of man have made to grow. Man and nature, man and the universe – this is the main thing for Chekhov; for him, it seems to me, this is much more important than the connections between people.[38]

The importance of the orchard, Stein's leading character, was established clearly in the first act. The nursery setting of Act I was in many ways similar to Stanislavsky's, with an angled wall at the back and three high windows. For the first part of the act these were curtained and shuttered, giving the room a somewhat forbidding aspect; despite the presence of children's furniture, the nursery was not a cozy room but a narrow passageway with multiple doors. Noting the number of characters who pass through the room on the way to somewhere else, Stein discerned a kind of "corridor dramaturgy" that governed much of the act. The multiple doors yielded much of the comedy, as in a Feydeau farce. Yasha dropped Dunyasha to the floor when their kiss was interrupted by Varya's sudden entrance. Later, Anya's overhearing of Gayev's disparaging remarks about Ranevskaya was plainly visible to the audience as she stood in one of the upstage doors. "These interrupted and broken-off conversations and actions as a new character enters or passes by, continue through the entire act," noted a critic of the *Bühnentechnische Rundschau*, a German technical theatre periodical. "The audience can hardly lean back in their seats, because they are carried along in a *mélange* of changing constellations and associated emotional outbursts."[39]

The emotional centerpiece of the act, however, involved not the doors but the windows: the revelation of the cherry orchard, a vision of beauty, alive with birdsong and glowing in the rising sun. The act had begun in near-darkness, with stage business, sound and lighting effects all combining to create an initially realistic portrayal of the early-morning arrival:

> As Ranevskaya and her entourage return home in the first act, everything is rivetingly specific: dogs yelp and bark in recognition, bookcases are sentimentally apostrophized, the romantic landowner herself dances on top of her old nursery-table. But when Firs recalls the ritual by which dried cherries were once shipped off by the cartload to Moscow, we hear a low stringed vibration that throughout symbolizes change. And when a muslin curtain parts to reveal the abundant white-blossomed orchard, the darkly silhouetted characters stand in front of it as if imposing their own private memories.[40]

Stein's stagecraft combined moments of subtle behavioral detail with broad strokes of symbolism. Just after Gayev poured his heart out to the bookcase, Yasha used its glass-fronted doors to check his appearance, preening his hair.[41] The eerie vibration sound called forth by Firs' memories both prefigured the breaking string of Act II and heralded the appearance of the orchard itself. Stein felt that this first glimpse of the orchard was a key moment of the play, and a choice of great audacity on Chekhov's part:

> By this device, the spectator "sees" the leading character, the orchard. It's really brilliant! In the theatre one cannot show real trees, one can only give a feeling of their beauty through the feelings of the characters. But Chekhov insists, "No, the audience has to see the orchard and believe that nothing is more beautiful!" It is hard to stage.[42]

Stein took no half measures in creating the symbolic beauty of the orchard. All of the light in the scene came from the white blossoms upstage, casting the speaking characters into shadow. Richard Eyre, director of Britain's National Theatre, noted that the scene was brilliantly lit, "but in a style we'd never tolerate: real dark, real shadow, real silhouette."[43] For Paul Taylor, it was "a vision of unearthly loveliness," an "other-worldly landscape" that might well be the domain of ghosts: "A magical blurring of the objective and the subjective, the spectacle brings home to you just why the Gayevs can't bear to part with their orchard and perhaps modifies your sense of their irritating fecklessness and inertia."[44]

The Act II setting was equally expressive. Following Stanislavsky and Simov, Karl-Ernst Hermann created a rather steeply sloping hillside surmounted by a bench, with an old chapel upstage left. Telegraph poles stood out against the cyclorama, on which, barely visible, were the unclear outlines of a city. Its smoking chimneys and onion domes became threateningly visible later in the act, in the light of an evening thunderstorm, at the moment of the breaking string. When Ranevskaya first entered she was rather drunk from her champagne luncheon, and lounged in a pile of fragrant hay, which could be smelled throughout the theatre. Jutta Lampe, Stein's leading lady at the Schaubühne and Masha in his *Three Sisters*, was a young and sensual Ranevskaya. She was forty-one when the production opened, older than Knipper when she first played the part, but younger than many Ranevskayas, and very beautiful and glamorous. John Peter found her "an unstable and sentimental woman, selfish and silly, but also kind, deeply sensual and ultimately tragic"; Catherine Lockerbie observed that "the fecund warmth and feckless generosity of this reckless, full, flawed woman are rendered in a performance of astonishing passion and depth."[45] The *Theater Heute* critic Michael Merschmeier found her "a person full of discontinuities," truth-seeking and dishonest, selfish and boundlessly loving, perceptive and narrow-minded. He thought her Act II "confession" rang false, perhaps because she had to deliver it while sitting on the haystack in white dress, veil and feather boa like a doll, "speaking in the miserable sing-song of a sufferer" – which Ranevskaya really isn't. "Her seraphic continual aria belies the fact that this woman has made her way out there in the world, beyond the protection of the nursery, and that her emotions are at least as much calculated as overpowering."[46] In other scenes she showed a surprising sobriety; although in the Act III party scene she suddenly revealed "how magnetic her public persona could be," according to David Murray.[47] While Stein insisted that no one character was at the center of the play, Lampe was very much at the center of the production.

For Act III, Stein and Herrmann used the same interior structure as they had for the nursery, except that three windows had been replaced by tall connecting doors revealing the ballroom beyond, where the party was taking place. Stein used the interaction between the two spaces continually and creatively; though much of the production was derived from Stanislavsky, the party scene was inspired by Meyerhold.[48] The flaming-red ballroom was populated by sinister figures in evening dress and masks. Grotesque dancers, short men and very tall women, leapt about to raucous Jewish folk music. While Ranevskaya quarreled with Trofimov, the guests all peered through the connecting doors like figures from Meyerhold's production of *The Inspector General*. But Stein's symbolist flair didn't preclude characteristic, tellingly observed details in the acting: when Trofimov could only offer her "platitudinous sympathy," Lampe "turn[ed] on him viciously while reapplying her make-up," a moment that for Antony Peattie represented the greatest acting he had ever seen.[49]

The contrast between the two rooms served the Chekhovian mix of the emotions of the scene, as well as Ranevskaya's disordered mental state, according to the *Bühnentechnische Rundschau* critic:

> In her tension, Ranevskaya can't stand the music, but she also can't escape it . . . The stage set mirrors her internal division – the ballroom, brightly lighted with a splendid chandelier and full of music and the murmur of voices, is a realization of her joy in life, the "waiting room" salon, with its modest lighting and the unrest of the constantly passing guests and slamming doors, shows her tension and fear of the future. Ranevskaya moves between the rooms and moods in her emotional outbreaks, until Lopakhin robs her of all her illusions with the news that he has bought the estate at auction.

The announcement of the sale was another *tour de force* moment for Lampe. Lopakhin (Michael König in Berlin and Daniel Friedrich on tour) was played as a vigorous but socially awkward man, clever and practical but physically graceless and unskilled in matters of the heart. His drunken account of the auction followed naturally from the character he had established. Ranevskaya's grief was a slow burn, a gradual outpouring of accumulated misery cruelly counterpointed by the indifference, not only of Lopakhin, but of the party guests. As Catherine Lockerbie described the moment, "The ball surges onwards in brutal merriment, Lopakhin . . . crashes about in drunken, compromised triumph, and Lampe as Ranevskaya weeps. Slowly, silently, gradually she weeps, and weeps. It is a moment matched in poignancy only by the long, long silence as, cases packed and galoshes found, the Ranevskayas gaze around the home which will soon be gone for ever."[50]

In Act IV, Stein took the traditional Russian custom of sitting down briefly before beginning a journey, one alluded to by Ranevskaya in Chekhov's text, and made it into one of the signature moments of the production. At the end of a performance that was already three and a half hours long, Stein had his cast sit in silence for a full minute, while "the audience held its breath, in presentiment of a calamity."[51] Once again unafraid to mix the heightened and symbolic with the mundane and specific, Stein interrupted the silence, from time to time, with Yasha's drunken hiccups and tasteless giggles.

When the family finally departed, Stein unleashed his final *coup de théâtre*. Lopakhin locked the doors with rattling finality, and the sound of the axes was audible on all sides of the auditorium. The stage was dark except for a grey light filtered through the shuttered windows upstage, as in the first moments of the play. Suddenly, the audience became aware of a slight, rustling noise and movement, and realized with a shock that Firs had been *onstage* throughout the scene, tucked away in an alcove down right, forgotten not only by the Ranevskys but by the audience. We were as complicit as they were in his certain death. A grey Beckettian figure, he shuffled with painful slowness around the stage, muttering to himself and trying every door in vain. When Firs had finished his last speech and settled himself in the middle of the stage to await the end, Stein played his final card. An eerie vibration portended the breaking string, but just as the terrifying sound rang out, one of the bare cherry trees came crashing through the tall shuttered windows, scattering broken glass and splintered wood about the stage, and letting in the frosty air that will ensure Firs' death. It was a heart-stopping moment, one that took Chekhov's inscrutable stage direction and made it frighteningly tangible and real. It provided a fitting conclusion to Stein's production: a moment that was realistically conceived, motivated, and executed, and yet one that carried sweeping dramatic and symbolic power.

As Michael Billington observed after watching the production's final incarnation at the Edinburgh Festival in 1997, "This is Chekhov presented in all his poetic realism and symbolic 'Sachlichkeit,' or factuality . . . in its sheer physical beauty and combination of realistic detail and rigorous form, it remains the most symphonic Chekhov production I have ever seen."[52] Stein and Brook, between them, carrying the torches respectively of Stanislavsky and Meyerhold, ended nearly a century of *Cherry Orchard* performances with productions representing fully the range, power, and beauty of the play.

CHAPTER 8

THE CHERRY ORCHARD AFTER ONE HUNDRED YEARS

As *The Cherry Orchard* approached its centenary, historical and social changes worldwide brought many of its themes and actions into sharp focus. The breakup of the Soviet Union, the anxieties over the new millennium, the terrorist attacks of 11 September 2001, and the ongoing political upheavals around the world: all served to highlight the play's concern with the often painful process of cultural change. In the UK, productions tended to remain in the elegiac mode, but with an increased sense of foreboding, especially in Adrian Noble's important RSC version. In the USA, directors made the play contemporary by confronting tensions in American society, notably race. Performances around the world experimented with a wide range of production styles as they applied the play's exploration of change to such diverse cultures as South Africa, Latin America, and China. And in Russia and the former Soviet states, the play was a potent metaphor for the uncertainties ahead and the haunting legacies of the past.

THE BRITISH CHEKHOV TRADITION

In Britain, *The Cherry Orchard* has remained a staple of the repertoire, appearing in major new productions every few years. While, in general, productions have followed a worldwide trend in playing up the comedy of the work and moving away from scenic realism, the British performance tradition has tended toward the conservative. As Vera Gottlieb has pointed out, productions are invariably in period dress, even when there is no specific historical interpretation; the costumes merely lend some heritage elegance to the generally affectionate portrait of the fading gentry.[1] More adventurous stagings have often come from outside England itself; the Abbey Theatre performed an Irish-accented version by Tom Murphy as part of its centenary celebration in 2004, while Philip Prowse directed a fast-paced farcical *Cherry Orchard* at the Glasgow Citizens' Theatre in 2002. This was an eclectic post-modern version that drew on many performance traditions that post-dated Chekhov, including "expressionism, silent film, Charlie Chaplin, Keystone Cops, farce, Marlene Dietrich (particularly in Anne Marie Timoney's performance as the governess), The Wizard of Oz, Brechtian alienation and the bleakly comic despair that was Beckett's speciality."[2]

One recent change in the English Chekhov tradition is that in contrast to the starry West End versions of the past, the play has been better served by ensemble productions by the subsidized national companies. The National Theatre and the Royal Shakespeare Company between them were responsible for three of the four most important *Cherry Orchard*s in the past twenty years, at the time of writing. Longer rehearsal periods, fully integrated designs, and strong ensemble casting have made *The Cherry Orchard* very much the province of the NT and the RSC, rather than the commercial theatre.

The National's 1985 production established this trend. Mike Alfreds, a creative and original director whose company Shared Experience was a leading force in the theatrical innovation of the 1970s, worked with an ensemble of actors formed within the larger structure of the NT. Ian McKellen and Edward Petherbridge had led a company of seventeen actors through a series of plays, collaborating with directors not ordinarily associated with the National, such as Philip Prowse, who directed *The Duchess of Malfi*. In *The Cherry Orchard*, Alfreds had a strong company already used to working together and open to experimentation. Using his own unique Stanislavsky-based process, Alfreds created a production that changed every night. The actors had neither pre-set blocking nor fixed emotional reactions, but were encouraged to live each scene afresh, responding in the moment based on the detailed psychological work they had done on their characters. When McKellen's Lopakhin announced his purchase of the estate, he might be either tender or destructive. The scene worked both ways, according to Michael Ratcliffe, who saw the production twice: he found the scene more moving when "the victorious and the defeated fell weeping into each other's arms, but it made equal theatrical sense . . . for the boorish Lopakhin to whirl the keys to the house around his head like a cowboy, kick over the daybed and scatter the vase of scarlet flowers, together with Ranevskaya (Sheila Hancock), to the very edge of the room" (*Observer*, 15 December 1985). Another strong point of Alfreds' production was that very good actors were cast in the minor roles; Greg Hicks was a solemn Yepikhodov, Selina Cadell a hysterical Dunyasha, and Jonathan Hyde a jackal-like Yasha, whose last-act theft of Pishchik's 400 rubles was one of many original touches. The most arresting performance came from Laurance Rudic, whose Trofimov was "no true idealist . . . but a cold-hearted, self-regarding humbug, certain to ruin Ranevskaya's ardent daughter Anya."[3] The overall tone of the play was bright and energetic, what Alfreds defined as "a light, elegant 'clown show.'"[4]

When Sam Mendes directed the play in the West End a few years later (Aldwych 1989), he did not have Alfreds' advantages. While Judi Dench gave a strong central performance as a sensual, tactile Ranevskaya, the rest of the casting was haphazard, and the production lacked consistency. Neither the white unit set nor the ad hoc company were able to define the Ranevsky household concretely. Peter Kemp noted that the "box-like set" and "unsubtle lighting," together with a lack of detail in the performances, contributed to "the persistent tendency of Sam Mendes' production to miss the play's fleetingly bleak intimations of mortality and transience."[5] Michael Gough, as Firs, was too young and urbane, Bernard Hill's Lopakhin "one-dimensional," the Anya "perfunctory and mechanical," according to Martin Hoyle of the *Financial Times* (26 October 1989). Michael Billington praised the light, ironic tone of the production, and especially Dench, who "never lets you forget that Ranevskaya is a woman dominated by sexual passion," but he felt that "there are depths in the play that no ad hoc cast, however brilliant, can ever fully sound within the limited span of a West End rehearsal period."[6]

The next major British *Cherry Orchard*, the RSC Stratford production by Adrian Noble in 1995, fared better. In place of a single dominant star, Noble had a strong company led by Penelope Wilton as Ranevskaya and Alec McCowen as Gayev. They played the landowners as snobbish, very English aristocrats, blinkered and self-centered, who were nonetheless moving in their utter inability to cope with the catastrophe overtaking them. As Nicholas De Jongh noted, "Rarely before can the Russian gentry who drift and dawdle their lives away in *The Cherry Orchard* have been so scathingly anatomized."[7]

The cast were dressed and lit in shades of pale green and grey, after the Danish painter Vilhelm Hammershoi. There was no set beyond a few pieces of furniture and the Swan theatre itself, a quasi-Elizabethan structure with wooden galleries and deep three-sided stage. As in Brook's production, the play inhabited the entire theatre, with actors moving through the house and behind the audience, the luggage for departure flung down from the galleries, and so forth. Lacking many possibilities for scenic expressiveness, Noble used movement to vivid effect. The Act III party, for instance, Noble conceived as comparable to the band playing on the sinking Titanic; accordingly, the dancers and the musicians careened in an off-balance way about the bare wooden stage as though they were on the deck of a ship.[8] While audience members didn't necessarily pick up the allusion, it gave the party scene a sense of desperate, frenzied gaiety entirely appropriate to the play.

David Troughton, who had recently played Caliban for the RSC, was a very coarse but warmhearted Lopakhin who worshipped Ranevskaya like a god. His clumsy attempts to interact with the gentry on their own terms were always rudely rejected, thus feeding his self-hatred. When he tried to talk about the theatre with Ranevskaya, and she sharply retorted that people shouldn't watch plays but should look at their own lives instead, he nodded vigorously in agreement and proceeded to berate himself viciously for his peasant brutishness. When he finally bought the orchard, his Caliban-like stamping dance of triumph ended with him groveling on the floor at Ranevskaya's feet, wiping his face on the hem of her dress.

While Noble offered some hope for the future, with Sean Murray's Trofimov taken quite seriously and Lucy Whybrow's Anya a radiant presence throughout, the overall effect of the production was chilling. Alec McCowen's sudden, startling sobs of "My sister . . . my sister!" had all the anguish of a lost child; Firs (Peter Copley) died in the middle of the stage floor of a realistic heart attack. The production was very powerful, and a success with both critics and audiences, but it pushed the play aggressively in the direction of ironic tragedy. As Irving Wardle commented, "Noble has penetrated deep into the play, and discovered ice."[9]

The most recent major English production, at the time of writing, was Trevor Nunn's at the Royal National Theatre in 2000. Like Noble's, it was a small-scale production, with the audience sitting around three sides of the National's Cottesloe Theatre. Real-life siblings Vanessa and Corin Redgrave played Ranevskaya and Gayev. Vanessa Redgrave's star status and tendency toward mannered acting were in some danger of unbalancing the play, but Nunn's taut direction and the strength of the company, together with the intimacy of the space, kept the play in proportion. Vanessa Redgrave, like Penelope Wilton, played a very English Ranevskaya, but Bloomsbury and Bohemian rather than lady of the manor. Corin Redgrave was a supercilious, unlikable Gayev. The central performance was the Lopakhin of Roger Allam. A Shakespearean actor famed for his verse-speaking and articulation, Allam cut a gentlemanly figure, betraying little of Lopakhin's peasant background beyond a slight accent. He explained his proposal for the cherry orchard with great enthusiasm, turning the tea-table into a map of the district, with sugar cubes standing in for the summer cottages he proposed to build. In a strong choice, Nunn made it clear that Gayev had concealed all knowledge of their financial problems from Ranevskaya, so that at first she thought Lopakhin was merely joking about cutting down the orchard; she laughed indulgently at his earnest demonstration.

The production, though quite somber in design and lighting, fully explored the comedy in the play, particularly with regard to the sexual mismatches. Overall, the production was more personal than political in emphasis. Charlotte Emerson's Anya was besotted with the Trofimov of Ben Miles, a contemptible intellectual who helped himself to Ranevskaya's picnic while bemoaning the starving workers. When Trofimov and Anya were left alone, her increasingly unsubtle attempts to seduce him were met only by oblivious and patronizing lectures. The courtship of Lopakhin and Varya was marked by similar moments of comic incongruity; for once the proposal scene was played almost entirely for laughs. Allam made three attempts to ask, "Will you marry me?" but the stuttered "w"-sounds finally resolved into "Where will you go now?" He crept forward from his chair as though about to kneel to Varya, but pulled up at the last moment, as though he had only intended to pick something up from the floor. When he resorted to talking about the weather, he put his hand over his face in comic mortification. As he finally fled the scene in embarrassment, Eve Best's Varya seemed to laugh at his foolishness; only after a moment did it become clear she was sobbing in anguish.

The originality and truthfulness of moments like these typified the production at its best. While the British tradition of Chekhov performance is not strikingly experimental or challenging, it continues to yield productions of high and consistent quality, and it has served *The Cherry Orchard* perhaps better than any of the other plays. John Stokes, discussing Adrian Noble's production in the *Times Literary Supplement*, concluded, "One hundred years after the plays were written in Russia, this is a golden age for Chekhov in England."[10]

12. *The Wisteria Trees*, Joshua Logan's Broadway adaptation of *The Cherry Orchard*, reset on a Louisiana plantation, with Helen Hayes in the Ranevskaya role. (Photofest.)

AMERICAN EXPERIMENTS

As *The Cherry Orchard* approached the end of its first century in the United States, directors seemed more willing to separate the play from its cultural context, and from the genteel Broadway performance tradition, in aggressive, usually politicized, reworkings. These often took the form of substantially rewritten adaptations; and they often dealt with specifically American concerns, particularly race.

Both of these tendencies actually surfaced quite early in American Chekhov production. Joshua Logan's Americanized *Cherry Orchard*, *The Wisteria Trees*, played in New York in 1950 and 1955, with Helen Hayes in the role of Lucy Andree Ransdell, a Southern belle losing her plantation. Logan, best known as the producer of *South Pacific*, had seen the MAT *Cherry Orchard* in Russia, and it had reminded him of his Louisiana childhood. His adaptation made the servants into former slaves, or the children of slaves; Lopakhin, or Yancy Loper, was a newly rich speculator played in the revival by Walter Matthau. Logan made overt the sublimated relationship between the estate's two owners; in the final act Lucy rejected a marriage proposal from Loper that would have saved the beloved wisteria trees. The play was tentative with regard to discussing race, though the Trofimov character had a monologue remembering his black and white "mothers." Nonetheless, it was the black actors who gained the most critical praise, especially Ossie Davis in the Yasha role and Alonzo Bosan as the Firs character, Scott, "who was so busy taking care of white people that he forgot to get himself freed from slavery."[11] While the play was in previews, Logan altered the ending to spare Scott from his entombment in the deserted house: "It seemed too darkly Russian to me. Besides, it was so cruel and heartless that it stole the show."[12] Brooks Atkinson read this change as one of anxiety over issues of race: "Note that Mr. Logan cannot dismiss his counterpart of Firs as brutally as Chekhov does" (*New York Times*, 3 February 1955). *The Wisteria Trees* was not a great success on the stage, but Hayes again played Ranevskaya, this time with Chekhov's text, in a television "Play of the Week" in 1959, opposite E. G. Marshall as Lopakhin.

Race was made even more central to *The Cherry Orchard* in a 1973 Public Theatre production with an all-black cast. The production was conceived by James Earl Jones (who played Lopakhin), produced by Joseph Papp, and directed by Michael Schultz. Gayev was Earle Hyman; Firs the great South African actor Zakes Mokae; and Ranevskaya Gloria Foster (now perhaps best remembered as the "Oracle" from the *Matrix* films). The play had period sets and costumes, and critics disagreed about the extent to which it was interpreted in racial terms. Richard Watts of the *New York Post* wrote, "After a few minutes you hardly notice . . . I doubt if [Papp and Jones] were concerned with making a racial gesture" (27 January 1973). William

Glover, by contrast, felt that the production had "amazing relevancy" and "seethe[d] with fresh vigor and value through a stroke of imaginative casting."[13] The *New York Times* interpreted the play in purely racialized terms, echoing the language of Malcolm X: "Even if the House Slaves were to take over the Big House but ape the decadence and dissolution of the Slavemaster, they would still not have their freedom" (4 February 1973). In a *Times* feature, Maya Angelou attacked the question of whether African-Americans should play Chekhov:

> Yes, Black actors not only should play Chekhov, it is imperative that Black actors do "The Cherry Orchard." For in a plethora of dull European classics, "The Cherry Orchard" takes the cake. The play desperately needs the rippling sensuosity of James Earl Jones and the exhausted languor of Gloria Foster. In fact, to make it come alive really, it could use a few impersonations by Sammy Davis Jr., "Young, Gifted and Black," sung by Nina Simone and a rousing sermon by the Reverend Jesse Jackson. Ray Charles and the Rayettes ought to be humming in the background.[14]

While few went so far as Angelou, many directors felt that the play was an outmoded European warhorse and needed the addition of a vital contemporary spirit from American culture, racially defined or otherwise. Joel Gersmann's postmodern travesty version, in 1986 at the Broome Street Theatre in Madison, Wisconsin, is perhaps the most extreme example. Gersmann's stated goal was to "honestly invigorate . . . a threadbare tradition," to liberate a play "strangled by decades of bad directing and soggy realism inherited from Stanislavsky."[15] Gersmann's strategy was to play *The Cherry Orchard* as a farce, as Chekhov intended; to eliminate intervals and pauses, keeping a very rapid pace throughout; and to create "a complete disjunction . . . between words and actions," so that "characters would never do what they said."[16]

The production clearly went beyond Gersmann's original goals, as some of the cast members "openly detested Chekhov's play."[17] Gersmann's company "attacked *The Cherry Orchard* like Red Guards discovering the Imperial wine cellar," as Laurence Senelick put it.[18] The production was set in the present, that is, in the materialistic world of Ronald Reagan's America, and took its style from prime-time soap operas like *Dallas, Falcon Crest,* and *Dynasty.* Gayev wasted his time with television rather than billiards; Anya was a coke-snorting transvestite (both Anya and Varya were played by men; Yasha and Pishchik by women). The sets were bleak, the costumes flashy and tasteless in a style Gersmann defined as "bankrupt chic." The production was accompanied by loud music throughout, including a raucous punk-rock elegy entitled "Grisha's Dead." In the final scene, Ranevskaya and Gayev left for their new life carrying a giant American Express card, while Lopakhin entered with a buzzing chainsaw to cut down the orchard. The end result was not an invigoration of the play but a cynical assault on it. Laurence Senelick compared the effect to *A Clockwork Orange*: "yahoos were trashing a gallery for no reason other than to proclaim their independence from responsibility, both artistic and humanitarian."[19]

A more faithful and in some ways more potent adaptation was that of playwright and director Emily Mann, at the MacArthur Theatre in Princeton in 2000. Mann cast African-American actors in the roles of Lopakhin, Varya, and Firs, so that the class politics of the play took on a distinctly American charge. Avery Brooks' Lopakhin longed for Jane Alexander's Ranevskaya and ignored Caroline Stephanie Clay's Varya; "her aching frustration . . . [was] given an added wrench by the racial implication," according to Bruce Weber.[20] As Lopakhin, Brooks conveyed the justifiable pride and social disorientation of the new black millionaire. His attitudes were tellingly juxtaposed with those of Firs (Roger Robinson), whose Act II scene with Charlotta, cut since Stanislavsky's day, Mann retained. "In the touching speech of [Firs'] arrest, decades earlier, for a killing he didn't commit, the American echoes are chilling," Weber wrote. "Indeed, you can't help but see the two actors together as bookends of a 100-year African-American journey."[21] Mann wrote her adaptation in modern colloquial speech, and though costumes and set pieces alluded to the play's original period, the emphasis was strongly on the present, making the play "contemporary and American without being literally an update."[22]

The American tendency toward adapting and revising *The Cherry Orchard* found repeated expression in the ChekhovNOW Festival in New York City, founded in 2000. The Festival stages adaptations and new plays inspired by Chekhov, and has included such works as *The Cherry Orchard: Firs' Dream* (featuring a female Firs recalling the events of the play); *Anya in Paris*, a sort of "prequel"; and *The Ghost of Firs Nicolaich*. The last of these, an original play by Sam Mossler, concerns the afterlife of the Ranevsky household. Apparently the villa has been spared, though the trees are cut down, and the new owners are troubled by Firs' ghost; a medium is called in, who turns out to be Varya, now mad. Among the other characters who turn up is Leon Trotsky, "who drops in with a hookah and some really good dope. Later, the Volga rises up and submerges everything."[23]

A similar tongue-in-cheek attitude was expressed in the Festival's 2004 production of *The Cherry Orchard*, directed by Darren Gobert for Jovial Crew. One critic complained that "the gags and gimmicks ricocheting randomly about this 'Orchard' seem at best the bleary-eyed result of a late-night undergrad dorm room beer bust."[24] The production had a high-tech Brechtian edge, with scenery, scene titles, and key quotations all flashed on projection screens. In a heavy-handed stroke of irony, "Clever people are so stupid" was projected throughout Trofimov's Act II monologue. Class differences were expressed through both costume and stage technology; the gentry wore beige costumes from the turn of the century and spoke without amplification, while the working classes were dressed in black and pink punk rock outfits and spoke through headset "Madonna microphones." The servants chewed gum and openly mocked their employers. Actress Kaitlin Kratter was the star of the production, a cross-dressing Lopakhin in tap shoes.[25]

The Classical Theatre of Harlem presented a racially inflected *Cherry Orchard* in 2005 that gained national critical attention. Lopakhin and all of the family members were black. Petronia Paley was a very beautiful, elegant, and self-deluded Ranevskaya; Roslyn Ruff a strict but sympathetic Varya. Earle Hyman, who had played Gayev at the Public in 1973, was a fiercely loyal Firs. Wendell Pierce was Lopakhin, "fat, tacky and loud . . . the archetype of the small-minded arriviste, and a hard man to like," according to Campbell Robertson in the *New York Times* (9 February 2005). But Lopakhin's scene of triumph in Act III hinted at a contemporary American reading, one backed up by the production's use of costumes that bridged the gap between period and modern. "In the middle of his near-hysterical drunken victory speech, Lopakhin raises his right fist into the air, and refers to his father and grandfather with a word that is used nowhere else: slaves." Though in many respects the production seemed merely to be using "color-blind" casting, the power of this moment reminded the audience of an urgent contemporary reading of Chekhov's play. In this regard the Classical Theatre of Harlem reflected American Chekhov production at its best.

INTERNATIONAL ECLECTICISM

Productions of *The Cherry Orchard* around the world at the end of the twentieth century reflected a wide range of styles, attitudes, and agendas. Transplanting the play from a Russian or European context resulted in many innovative productions, and brought Chekhov into contact with receptive new audiences. In 2000, actress Janet Suzman wrote a contemporary adaptation called *The Free State* that set the play just after the first democratic elections in South Africa in 1994. Ranevskaya (played by Suzman herself) became Lulu Rademeyer, widow of a liberal Afrikaans lawyer, who has adopted his illegitimate half-black child Maria (Varya), and borne him a daughter, Anna, and a boy, Gerrie, who drowned. She has returned to her country from Paris in the wake of the elections, and eventually loses her estate to Leko Lebaka, a black businessman whose education she and her husband paid for. Suzman's version, which was performed both in South Africa and Britain, is in many cases nearly a line-by-line adaptation. Lulu sees the ghost of her mother in Act I: "Oh look, Mama all in white walking in the orchard! Look . . . To the left, by the path to the tennis courts – the little white tree bending over – looks just like a woman stooping to kiss a little child."[26] However, Suzman made some telling changes that brought the contemporary South African setting into sharp focus. At the beginning of the play, for instance, Leko dozed in front of the television, rather than falling asleep reading a book; his yellow boots became Guccis, while Yepikhodov's squeaky shoes were worn-out trainers; in frustration at Dunyasha's airs and graces, Leko snapped, "Now, Kele, don't you go all 'white' on me."[27] In keeping with her hopes for South Africa, Suzman's version was basically hopeful, with Anna working for the future with her lover Pitso Thekiso, an activist black student. When Lulu leaves the house behind, she shakes Leko's hand and says, "Leko. I think it's thank you."[28] As Suzman writes, "The burden of living with apartheid has been lifted from her shoulders."[29]

Singaporean playwright Chay Yew adapted the play to the Shanxi province of Northern China in 1934 in his 2002 play *The Morning People*, later produced in the USA as *A Winter People*. In Yew's adaptation, Ranevskaya became Madam Siet, a Chinese woman who has been living in London as a chanteuse but returns to her family's cherry estate on the eve of the Nationalist Revolution. Yew's resetting of the play emphasized the historical ironies: the Lopakhin character will lose his new estate to the communists within a year. Neo Swee Lin, as Madam Siet, made it clear that her reason for leaving China was neither the drowning of her son, nor a foreign lover, but dissatisfaction with her life in China and a dream of success in the West; her return is the result of her disenchantment.[30] Janice Koh gave a nuanced performance of the Varya character, a mixture of no-nonsense practicality, fragility, and thwarted love. As a Singaporean critic noted, "Even her character's name, Mei – a Mandarin homonym of both 'plum blossom' and 'nothing' – reinforces her star-crossed destiny as the cherry orchard which she believes is her birthright slips out of her grasp."[31]

In spite of the politically charged nature of the resetting, critics viewed *The Morning People* as apolitical, or rather anti-political: "Is this theatre in fact totally apolitical? Not at all," wrote Kalina Stefanova in *The European Review*. "Because it also has a clear protest-vote statement: we are fed up with politics and all it's done to people, it says. In the end political and economic systems come and go, and it's humanity that stays and defines us as people."[32]

A similar disavowal of politics characterized a Nicaraguan production directed by Adolph Shapiro in 1988, near the end of the civil conflict there. The distinguished Estonian director was invited to Managua to direct *The Cherry Orchard* with a Nicaraguan cast, working along with a Russian designer and movement teacher. Though the production was co-sponsored by the Soviet embassy, "no flags or political emblems were on the stage, and the text contained no call to the barricades, no inflammatory language," according to the *New York Times*. "For many Nicaraguan theatergoers, that was novel."[33] Since the 1979 Revolution, virtually all theatre in the country had been overtly didactic. "I saw that these Nicaraguan actors wanted to go beyond propaganda, toward the higher cultural level of theater on a world scale," Shapiro said. "For them, this is an encounter with Chekhov, an introduction to psychological drama and a course in the Stanislavsky method all rolled into six weeks."[34] The production was hardly without political significance – the Soviet Ambassador attended the premiere, along with several Sandinista artists – but no senior government officials attended. Ranevskaya was played by Socorro Bonilla Castellon, head of the National Comedy Company, one of Nicaragua's few professional theatre groups. "I didn't want to miss the chance of working with Shapiro," she said. "This is the kind of thing we have to be doing in Nicaragua if we want to connect our people to universal culture."[35] The Nicaraguans used the play, not to make a specific political statement about land ownership, but to link themselves to a universally respected playwright, and to their Soviet allies. Ironically, the Soviet Union would collapse within a year, and the Sandinistas would lose power a year later.

13. Suzuki Tadashi's Japanese adaptation *The Chekhov*, with Ranevskaya (Shiraishi Kayoko) making a grand entrance watched by Lopakhin (Tsutamori Kôsuke), Gayev (Sakato Toshihiro), and Anya (Takemori Yôichi). (Toga Sanbô, 1986.)

The most distinctive and eclectic international production of the play in recent years was the Japanese version by Suzuki Tadashi, part of his 1986 adaptation, *The Chekhov*. From the beginning, Chekhov had been at the heart of the Japanese Shingeki, or "new drama," western-oriented theatre that sought to distinguish itself from more traditional forms like Noh and Kabuki. In 1912, Osanai Kaoru, the founder of Shingeki, went to Russia to observe Stanislavsky direct at the Moscow Art Theatre, and he brought the MAT's methods back to productions in Japan. Senda Koreya, his successor, produced *The Cherry Orchard* to symbolize the rebirth of Japanese progressive theatre after the war ended in 1945. With the theatrical experimentation of the 1960s and 70s, Suzuki Tadashi began to reincorporate elements of Noh and Kabuki into Shingeki, along with influences from Brecht, Beckett, and the New York avant garde. "But one of Suzuki's greatest subversive achievements," according to Takahashi Yasunari, "was to undermine the privileged position of the written text provided by the playwright," giving priority instead to the actor.[36] Nonetheless, Suzuki retained a fondness for Chekhov, from his very first production, of Chekhov's farce *The Jubilee* in 1959, throughout his career.

The Chekhov was initially a double bill of very short adaptations of *Three Sisters* and *The Cherry Orchard*; *Uncle Vanya* was added in 1988. The whole performance ran only an hour and a half or so; Suzuki used only about one-fifth of Chekhov's *Cherry Orchard* text. The performance used a unit set of shoji screens, tatami mats, Western-style armchairs, and Japanese reed baskets; these were used to contain the characters like Beckett's urns in *Play*. For *The Cherry Orchard* section of the performance, dustsheets were thrown over the furniture, suggesting the final closing of Ranevskaya's household. The play itself was a dreamlike montage centered on Ranevskaya (the celebrated Suzuki actress Shiraishi Kayoko); Lopakhin, Gayev, Anya, Yasha, and Firs had only supporting parts, and all of the other characters were cut. The supporting players had eclectic costumes mixing cultural elements; Lopakhin, for instance, wore a bright red western businessman's hat together with the traditional work clothes of a Japanese peasant, suggesting his divided persona. Anya, played by a male actor, wore an untucked white shirt over blue stockings and white gym shorts, together with round-rimmed glasses and a blue-and-white baseball cap, worn backwards. Ranevskaya herself wore an elegant, sexy black dress and a black pillbox hat hung with strips of silver tinsel, "which signify something between grey hair and a headdress designed to allure." Music was a large feature of her performance. She made a grand entrance to the waltz from Gounod's *Faust*, and the dancing at the party was replaced by her singing of a popular karaoke song, "Drinking sake alone," which drew laughter and applause from the audience. Apart from these bursts of animation, however, Ranevskaya was a restrained figure suggesting the doomed heroine of a Noh play, according to Ian Carruthers: "her face is a tragic, totally impassive Noh mask; and when having finally lost her home, she says 'Let us go,' she, like Beckett's tramps, does not move. It is as if she has become the ghost of the place."[37]

The influences of Noh and Beckett were even more prevalent in Suzuki's television adaptation of *The Cherry Orchard*, also with Shiraishi, in 1989. This reduced the play to Ranevskaya's interior monologue, now only one-tenth of Chekhov's original text. The play consisted merely of an old woman, sitting in a chair, waiting for death, suggesting the heroines of *Not I* and *Rockaby* or the mad ghosts of the Noh. Apart from a few, mainly off-screen voices, all the text was hers, replaying the events of *The Cherry Orchard* as a dying memory. From time to time she loudly blew her nose, dropping the crumpled pink tissues into a waste-basket: in Carruthers' words, "The fall of cherry blossom from the trees in the orchard, symbolizing the beauty of transience, had been replaced by Suzuki with the grotesque dropping of waste matter."[38] Her only moment of animation came during the party, when she transformed briefly into her younger self to sing her karaoke song in the pink light of a dream sequence. At the end of the play, she suffered a fatal heart attack. Two heads rose from the baskets behind her, commenting on her passing with a distorted version of Firs' final lines: "My life's gone . . . I'm an empty shell. Oh you, you're just a used tissue."[39] Suzuki's television *Cherry Orchard* went even farther than *The Chekhov* in reducing the play to a bleak expression of the futility of life.

There have been a number of other film and television adaptations of the play around the world, in addition to the British and American versions already mentioned. Both Strehler's Milan *Orchard* and Brook's Paris version were broadcast in their home countries. An Australian TV production, with Googie Withers as Ranevskaya, aired in 1974. An Italian film, *Il Giardino dei Ciliegi*, directed by Antonello Aglioti, played at the San Sebastian Film Festival in 1992, but was widely panned. Filmed in Italian and updated to contemporary Europe, it featured Susan Strasberg, daughter of Lee Strasberg, as Ranevskaya (Susan Strasberg had played Anya opposite Helen

Hayes in an American TV version in 1959). Marisa Berenson played Charlotta.

A 1990 Japanese film, *Sakura no Sono*, used a production of *The Cherry Orchard* at an all-girls' school as a metaphor for exploring the students' experiences of growth, change, and loss. The 1979 Bulgarian film *Chereshova Gradina* (*The Cherry Orchard*), while not following Chekhov's plot, used a conflict over a cherry orchard to explore conflicts between old and new ways of life (in this case, between the orchard's manager and a communist party official). A 1993 Russian film directed by Anna Tchernakova used a period setting, but necessarily resonated with the changes in Russia after the fall of the Soviet Union. The most widely distributed film version of the play was Michael Cocoyannis' Greek/Cypriot/French-produced version of 1999, which used primarily British actors. Charlotte Rampling played Ranevskaya, Alan Bates Gayev; more vital performances came from Katrin Cartlidge as Varya and the Welsh actor Owen Teale as Lopakhin. The film made some attempts to open up the play cinematically, including a prologue showing Anya's embassy to Paris, a scene of the luncheon in Gayev's favorite restaurant, and an episode from the auction, which undermined the effect of Lopakhin's Act III account. In general, *The Cherry Orchard* has resisted translation to television and film; despite various attempts, there has never been a particularly successful or influential version comparable to Louis Malle's *Vanya on 42nd Street*.

"ALL RUSSIA IS OUR ORCHARD"

The breakup of the Soviet Union in 1989 brought sweeping changes to the Russian theatre. Chekhov, long associated with Soviet traditions and socialist realism, was temporarily put aside as outmoded, while directors eagerly performed glasnost-era playwrights like Alexander Galin and Lyudmila Petrushevskaya, or writers like Bulgakov who had been previously banned. Soon, however, theatres in Russia and the former Soviet states began to reclaim Chekhov, and *The Cherry Orchard* in particular became relevant to a country in which the old order was once again fading in the face of uncertain hopes for the future.

Leonid Trushkin, a young post-Soviet director, opened his career with an aggressively avant-garde *Cherry Orchard* in 1990. The stage was dominated by an enormous bookcase, "which opened like a peep-show to reveal the locales of the play," according to Laurence Senelick.[40] A violin-playing clown marionette announced the play as "*The Cherry Orchard*: A Comedy," and the whole piece had the frenetic energy of a Punch and Judy show. Tatiana Vasileva was a worldly Ranevskaya, unconcerned with the orchard; her eagerness to return to Paris "implied in this context that Russia was keen to move on to other things."[41]

Lev Dodin's Maly Drama Theatre in St. Petersburg rose to prominence with the decline of the Soviet Union, with plays exploring the lives of those who suffered under the Soviet system: Moscow prostitutes in Galin's *Stars in the Morning Sky*, military recruits in *Gaudeamus*, collective farmers in *Brothers and Sisters*. Dodin directed *The Cherry Orchard* in 1994 because, as he put it, "Like Chekhov's characters, we live today between two eras. One thing is replaced by another. We can't yet understand what is fading into the past. We can't yet conceive what is coming. But it is at these fateful moments that we begin to hear the rustle of time flying. Every moment of life takes on a taste, a value, and becomes an object of desire. We swallow each moment with an almost comical greed and an almost tragic edge."[42] His production of the play reflected this heightened sense of time, and these sometimes violently contradictory emotions about the changes taking place. Running just over two hours without an interval, Dodin's *Cherry Orchard* had a rapid pace and almost ceaseless movement, particularly in the ballroom scene. The setting facilitated these rapid transitions. Tall, free-standing window panels, incorporating cherry branches, created a spare, indoor–outdoor set. Each act merged seamlessly into the next: at the end of Act II (Chekhov's original version with Charlotta and Firs), Charlotta's firing of her gun served as a pistol-start for vigorous dancing that instantly began Act III; at the end of the party, the glowing chandelier was lowered into an ornamental pond, extinguishing its candles and setting the mood for the final act. Dodin's mostly young actors, many of them his former students, performed with physical abandon; Arkady Koval's spectacularly accident-prone Yepikhodov at one point fell headfirst into the pond. Igor Ivanov's "gritty, driven performance of Lopakhin" gave the production a post-Soviet edge, according to *Moscow Times* critic John Freedman; this was "no nostalgic portrait of the dying aristocracy, but a rough, gruff exploration of a middle class emerging from a class of slaves."[43] Tatiana Shestakova was an unusually young and sensual Ranevskaya, heedlessly flinging herself at all of the other characters, passionately kissing Lopakhin even after his purchase of the estate. When the Maly *Cherry Orchard* played in London, Michael Billington wrote, "The moment I shall long remember is in the final act when she licks her brother's face with lascivious glee and they play a last game of hide-and-seek around the dwindling furniture as if there were no tomorrow."[44] The Maly's tours to the West were related to its tenuous position in the new Russia; the theatre itself had the same kind of economic vulnerability as the Ranevsky estate. As Dodin admitted, "There are people at the Maly that we can only support by working [in the West]. We have to send a lot of money home; and this is getting harder."[45]

Another prominent Russian *Cherry Orchard* that toured to the West was Galina Volchek's production from Moscow's Sovremennik (contemporary) Theatre. Volchek had been a founding member of the Sovremennik in 1956, and took it over in 1972 after Oleg Yefremov left for the MAT. She had directed *The Cherry Orchard* several times before her 1997 production, which played on Broadway before becoming a staple of the Sovremennik repertoire. For this production, Volchek reconceived the play for the post-Soviet world. In her first *Cherry Orchard* in Moscow in 1976, she had presented Lopakhin negatively: "The Russian intelligentsia wanted to escape from the coming of Lopakhins," she recalled.[46] In 1997, Sergei Garmash's handsome, earnest Lopakhin was a positive figure, trying to find a way to preserve what was good in the past while building a better Russia for the future. Marina Neyolova made a tragic, doomed Ranevskaya, "a faded bird of luxury mourning the life she can't quite believe she has been compelled to sign away."[47] The play ended, not with Firs alone onstage, but with the company surrounding him in a final dance.

While full productions of *The Cherry Orchard* were common in post-Soviet Russia, there were also more radical reworkings. Igor Larin made the play into a one-man show called *A Dream about the Cherry Orchard*. The estate was a ruined castle in a snow globe; Larin, as Lopakhin, played a kind of Prince Charming trying to wake the sleeping beauty Ranevskaya. Failing to do so, he transformed into a "crude businessman with a briefcase" loudly promoting "the advancement of the trade."[48] Larin's iconoclastic vision included an outraged spectator planted in the audience, who walked out every night.

Interestingly, many of the most striking productions of the play seen in Moscow and St. Petersburg were by non-Russian directors from other former Soviet states. The Lithuanian Eimuntas Nekrosius and the Estonian Adolph Shapiro both directed *The Cherry Orchard* in Moscow in its centenary year, 2004. Nekrosius' production was six hours long. It featured the kind of detailed, idiosyncratic theatrical invention for which the Lithuanian director was famous, according to John Freedman of the *Moscow Times*: "It certainly could not be mistaken for the work of any other director. The actors' improvisations that transform into self-sufficient mini-dramas; the unexpected visual metaphors involving props; the hurricane-like energy of young actresses hurtling about the stage – Nekrosius has brought all of this into his Russian version of *The Cherry Orchard*."[49] Before the play even began, Firs slowly, inexplicably pulled a dozen coats off a chair. Ranevskaya (Lyudmila Maksakova) entered and lay down like a corpse, to be carried out as if to her funeral; she remained a spectre throughout the performance, absorbed in her own griefs and complexes. Yevgeny Mironov made Lopakhin a menacing figure from Putin's Moscow: "a guy you will certainly like, a future gangster with the makings of a tycoon, an ugly symbol of the new life in Russia."[50] All the other characters were heartsick and doomed.

The cherry orchard was composed of clumped weather vanes; at the end of the play the characters were all herded into it like hunted rabbits. The costumes were in drab shades of grey and brown; the chief set-pieces were "two dirty structures that could be anything from unmarked graves to tiny policemen's booths."[51] The discordant soundtrack began with a Mahlerian death march and included painfully loud cricket sounds, an ironic wink at Stanislavsky. The dance beginning Act III was a hellish saturnalia after Hieronymus Bosch, filled with cripples, monsters, and witches. The whole production was saturated with dread about life in the new Russia, according to Arkady Petrov:

> In his own cherry orchard drama, Eimuntas Nekrosius . . . plunged us into an abyss of horrors by opening our eyes on how little the start of last century differed from the beginning of this one, and how much in common we share with "them". The implication was that "their" disasters could befall us, with the complicity and connivance of "their" new reincarnations living among us.[52]

The Moscow Art Theatre itself staged *The Cherry Orchard* as part of the Chekhov centenary. In fact, it staged two *Cherry Orchards*. The MAT had split, in 1987, into two theatres, both of which persisted into the twenty-first century. The theatre named for Gorky was run by Tatiana Doronina, a Soviet throwback and dedicated communist. She played Ranevskaya in a 1988 socialist realist production that was still in the repertoire in 2005, in the imposing concrete building on Tverskoi Boulevard inhabited by the Gorky MAT. The other

MAT, named for Chekhov, remained in the art nouveau theatre on Kamergersky Pereulok where *The Cherry Orchard* was first performed. Considered by most Russians to be the true MAT, it was run by Oleg Yefremov from 1978 until his death in 2000, when his former student Oleg Tabakov succeeded him. The Chekhov Art Theatre introduced a new production by Adolph Shapiro in 2004 to commemorate the 100th anniversary of the play's premiere and the playwright's death.

Shapiro's production reflected on the importance of the play to the Art Theatre while also relating it to the new Russia. The principal feature of David Borovsky's set was a divided curtain, a copy of the original art nouveau curtain, with its Seagull logo, that the theatre used when it opened in 1902. The curtain could divide and move in all directions, or part to reveal lighter curtains of white gauze; in this way it created both house and orchard. The moving curtain alluded not only to the MAT but to one of Russia's most famous modern theatre productions, Lyubimov's 1971 Taganka *Hamlet* with Vladimir Vysotsky, which Borovsky also designed. As in *Hamlet*, the moving curtain, suspended in front of a black void and sweeping characters on and off the stage, was a potent symbol of history.

The tone of Shapiro's *Cherry Orchard* was dark and reflective. The dominant presence was Andrei Smolyakov's Lopakhin, a handsome, pensive, surprisingly intellectual figure who clearly foresaw the dangerous course of future events. He was not an unhopeful emblem for the new Russia. A deep thinker as well as a man of action, he suffered as much as anyone at the spoliation of the orchard. Ranevskaya, the film actress Renata Litvinova, was a bored and pampered beauty, unable to work up any real concern with the estate or any connection with the other characters. Dressed in the manner of a forties movie star, with platinum blonde hair, long cigarette holder, purple silk gown, and fur stole, she had a flat, toneless delivery and a dead-eyed somnolent demeanor. Her performance, though not ineffective, was deeply unsympathetic; her best moment came in Act III when she teased and tormented Trofimov with the idea of her lover in Paris, sensually caressing the telegram. Otherwise, none of the relationships had much heat. Trofimov was an earnest dreamer, not much interested in Anya, who was a spoiled child. Varya was too vital, practical and confidently attractive to be crushed by missing out on Lopakhin. Her final line to him, "*Ya i ne dumala*" – "I never thought of it" – referred not to a blow with the umbrella, but to the missed proposal; she was letting him know she hadn't really wanted him and wasn't too badly hurt.

Gayev was played by Sergei Dreiden, a leading St. Petersburg actor, as a relatively serious man: a cranky philosopher like Astrov rather than an overgrown child or snobbish aristocrat. While he had flights of playfulness, riding a bicycle around the stage at one point, he mostly came across as a thoughtful if rather quirky observer, not unlike Chekhov himself. When his nieces hushed him at the end of the play, preventing him from making a farewell speech to the house, the scene conveyed their shallowness rather than his volubility; he seemed to have earned the right to speak.

One of Dreiden's more striking moments as Gayev may provide a fitting place to conclude this study of *The Cherry Orchard*'s production history. It was one of several points where the MAT production seemed to reflect on Chekhov's position in Russian culture as his play entered its second century. During his speech to the bookcase, Dreiden as Gayev moved down to the footlights and addressed the Moscow Art Theatre itself. Words that Chekhov clearly intended to sound ridiculous took on a new seriousness as Dreiden/Gayev meditated on the value of a storehouse of culture that had endured a painful century of life:

> I salute your existence, which for more than a hundred years now has been directed toward the shining ideals of goodness and of truth.[53]

Gayev's absurd panegyric may be as good a way as any to acknowledge the achievement of *The Cherry Orchard* itself, which has now endured a century of exploration, both tragic and ridiculous, both painfully realistic and poetically abstract, both despairing and alive with hope.

For a hundred years your unspoken summons to fruitful labor has never faltered, upholding, through all the generations of our family, wisdom and faith in a better future, and fostering within us ideals of goodness and of social consciousness.

Whatever ideals *The Cherry Orchard* has fostered in the first century of its existence, the play is certain to be challenged, reinvented, and rediscovered in the years to come. The axes may be ringing in the orchard, but the new life is always beginning.

NOTES

Introduction

1. Anton Chekhov, letter to Olga Knipper, 7 March 1901, in *The Oxford Chekhov*, trans. and ed. Ronald Hingley, vol. III (London: Oxford University Press, 1964), p. 317.
2. Chekhov to Knipper, 22 April 1901, Hingley, *Oxford Chekhov*, p. 317.
3. Chekhov to Lilina, 15 September 1903, Hingley, *Oxford Chekhov*, p. 319.
4. Stanislavsky to Chekhov, 22 October 1903, *The Moscow Art Theatre Letters*, trans. and ed. Jean Benedetti (London: Methuen, 1991), p. 162.
5. Chekhov to Knipper, 29 March 1904 and 10 April 1904, Hingley, *Oxford Chekhov*, pp. 330, 331.
6. Constantin Stanislavsky, *My Life in Art*, trans. J. J. Robbins (London: Methuen, 1985), p. 420.
7. Meyerhold to Chekhov, 8 May 1904, quoted in *A Sourcebook on Naturalistic Theatre*, ed. Christopher Innes (London: Routledge, 2000), p. 179.
8. Vsevolod Meyerhold, "The Naturalistic Theatre and the Theatre of Mood" (1906), trans. Nora Beeson, in *Anton Chekhov's Plays*, ed. Eugene Bristow (New York: Norton, 1977), p. 318.
9. Trevor Griffiths, Introduction, *The Cherry Orchard, by Anton Chekhov, a New English Version by Trevor Griffiths*; from a translation by Helen Rappaport (London: Pluto Press, 1978), p. 14.

1. *The Cherry Orchard*: text and performance

1. Quoted in Maurice Valency, *The Breaking String: The Plays of Anton Chekhov* (Oxford: Oxford University Press, 1966), p. 249.

2. J. L. Styan, "Chekhov on the British Stage: Differences," in *Chekhov on the British Stage*, ed. Patrick Miles (Cambridge: Cambridge University Press, 1993), p. 14.

3. Quoted in *ibid.*, p. 15.

4. Anton Chekhov, *The Cherry Orchard*, trans. Michael Frayn (London: Methuen, 1995), p. 1. Unless otherwise specified, all quotations of the text of *The Cherry Orchard* are from Frayn's translation.

5. 5 February 1903, Hingley, *Oxford Chekhov*, p. 318.

6. Vladimir Kataev, *If Only We Could Know!: An Interpretation of Chekhov*, trans. and ed. Harvey Pitcher (Chicago: Ivan R. Dee, 2002), p. 274.

7. David Magarshack, *Chekhov the Dramatist*, Dramabooks edn. (New York: Hill and Wang, 1960), p. x.

8. Nick Worrall, "Commentary," *The Cherry Orchard*, trans. Michael Frayn (London: Methuen 1995), p. xli.

9. Donald Rayfield, *The Cherry Orchard: Catastrophe and Comedy* (New York: Twayne, 1994), p. 55.

10. Hingley, *Oxford Chekhov*, p. 322.

11. John Gielgud, *Gielgud on Gielgud* (London: Hodder and Stoughton, 2000), pp. 71–2.

12. Chekhov to Nemirovich-Danchenko, 22 August 1903, Hingley, *Oxford Chekhov*, p. 319.

13. Frayn's translation says Charlotta doesn't have "proper papers." She is referring to the internal passport used for travel within Russia, but most translators use the direct English cognate for the Russian "*pasport*." I find "passport" a more evocative, if slightly misleading, translation.

14. Chekhov to Knipper, 25 September 1903, Hingley, *Oxford Chekhov*, p. 320.

15. J. L. Styan, *Chekhov in Performance* (Cambridge: Cambridge University Press, 1971), p. 279.

16. Kataev, *If Only We Could Know!*, p. 273.

17. Harvey Pitcher, *The Chekhov Play: A New Interpretation* (London: Chatto and Windus, 1973), p. 180.

18. Hingley, *Oxford Chekhov*, p. 322. Chekhov originally had additional dialogue here, with Varya proposing that Yepikhodov be fired in order to save money; by removing these lines Chekhov preserved the meditative nature of the scene.

19. Rayfield, *The Cherry Orchard*, p. 74.
20. Magarshack, *Chekhov the Dramatist*, Dramabooks ed., p. 286.
21. Francis Fergusson, "*The Cherry Orchard*: A Theatre-Poem of the Suffering of Change," from *The Idea of a Theatre* (Princeton: Princeton University Press, 1949), p. 170; Valency, *The Breaking String*, p. 286.
22. Pitcher, *The Chekhov Play*, p. 183.
23. Laurence Senelick, *Anton Chekhov* (London: Macmillan, 1985), p. 26.
24. Andrey Bely, "*The Cherry Orchard*," in *Russian Dramatic Theory from Pushkin to the Symbolists*, trans. and ed. Laurence Senelick (Austin: University of Texas Press, 1981), p. 92.
25. Meyerhold, "The Naturalistic Theatre," p. 317.
26. Rayfield, *The Cherry Orchard*, p. 81.
27. Styan, *Chekhov in Performance*, p. 295.
28. Senelick, *Anton Chekhov*, p. 130.
29. Meyerhold to Chekhov, 8 May 1904, quoted in Christopher Innes, *A Sourcebook on Naturalistic Theatre* (London: Routledge, 2000), p. 179.
30. Rayfield, *The Cherry Orchard*, p. 81.
31. David Mamet, "Notes on *The Cherry Orchard*," in *The Cherry Orchard*, by Anton Chekhov, adapted by David Mamet (New York: Grove Press, 1985), p. vii.
32. Hingley, *Oxford Chekhov*, p. 325.
33. Styan, *Chekhov in Performance*, p. 308.
34. Nick Worrall, "Stanislavsky's Production Score for Chekhov's *The Cherry Orchard* (1904): A Synoptic Overview," *Modern Drama* 42.4 (Winter 1999), p. 534.
35. David Magarshack, *Chekhov the Dramatist* (London: J. Lehmann, 1952), p. 281.
36. My translation. Frayn, unlike Chekhov, does not repeat the verbs: his Lopakhin says, "It is," and "I did."
37. Pitcher, *The Chekhov Play*, p. 190.
38. In the original text Act IV was set merely in a room on the ground floor. Before rehearsals began, Stanislavsky suggested to Chekhov that Act IV use the same set as Act III. Chekhov agreed, but at some point it was decided to return to the set for Act I: much the most effective of the three options.

39. Chekhov to Knipper, 29 March 1904, Benedetti, *The Moscow Art Theatre Letters*, p. 189.

40. Chekhov apparently added these important lines during rehearsals or after the opening; they are not in the original manuscript. Hingley, *Oxford Chekhov*, p. 325.

41. Rayfield, *The Cherry Orchard*, p. 88.

42. Styan, *Chekhov in Performance*, p. 321.

43. Pitcher, *The Chekhov Play*, p. 206.

44. *Ibid.*

2. The Moscow Art Theatre production, 1904

1. Chekhov to Knipper, 29 March 1904, Hingley, *Oxford Chekhov*, p. 330.

2. Quoted in Magarshack, *Chekhov the Dramatist*, p. 14.

3. Nemirovich-Danchenko to Stanislavsky, after 26 July 1904, Benedetti, *The Moscow Art Theatre Letters*, pp. 206–7.

4. Nemirovich-Danchenko to Chekhov, 2 December 1902, 16 February 1903, Benedetti, *The Moscow Art Theatre Letters*, pp. 145, 148.

5. Knipper to Chekhov, 20 October 1903, Benedetti, *The Moscow Art Theatre Letters*, p. 161.

6. Nemirovich-Danchenko to Chekhov, 18 October 1903, Benedetti, *The Moscow Art Theatre Letters*, p. 160.

7. Chekhov to Nemirovich-Danchenko, 23 October 1903, Hingley, *Oxford Chekhov*, pp. 326–7.

8. Chekhov to Knipper, 11 February 1903, Hingley, *Oxford Chekhov*, p. 318.

9. Chekhov to Nemirovich-Danchenko, 2 November 1903, Benedetti, *The Moscow Art Theatre Letters*, p. 176.

10. Chekhov to Olga Knipper, 14 October 1903, Hingley, *Oxford Chekhov*, p. 327.

11. Chekhov to Olga Knipper, 25 October 1903, Hingley, *Oxford Chekhov*, p. 327.

12. Chekhov to Olga Knipper, 30 October 1903, Benedetti, *The Moscow Art Theatre Letters*, p. 171.

13. Chekhov to Stanislavsky, 30 October 1903, *The Moscow Art Theatre Letters*, p. 171. Benedetti translates *kulachok* as "farmer," which doesn't give the sense of a grasping peasant Chekhov implies.

14. Sharon Carnicke, "Stanislavsky's Production of *The Cherry Orchard* in the US," in *Chekhov Then and Now: The Reception of Chekhov in World Culture*" (New York: Peter Lang, 1997), p. 28, n. 25.

15. Stanislavsky to Chekhov, 31 October 1903, Benedetti, *The Moscow Art Theatre Letters*, p. 174.

16. Laurence Senelick, *The Chekhov Theatre* (Cambridge: Cambridge University Press, 1997), p. 71.

17. Chekhov to Knipper, 21 October 1903, Benedetti, *The Moscow Art Theatre Letters*, p. 161.

18. Chekhov to Nemirovich-Danchenko, 2 November 1903, Hingley, *Oxford Chekhov*, p. 328.

19. Chekhov to Nemirovich-Danchenko, 2 November 1903, Benedetti, *The Moscow Art Theatre Letters*, p. 175.

20. Anton Chekhov, letter to Olga Knipper, 27 February 1904, quoted in Senelick, *The Chekhov Theatre*, p. 70.

21. Chekhov to Stanislavsky, 5 November 1903, Hingley, *Oxford Chekhov*, p. 328.

22. Nick Worrall, *The Moscow Art Theatre* (London: Routledge, 1996), p. 159.

23. David Allen, *Performing Chekhov* (London: Routledge, 2000), p. 29.

24. Worrall, *The Moscow Art Theatre*, p. 156.

25. *Ibid.*

26. Chekhov to Knipper, 20 November 1903, quoted in *Chekhov in Performance in Russia and Soviet Russia*, companion volume to slide collection, by Vera Gottlieb (London: Chadwyck Healey, 1984), p. 27.

27. Chekhov to Nemirovich, 2 November 1903, Hingley, *Oxford Chekhov*, p. 328.

28. L. M. Leonidov, quoted in Hingley, *Oxford Chekhov*, p. 330.

29. Worrall, "Stanislavsky's Production Score," p. 522.

30. Hugh Walpole, "Epikhodov, Notes on a Russian Character," in *The Soul of Russia*, ed. Winifred Stephens (London: Macmillan, 1916), p. 37.

31. Senelick, *The Chekhov Theatre*, p. 373, n. 91.

32. Lilina to Chekhov, 11 November 1903, Benedetti, *The Moscow Art Theatre Letters*, p. 181.

33. Chekhov to Knipper, 25 October 1903, Hingley, *Oxford Chekhov*, p. 327.

34. M. Turovskaya, quoted in Harvey Pitcher, *Chekhov's Leading Lady* (New York: Franklin Watts, 1980), p. 196.
35. *Ibid.*, p. 197.
36. *Ibid.*, pp. 197–8.
37. *Ibid.*, p. 198.
38. Quoted in David Magarshack, *Stanislavsky, A Life* (London: Faber, 1986), p. 256.
39. Pitcher, *Chekhov's Leading Lady*, p. 198.
40. Allen, *Performing Chekhov*, p. 30.
41. Quoted in Magarshack, *Stanislavsky*, p. 256.
42. Allen, *Performing Chekhov*, p. 31.
43. Carnicke, "Stanislavsky's Production," p. 24.
44. *Ibid.*, p. 29, n. 38.
45. Worrall, "Stanislavsky's Production Score," p. 524.
46. *Ibid.*
47. *Ibid.*
48. Allen, *Performing Chekhov*, p. 31.
49. Worrall, "Stanislavsky's Production Score," p. 524.
50. *Ibid.*
51. Allen, *Performing Chekhov*, p. 31.
52. Chekhov to Stanislavsky, 5 November 1903, in Benedetti, *The Moscow Art Theatre Letters*, p. 178.
53. Stanislavsky to Chekhov, 19 November 1903, in Benedetti, *The Moscow Art Theatre Letters*, p. 185.
54. Quoted in Allen, *Performing Chekhov*, p. 17.
55. *Ibid.*, p. 44.
56. *Ibid.*, p. 37.
57. *Ibid.*
58. Worrall, "Stanislavsky's Production Score," p. 526.
59. Allen, *Performing Chekhov*, p. 30.
60. Quoted in S. S. Koteliansky, trans. and ed., *Anton Tchekhov: Literary and Theatrical Reminiscences* (London: Routledge, 1927), p. 170.
61. Nemirovich to Stanislavsky, 26 October 1899, in Benedetti, *The Moscow Art Theatre Letters*, p. 60.
62. Worrall, "Stanislavsky's Production Score," p. 527.
63. *Ibid.*

64. Knipper to Chekhov, 23 November 1903, in Benedetti, *The Moscow Art Theatre Letters*, p. 186.
65. Chekhov to Knipper, 19 October 1903, Hingley, *Oxford Chekhov*, p. 326.
66. Senelick, *The Chekhov Theatre*, p. 93.
67. Worrall, "Stanislavsky's Production Score," p. 527.
68. Chekhov to Knipper, 18 March 1904, Hingley, *Oxford Chekhov*, p. 330.
69. Worrall, "Stanislavsky's Production Score," p. 528.
70. Quoted in Senelick, *The Chekhov Theatre*, p. 76.
71. Quoted in Innes, *A Sourcebook on Naturalist Theatre*, p. 174.
72. Quoted in Koteliansky, *Anton Tchekhov*, p. 132.
73. Worrall, "Stanislavsky's Production Score," p. 532.
74. *Ibid.*
75. Quoted in Koteliansky, *Anton Tchekhov*, p. 169.
76. Meyerhold to Chekhov, 8 May 1904, quoted in Innes, *Sourcebook on Naturalistic Theatre*, p. 179.
77. Meyerhold, "The Naturalistic Theatre," p. 318.
78. *Ibid.*
79. Allen, *Performing Chekhov*, p. 39; see also Worrall, *The Moscow Art Theatre*, p. 164.
80. Allen, *Performing Chekhov*, p. 40; Worrall, "Stanislavsky's Production Score," p. 529.
81. Quoted in Senelick, *The Chekhov Theatre*, p. 77.
82. Worrall, "Stanislavsky's Production Score," p. 533.
83. Nemirovich to Knipper, before 17 January 1904, Benedetti, *The Moscow Art Theatre Letters*, pp. 186–7.
84. Worrall, "Stanislavsky's Production Score," p. 533.
85. Michel Saint-Denis, "Style and Reality," *Theatre: The Rediscovery of Style* (London: Heinemann, 1960), p. 42.
86. Stanislavsky, *My Life in Art*, p. 422.
87. Jean Benedetti, *Stanislavski* (London: Methuen, 1988), p. 131.
88. *Ibid.*, p. 131.
89. *Ibid.*, p. 132.
90. *Ibid.*
91. *Ibid.*

92. "Nemirovich to Leonidov," January 1904, Benedetti, *The Moscow Art Theatre Letters*, pp. 187–8.
93. Benedetti, *Stanislavski*, p. 133.
94. Quoted in Benedetti, *Stanislavski*, p. 133.
95. Cheryl Crawford, *One Naked Individual: My Fifty Years in the Theatre* (New York: Bobbs-Merrill, 1977), p. 86.
96. Worrall, "Stanislavsky's Production Score," p. 535.
97. "Chekhov to Knipper," 29 March 1904, Benedetti, *The Moscow Art Theatre Letters*, p. 189.
98. Worrall, "Stanislavsky's Production Score," p. 537.
99. Oliver Sayler, *The Russian Theatre* (New York: Brentano's, 1922), p. 58.
100. Worrall, "Stanislavsky's Production Score," p. 538.
101. I. N. Soloviova, ed., *Rezhissërskiye èkzemplyary K. S. Stanislavskogo*, vol. III, 1901–1904 (Moscow: Iskusstvo, 1983), p. 457.
102. Heywood Broun, *New York World*, 23 January 1923, quoted in Carnicke, "Stanislavsky's Production," p. 24.
103. Carnicke, "Stanislavsky's Production," p. 25.
104. Stanislavsky, *My Life in Art*, p. 422.
105. Quoted in Worrall, *The Moscow Art Theatre*, p. 161.
106. *Ibid.*
107. *Ibid.*, p. 162.
108. Quoted in Senelick, *The Chekhov Theatre*, p. 84.
109. Quoted in Worrall, *The Moscow Art Theatre*, p. 161.
110. Senelick, *The Chekhov Theatre*, p. 78.
111. Stanislavsky, *My Life in Art*, p. 554.

3. Russian and Soviet performances, 1904–1953

1. Quoted in Konstantin Rudnitsky, *Russian and Soviet Theatre: Tradition and the Avant-Garde*, trans. Roxanne Permar (London: Thames and Hudson, 1988), p. 51.
2. Nemirovich-Danchenko to Stanislavsky, 25 July 1904, Benedetti, *The Moscow Art Theatre Letters*, p. 203.
3. Stanislavsky to Nemirovich-Danchenko, 13 July 1904, Benedetti, *The Moscow Art Theatre Letters*, p. 202.

4. Meyerhold, "The Naturalistic Theatre," p. 318.
5. Edward Braun, *The Theatre of Meyerhold* (New York: Drama Book Specialists, 1979), p. 33.
6. Quoted in Senelick, *The Chekhov Theatre*, p. 92.
7. Meyerhold to Chekhov, 8 May 1904, in Innes, *A Sourcebook on Naturalistic Theatre*, p. 179.
8. Quoted in Senelick, *The Chekhov Theatre*, p. 88.
9. *Ibid.*
10. *Ibid.*, p. 93.
11. *Ibid.*, p. 94.
12. *Ibid.*, p. 96.
13. *Ibid.*
14. André Van Gyseghem, *Theatre in Soviet Russia* (London: Faber, 1940), pp. 52–5.
15. Allen, *Performing Chekhov*, p. 70.
16. Senelick, *The Chekhov Theatre*, p. 111.
17. *Ibid.*, p. 122.
18. Stanislavsky, *My Life in Art*, p. 555.
19. Van Gyseghem, *Theatre in Soviet Russia*, p. 54.
20. Quoted in Anatoly Smeliansky, "Chekhov at the Moscow Art Theatre," in *The Cambridge Companion to Chekhov*, ed. Vera Gottlieb and Paul Allain (Cambridge: Cambridge University Press, 2000), p. 30.
21. Quoted in Senelick, *The Chekhov Theatre*, pp. 114–15.
22. *Ibid.*, p. 115.
23. Quoted in Allen, *Performing Chekhov*, pp. 73–4.
24. Quoted in Rudnitsky, *Russian and Soviet Theatre*, p. 47.
25. Sergei Ostrovsky, "Germanova and the MAT Prague Group," in *Wandering Stars, Russian Émigré Theatre: 1905–1940*, ed. Laurence Senelick (Iowa City: Iowa University Press, 1992), p. 88.
26. James Agate, *Sunday Times*, 15 April 1928.
27. Anatoly Smeliansky, "In Search of El Dorado: America in the Fate of the Moscow Art Theatre," in Senelick, *Wandering Stars*, p. 49.
28. Jean Benedetti, editor's note, *The Moscow Art Theatre Letters*, p. 316.
29. Carnicke, "Stanislavsky's Production," p. 19.
30. Magarshack, *Stanislavsky*, p. 364.
31. *Ibid.*, pp. 358–9.

32. Oliver M. Sayler, ed., *The Moscow Art Theatre Series of Russian Plays*, trans. Jennie Covan (New York: Brentano's, 1923), p. v.

33. Quoted in Carnicke, "Stanislavsky's Production," p. 27, n. 19.

34. Christine Edwards, *The Stanislavsky Heritage, Its Contribution to the Russian and American Theatre* (New York: New York University Press, 1965), p. 226.

35. Carnicke, "Stanislavsky's Production," p. 25.

36. John Corbin, *New York Times*, 23 January 1923.

37. John V. A. Weaver, "A 100 Per Cent. American Speaks," *New York Times*, reprinted in *Literary Digest*, 3 March 1923; clipping in the Billy Rose Theatre Collection, New York Public Library.

38. Quoted in Carnicke, "Stanislavsky's Production," p. 24.

39. Nemirovich-Danchenko to Olga Bokshanskaya, 9 March 1924, quoted in Smeliansky, "In Search of El Dorado," p. 64.

40. Quoted in Senelick, *The Chekhov Theatre*, p. 122.

41. Quoted in Smeliansky, "Chekhov at the Moscow Art Theatre," p. 31.

42. Quoted in Senelick, *The Chekhov Theatre*, p. 123.

43. *Ibid.*

44. Worrall, "Commentary," *The Cherry Orchard*, trans. Frayn, p. xxxiv.

45. Quoted in Senelick, *The Chekhov Theatre*, p. 123.

46. Rudnitsky, *Russian and Soviet Theatre*, p. 59.

47. Senelick, *The Chekhov Theatre*, p. 124.

48. Worrall, "Commentary," *The Cherry Orchard*, trans. Frayn, p. xxxiv.

49. Senelick, *The Chekhov Theatre*, p. 124.

50. *Ibid.*, p. 125.

51. Allen, *Performing Chekhov*, pp. 85–6.

4. *The Cherry Orchard* in English: early productions

1. *The World*, 6 June 1911, quoted in Senelick, *The Chekhov Theatre*, p. 132.

2. Patrick Miles, *Chekhov on the British Stage, 1909–1987* (Cambridge: SAM and SAM, 1987), p. 4; Allen, *Performing Chekhov*, p. 161.

3. Miles, *Chekhov on the British Stage, 1909–1987*, p. 4.

4. George Calderon, *Two Plays by Tchekhof* (New York: M. Kennerley, 1912), p. 10.

5. Walpole, "Epikhodov," p. 37.
6. Calderon, *Two Plays*, p. 10.
7. *Ibid.*, p. 101, n. 1.
8. *Ibid.*, p. 128, n. 1.
9. Calderon, *Two Plays*, p. 138, n. 1.
10. Arnold Bennett, "Jacob Tonson," *New Age*, 8 June 1911, p. 132.
11. Jan McDonald, "Naturalism and the Drama of Dissent," in Miles, *Chekhov on the British Stage*, p. 31.
12. Calderon, "The Russian Stage," *Quarterly Review*, 1912, p. 31.
13. Bennett, "Jacob Tonson," p. 132.
14. H. W. Massingham, *Nation*, 3 June 1911.
15. J. T. Grein, *Sunday Times*, 4 June 1911.
16. Bennett, "Jacob Tonson," p. 132.
17. J. Middleton Murry, *New Republic*, 8 September 1920, quoted in Charles W. Meister, *Chekhov Criticism: 1880 Through 1986* (Jefferson, North Carolina: MacFarland, 1988), p. 269.
18. Margaret Webster, *The Same Only Different: Five Generations of a Great Theatre Family* (New York: Knopf, 1969), p. 316.
19. Senelick, *The Chekhov Theatre*, pp. 134, 137–8.
20. Gielgud, *Gielgud On Gielgud*, p. 71.
21. Hal Burton, *Great Acting* (New York: Hill and Wang, 1967), p. 136; quoted in Senelick, *The Chekhov Theatre*, p. 141.
22. Jonathan Croall, *Gielgud, A Theatrical Life* (London: Methuen, 2000), p. 68.
23. John Gielgud, *Stage Directions* (London: Heinemann, 1963), p. 85.
24. Croall, *Gielgud*, p. 61.
25. *Ibid.*
26. Nigel Playfair, *The Lyric Theatre, Hammersmith* (London, 1925), p. 217.
27. *Star*, 26 May 1925; *Times*, 26 May 1925.
28. Francis Birrell, *Nation and Athenaeum*, 30 May 1925; Don Chapman, "James Bernard Fagan and Chekhov," *Theatre Notebook* 56.1 (2002), p. 15.
29. C. Nabokoff, *Contemporary Review*, January–June 1926.
30. Desmond MacCarthy, *New Statesman and Nation*, 21 October 1933.
31. Frances Birrell, *Nation and Athenaeum*, 30 May 1925.
32. *Spectator*, 6 June 1925.

33. *Daily News*, 26 May 1925.

34. Birrell, *Nation and Athenaeum*, 30 May 1925.

35. Theodore Komisarjevsky, *Myself and the Theatre* (London: Heinemann, 1929), pp. 135–6.

36. Komisarjevsky, *Myself*, p. 67.

37. Alexei Bartoshevich, "Theodore Komisarjevsky, Chekhov, and Shakespeare," in Senelick, *Wandering Stars*, p. 106.

38. Komisarjevsky, *Myself*, p. 139.

39. Allen, *Performing Chekhov*, p. 165.

40. Gielgud, *Stage Directions*, p. 3.

41. *Ibid.*, p. 87.

42. Robert Tracy, "Komisarjevsky's 1936 *Three Sisters*," in Miles, *Chekhov on the British Stage*, p. 65.

43. Komisarjevsky, *Myself*, p. 149.

44. *Ibid.*, p. 172.

45. *New Statesman and Nation*, 6 March 1926.

46. Miles, *Chekhov on the British Stage*, p. 19.

47. *Nation and Athenaeum*, 9 October 1926.

48. *Observer*, 3 October 1926; *Sunday Times*, 15 April 1928.

49. *Times*, 29 September 1926.

50. Victor Borovsky, *A Triptych from the Russian Theatre: An Artistic Biography of the Komissarzhevskys* (London: Hurst and Co., 2001), p. 368.

51. Simon Callow, *Charles Laughton, A Difficult Actor* (London: Methuen, 1987), p. 15.

52. Quoted in Callow, *Charles Laughton*, p. 64.

53. *New Statesman and Nation*, 21 October 1933.

54. *Era*, 11 October 1933.

55. *Daily Telegraph*, 10 October 1933.

56. Janet Dunbar, *Flora Robson* (London: Harrap, 1960), p. 163.

57. *Sunday Times*, 15 October 1933.

58. *New Statesman and Nation*, 21 October 1933.

59. Tyrone Guthrie, *A Life in the Theatre* (New York: McGraw-Hill, 1959), p. 126.

60. *Observer*, 9 October 1933.

61. Quoted in Callow, *Charles Laughton*, p. 64.

62. *Daily Telegraph*, 10 October 1933.

63. Guthrie, *A Life in the Theatre*, p. 126.
64. *New Statesman and Nation*, 21 October 1933.
65. Guthrie, *A Life in the Theatre*, p. 126.
66. *New Statesman and Nation*, 21 October 1933; *Sunday Times*, 15 October 1933.
67. Dunbar, *Flora Robson*, p. 163.
68. *New Statesman and Nation*, 21 October 1933; *Observer*, 9 October 1933; *Times*, 10 October 1933; *Sunday Times*, 15 October 1933.
69. *Sunday Times*, 15 October 1933; *New Statesman and Nation*, 21 October 1933.
70. *Times*, 10 October 1933.
71. Guthrie, *A Life in the Theatre*, p. 120; *Observer*, 9 October 1933.
72. *Era*, 11 October 1933.
73. *Ibid.*
74. "F.S.," *Theatre World*, September 1941, p. 44.
75. *Spectator*, 5 September 1941, p. 235.
76. *The World*, 6 March 1928.
77. Eva Le Gallienne, Preface, *The Plays of Anton Chekhov*, trans. Constance Garnett (New York: Carlton House, 1930), ix.
78. Le Gallienne, Preface, x.
79. Quoted in Robert Schanke, "The Legend of Alla Nazimova," *Central States Speech Journal* 29 (Spring 1978), p. 40.
80. Helen Sheehy, *Eva Le Gallienne* (New York: Alfred A. Knopf, 1996), p. 181.
81. Gavin Lambert, *Nazimova* (New York: Alfred A. Knopf, 1997), p. 263.
82. Lambert, *Nazimova*, pp. 263, 264.
83. John Mason Brown, *Dramatis Personae* (New York: Viking, 1963), p. 10.
84. Brooks Atkinson, *New York Times*, 18 November 1928.
85. Lambert, *Nazimova*, p. 311.
86. Eva Le Gallienne, *At 33* (London: Bodley Head, 1934), p. 224.
87. Robert Schanke, *Shattered Applause: The Lives of Eva Le Gallienne* (Carbondale: Southern Illinois University Press, 1992), p. 81.
88. Sheehy, *Eva Le Gallienne*, p. 182.
89. John Mason Brown, *Two on the Aisle* (New York: Norton, 1938), pp. 86, 87.

90. *New York Times*, 18 November 1928.
91. John Chapman, *New York Daily News*, 26 January 1944.
92. George Jean Nathan, *The Theatre Book of the Year, 1943–44* (New York: Knopf, 1944).
93. Wilella Waldorf, *New York Post*, 26 January 1944; Rosamund Gilder, *Theatre Arts Monthly*, April 1944.
94. *Commonweal*, 11 February 1944.
95. Sheehy, *Eva Le Gallienne*, p. 275.
96. Rosamund Gilder, *Theatre Arts Monthly*, April 1944.
97. Walter Kerr, *Thirty Plays Hath November* (New York: Simon and Schuster, 1969), pp. 147–8.
98. Rosamund Gilder, *Theatre Arts Monthly*, April 1944.
99. Le Gallienne, *With a Quiet Heart* (New York: Viking, 1953), pp. 234–5.
100. Lewis Nichols, *New York Times*, 26 January 1944.
101. Rosamund Gilder, *Theatre Arts Monthly*, April 1944.
102. Schanke, *Shattered Applause*, p. 170.
103. *New York World-Telegram*, 26 January 1944.
104. Sheehy, *Eva Le Gallienne*, p. 384.
105. Schanke, *Shattered Applause*, p. 229.
106. Sheehy, *Eva Le Gallienne*, p. 385.
107. *New York Times*, 20 March 1968.
108. Schanke, *Shattered Applause*, p. 229.
109. Richard P. Cooke, *Wall Street Journal*, 21 March 1968.
110. John Chapman, *Daily News*, 20 March 1968; Clive Barnes, *New York Times*, 20 March 1968; Martin Gottfried, *Women's Wear Daily*, 20 March 1968.

5. *The Cherry Orchard* at mid-century: Barrault, Saint-Denis, Strehler

1. "F.S." in *Theatre World*, September 1941, p. 44.
2. Olga Knipper-Chekhova, *New York Times*, 19 March 1944.
3. Senelick, *The Chekhov Theatre*, pp. 165–6.
4. *Le Peuple*, 22 April 1921, quoted in David Whitton, *Stage Directors in Modern France* (Manchester: Manchester University Press, 1987), p. 108.

5. Georges Pitoëff, *Notre Théâtre* (Paris: Messages, 1949), p. 14, quoted in Whitton, *Stage Directors*, p. 109.

6. *France-Soir*, 9 October 1954.

7. *France-Soir*, 9 October 1954 (my translation).

8. Jean-Louis Barrault, "Why *The Cherry Orchard*?" in *The Theatre of Jean-Louis Barrault*, trans. Joseph Chiari (London: Barrie and Rockliff, 1959, reprinted 1961), p. 104.

9. *Ibid.*, p. 105.

10. *Ibid.*, p. 106.

11. Senelick, *The Chekhov Theatre*, p. 274.

12. *France-Soir*, 9 October 1954.

13. Barrault, "Why *The Cherry Orchard*?", p. 108.

14. Guy Demur, "Lioubov et Madeleine Renaud" (trans. Kendle Wade and James Loehlin), *Théâtre en Europe* 2 (1984), p. 78.

15. *Ibid.*, p. 78.

16. Undated clipping, Billy Rose Theatre Collection, New York Public Library.

17. Barrault, "Why *The Cherry Orchard*?", p. 108.

18. Undated clipping, Billy Rose Theatre Collection, New York Public Library.

19. Senelick, *The Chekhov Theatre*, p. 276.

20. Undated clipping, Billy Rose Theatre Collection, New York Public Library.

21. *Ibid.*

22. Senelick, *The Chekhov Theatre*, p. 275.

23. Gabriel Marcel, *Nouvelles Littéraires* (28 October 1954), quoted in Senelick, *The Chekhov Theatre*, p. 400, n. 34; Kenneth Tynan, *Curtains* (New York: Atheneum, 1961), p. 385.

24. Barrault, "Why *The Cherry Orchard*?", p. 111.

25. Michel Saint-Denis, "Introduction," *The Cherry Orchard*, trans. John Gielgud (New York: Theatre Arts Book, 1963).

26. Quoted in Gordon McVay, 'Peggy Ashcroft and Chekhov,' in Miles, *Chekhov on the British Stage*, p. 85.

27. *Ibid.*, p. 86.

28. Kenneth Tynan, *Observer*, 18 May 1958.

29. Saint-Denis, *Theatre*, p. 41.

30. By a historical irony, Tarasova, in the late fifties, was playing the "dull matron" Ranevskaya of the Stanitsyn MAT *Cherry Orchard*. By another irony, Dench suffered so much in perfecting Anya's sofa-leaping entrance that she transferred this business to Ranevskaya when she played that role in the 1990s.

31. Jane Baldwin, "Chekhov, the Rediscovery of Realism: Michel Saint-Denis' productions of *Three Sisters* and *The Cherry Orchard*," *Theatre Notebook* 53.2 (1999), p. 108.

32. Quoted in Baldwin, "Chekhov," p. 108.

33. *Birmingham Post*, 15 December 1961, quoted in Baldwin, "Chekhov," p. 111.

34. Undated clipping, *Stratford-Upon-Avon Herald*, Theatre Museum, Covent Garden.

35. *Punch*, 27 December 1961.

36. *Tatler*, 3 January 1962.

37. *Guardian*, 15 December 1961.

38. Michel Saint-Denis, "Chekhov and the Modern Stage," *Drama Survey* 3 (1963), p. 80.

39. Eric Keown, *Punch*, 27 December 1961.

40. Croall, *Gielgud*, p. 424.

41. Baldwin, "Chekhov," p. 110.

42. Edmund Gardner, undated clipping, *Stratford-Upon-Avon Herald*, Theatre Museum, Covent Garden.

43. Saint-Denis, "Chekhov," p. 80.

44. Baldwin, "Chekhov," p. 112.

45. Clancy Sigal, *Queen*, 3 January 1961.

46. Edmund Gardner, undated clipping, *Stratford-Upon-Avon Herald*, Theatre Museum, Covent Garden.

47. Giorgio Strehler, "La Cerisaie, Enquête Sur Le Temps", *Théâtre en Europe* 2 (1984), p. 49.

48. Giorgio Strehler, *Per un Teatro Umano* (Milan: Giangiacomo Feltrinelli: 1974), trans. Laurence Senelick, in Senelick, ed., *Anton Chekhov's Selected Plays* (New York: Norton, 2005), p. 614.

49. Giorgio Strehler, *Per un Teatro Umano*, in Senelick, *Anton Chekhov's Selected Plays*, p. 615.

50. Senelick, *The Chekhov Theatre*, p. 154.

51. *Ibid.*, pp. 264–5.
52. Franco Zeffirelli, quoted in Senelick, *The Chekhov Theatre*, p. 266.
53. David L. Hirst, *Giorgio Strehler* (Cambridge: Cambridge University Press, 1993), p. 25.
54. Strehler, *Per un Teatro Umano*, in Senelick, *Anton Chekhov's Selected Plays*, p. 619.
55. Senelick, *The Chekhov Theatre*, p. 272.
56. Pia Kleber, "The Whole of Italy is our Orchard: Strehler's *Cherry Orchard*," *Modern Drama* 42 (Winter 1999), p. 590.
57. Quoted in Maurizio Porro, "Lioubov et Valentina Cortese," *Théâtre en Europe* 2 (1984), p. 80.
58. Senelick, *The Chekhov Theatre*, p. 270.
59. Strehler, *Per un Teatro Umano*, in Senelick, *Anton Chekhov's Selected Plays*, p. 619.
60. Kleber, "The Whole of Italy," p. 586.
61. *Ibid.*, p. 591.
62. Quoted in Hirst, *Giorgio Strehler*, p. 32.
63. *Ibid.*, p. 29.
64. Quoted in Kleber, "The Whole of Italy," p. 584.
65. Senelick, *The Chekhov Theatre*, p. 271.
66. *Ibid.*, p. 272.

6. Radical revisions, 1975–1977

1. Anatoly Smeliansky, *The Russian Theatre After Stalin*, trans. Patrick Miles (Cambridge: Cambridge University Press, 1999), p. 60.
2. *Ibid.*, p. 64.
3. Tatiana Shakh-Azizova, "Chekhov on the Russian Stage," in *The Cambridge Companion to Chekhov*, ed. Vera Gottlieb and Paul Allain (Cambridge: Cambridge University Press, 2000), p. 169.
4. Gottlieb, *Chekhov in Performance*, p. 66.
5. Quoted in John D. Mitchell, *Staging Chekhov: Cherry Orchard* (New York: Institute for Advanced Studies in the Theater Arts, 1991), p. 232.
6. Maria Knebel, quoted in Senelick, *The Chekhov Theatre*, p. 219.
7. *Ibid.*, p. 220.

8. Emma Polotskaya, *Vishnyovy Sad: Zhizin vo Vremeni*, trans. Tatiana Segura and James Loehlin (Moscow: Nauka, 2003), p. 293.
9. Shakh-Azizova, "Chekhov on the Russian Stage," p. 168.
10. Anatoly Efros, "Everything to Do with Chekhov," in Senelick, *Chekhov's Selected Plays*, p. 644.
11. Spencer Golub, "Acting on the Run: Efros and the Contemporary Soviet Theatre," *Theatre Quarterly* 7. 26 (Summer 1977), p. 25.
12. *Ibid.*, p. 24.
13. Kirsikka Siikala, "La Cerisaie d'Efros: Le Carrousel des Ames Perdues," *Théâtre en Europe* 2 (1984), pp. 33–5. Siikala's article deals with Efros' restaging of the play in Helsinki, but the set and the movement were the same.
14. Alla Demidova, "Repetitsii *Vishnyovovo Sada*," in *Teatr Anatolia Efrosa*, ed. M. G. Zaionts (Moscow: "Artist. Rezhisser. Teatr", 2000), pp. 97–8.
15. Tatiana Shakh-Azizova, "Chekhovskaya Trilogia," in Zaionts, *Teatr Anatolia Efrosa*, p. 391.
16. *Ibid.*, p. 382.
17. Golub, "Acting on the Run," p. 25.
18. Demidova, "Repetitsii *Vishnyovovo Sada*," p. 100.
19. Golub, "Acting on the Run," p. 25.
20. Maria Szewcow, "Anatolij Efros Directs Chekhov's The Cherry Orchard and Gogol's The Marriage," *Theatre Quarterly* 7. 26 (Summer 1977), p. 36.
21. *Ibid.*
22. *Ibid.*
23. Demidova, "Repetitsii *Vishnyovovo Sada*," p. 99.
24. Smeliansky, *Russian Theatre*, p. 122.
25. *Ibid.*, p. 121.
26. Golub, "Acting on the Run," p. 25.
27. Shakh-Azizova, "Chekhovskaya Trilogia," pp. 382–3.
28. Smeliansky, *Russian Theatre*, p. 122.
29. Senelick, *The Chekhov Theatre*, p. 248.
30. Otomar Krejca, "Chekhov's Plays," trans. Laurence Senelick, in Senelick, *Anton Chekhov's Selected Plays*, p. 607.
31. Senelick, *The Chekhov Theatre*, p. 249.

32. Austin Pendleton, "An Appetite for Joy," interview in Jean Hackett, ed., *The Actor's Chekhov: Nikos Psacharopoulos and the Company of the Williamstown Theatre Festival, on the Plays of Anton Chekhov* (Newbury, VT: Smith and Kraus, 1992), p. 2.

33. Pendleton, "An Appetite for Joy," p. 2.

34. Olympia Dukakis, quoted in Hackett, *The Actor's Chekhov*, p. 275.

35. Pendleton, "An Appetite for Joy," p. 15.

36. Quoted in Senelick, *The Chekhov Theatre*, p. 250.

37. *Ibid.*

38. Brendan Gill, *New Yorker*, 28 February 1977.

39. *Ibid.*

40. Jack Kroll, *Newsweek*, 28 February 1977.

41. Martin Gottfried, *New York Post*, 26 February 1977.

42. Christopher Porterfield, *Time*, 28 February 1977.

43. Julius Novick, *Village Voice*, 7 March 1977.

44. Edwin Wilson, *Wall St. Journal*, 1 March 1977.

45. See reviews in *Variety*, 23 February 1977, and *Soho Weekly News*, 3 March 1977.

46. Erika Munk, *Village Voice*, 7 March 1977; Rocco Landesmann, "Comrade Serban in the Cherry Orchard," *Yale/Theatre* 8.2–3 (1977), p. 141.

47. Senelick, *The Chekhov Theatre*, p. 344.

48. Griffiths, *The Cherry Orchard*, p. vi.

49. Harold Hobson, *Sunday Times*, 24 July 1966.

50. Richard Eyre, quoted in David Allen, "*The Cherry Orchard*: a New English Version by Trevor Griffiths," in Miles, *Chekhov on the British Stage*, pp. 156–7.

51. Griffiths, *The Cherry Orchard*, p. 14.

52. *Ibid.*

53. *Ibid.*, p. 21.

54. *Ibid.*, p. 26.

55. Quoted in Allen, "*The Cherry Orchard*," p. 159.

56. Griffiths, *The Cherry Orchard*, p. 30.

57. Quoted in Allen, "*The Cherry Orchard*," p. 157.

58. *Ibid.*, p. 162.

59. Griffiths, *The Cherry Orchard*, p. 13.

60. Allen, "*The Cherry Orchard*," p. 165.

61. Irving Wardle, *Times*, 15 March 1977.
62. Allen, "*The Cherry Orchard*," p. 161.
63. Benedict Nightingale, *New Statesman*, 18 March 1977.
64. Griffiths, *The Cherry Orchard*, p. 28.
65. Vera Gottlieb, "Chekhov in Limbo: British Productions of the Plays of Chekhov," in *The Play Out of Context: Transferring Plays from Culture to Culture*, ed. Hanna Scolnicov and Peter Holland (Cambridge: Cambridge University Press, 1989), p. 164; John Tulloch, "'Going to Chekhov': Cultural Studies and Theatre Studies," *Journal of Dramatic Theory and Criticism*, 13.2 (Spring 1999), pp. 35–40.
66. Frank Marcus, *Sunday Telegraph*, 19 February 1978.
67. Peter Hall, interview with the author, London, 18 November 2003.
68. Bernard Levin, *Sunday Times*, 22 January 1978.
69. Sheridan Morley, *Punch*, 22 February 1978.

7. Brook and Stein, 1981–1997

1. Peter Brook, *The Empty Space* (New York: Avon, 1968), p. 72.
2. *Ibid.*, p. 9.
3. Peter Brook, interview with Mel Gussow, *New York Times*, 9 August 1981.
4. Jane Kramer, "Letter from Europe," *The New Yorker*, 31 October 1983, p. 132.
5. Peter Brook, interview with Mel Gussow, *New York Times*, 9 August 1981.
6. Peter Brook, *Threads of Time: A Memoir* (London: Methuen, 1998), p. 160.
7. Quoted in Andrew Todd and Jean-Guy LeCat, *The Open Circle: Peter Brook's Theatre Environments* (London: Faber, 2003), p. 80.
8. Barbara Bray, "Brook in Paris," *Times Literary Supplement*, 3 April 1981.
9. Quoted in Todd and LeCat, *The Open Circle*, p. 80.
10. *Ibid.*, p. 78.
11. Jane Kramer, "Letter from Europe," p. 133.
12. *New York Times*, 2 April 1981.
13. Peter Brook, "*The Cherry Orchard*: An Immense Vitality," in Senelick, *Anton Chekhov's Selected Plays*, p. 629.

14. Quoted in Albert Hunt and Geoffrey Reeves, *Peter Brook* (Cambridge: Cambridge University Press, 1995), p. 236.
15. *Ibid.*, p. 237.
16. *Ibid.*
17. Richard Christiansen, *Chicago Tribune*, 25 January 1988.
18. *Village Voice*, 2 February 1988; *West Side Spirit*, 14 February 1988; *New York Times*, 9 August 1981.
19. *New York Times*, 9 August 1981; 25 January 1988.
20. Mel Gussow, *New York Times*, 9 August 1981.
21. *New York Times*, 2 April 1981.
22. *Wall St. Journal*, 26 January 1988; *Village Voice*, 2 February 1988.
23. *New York Times*, 25 January 1988.
24. Brook, "*The Cherry Orchard*," in Senelick, *Anton Chekhov's Selected Plays*, p. 630.
25. *Village Voice*, 2 February 1988.
26. Quoted in *New York Times*, 9 August 1981.
27. *New York Times*, 2 April 1981.
28. *New York Times*, 9 August 1981.
29. Hunt and Reeves, *Peter Brook*, p. 240.
30. Quoted in *New York Times*, 6 March 1989.
31. *Ibid.*
32. Peter Stein, "My Chekhov," trans. Laurence Senelick, in Senelick, *Anton Chekhov's Selected Plays*, p. 633.
33. John Freedman, *Moscow Performances: The New Russian Theatre 1991–1996* (London: Routledge, 1997), p. 226.
34. Stein, "My Chekhov," in Senelick, *Anton Chekhov's Selected Plays*, p. 639.
35. *Ibid.*, p. 633.
36. *Ibid.*, p. 631.
37. *Ibid.*, p. 638.
38. *Ibid.*, pp. 633–4.
39. "*Der Kirschgarten* von Anton Tschechow: Das Bühnenbild als dramaturgisches Gestaltungselement", *Bühnentechnische Rundschau* 6 (1989), p. 11. Translated by Jennifer Loehlin.
40. Michael Billington, *Guardian*, 30 August 1997.
41. Jeremy Kingston, *Times*, 30 August 1997.

42. Stein, "My Chekhov," in Senelick, *Anton Chekhov's Selected Plays*, p. 634.

43. Richard Eyre, *National Service: Diary of a Decade* (London: Bloomsbury, 2003), p. 78.

44. Paul Taylor, *Independent*, 30 August 1997.

45. John Peter, *Sunday Times*, 2 July 1989; Catherine Lockerbie, *Scotsman*, 29 August 1997.

46. Michael Merschmeier, "Zu Schön, um Wahr zu Sein," *Theater Heute*, July 1989, p. 5. Translated by Jennifer Loehlin.

47. David Murray, *Financial Times*, 13 September 1996.

48. Senelick, *The Chekhov Theatre*, p. 343.

49. Antony Peattie, *Independent*, 3 August 1995.

50. Lockerbie, *Scotsman*, 29 August 1997.

51. Senelick, *The Chekhov Theatre*, p. 343.

52. Michael Billington, *Guardian*, 30 August 1997.

8. The Cherry Orchard after one hundred years

1. Vera Gottlieb, "Chekhov in Limbo," p. 164.

2. Elisabeth Mahoney, *Guardian*, 20 March 2002.

3. Francis King, *Sunday Telegraph*, 15 December 1985.

4. Quoted in Allen, *Performing Chekhov*, p. 194.

5. Peter Kemp, *Independent*, 26 October 1989.

6. Michael Billington, *Guardian*, 26 October 1989.

7. Nicholas De Jongh, *Evening Standard*, 5 July 1995.

8. Tulloch, "'Going to Chekhov,'" p. 41.

9. Irving Wardle, *Independent*, 9 July 1995.

10. John Stokes, *Times Literary Supplement*, 21 July 1995.

11. John Chapman, *Daily News*, 3 February 1955.

12. Joshua Logan, *Josh* (New York: Delacorte Press, 1976), p. 319.

13. William Glover, Associated Press wire story, 1973.

14. Maya Angelou, *New York Times*, 4 February 1973.

15. Quoted in Ronald LeBlanc, "Liberating Chekhov or Destroying Him? Joel Gersmann's Farcical Production of The Cherry Orchard," in *Chekhov Then and Now: The Reception of Chekhov in World Culture*, ed. J. Douglas Clayton (New York: Peter Lang, 1997), p. 55.

16. *Ibid.*
17. *Ibid.*, p. 59.
18. Senelick, *The Chekhov Theatre*, p. 336.
19. *Ibid.*
20. Bruce Weber, *New York Times*, 11 April 2000.
21. *Ibid.* The Firs/Charlotta scene had also been included in Lucian Pintilie's 1988 production at the Arena Stage, Washington DC.
22. *Ibid.*
23. Brook Stowe, online review, *t2k*, http://www.theater2k.com/Chekhov111802.html.
24. *Ibid.*
25. Jade Esteban Estrada, online review, *Off-Off-Broadway Review*, http://www.oobr.com/top/volNine/seventeen/1123cherry.htm.
26. Janet Suzman, *The Free State: A South African Response to Chekhov's The Cherry Orchard* (London: Methuen, 2000), p. 21.
27. *Ibid.*, p. 3.
28. *Ibid.*, p. 73.
29. *Ibid.*, p. xxxiii.
30. Richard Lord, "Cherry Blossoms in China," *Quarterly Literary Review Singapore* 1.4 (July 2002), http://www.qlrs.com/emedia.asp?id=235.
31. Clara Chow, *The Straits Times*, Singapore, 8 June 2002.
32. Kalina Stefanova, "Arts Renaissance on the Asian Equator," *European Review*, http://www.mediaguide.hu/eufuzetek/en/13stefanova.php.
33. Stephen Kinzer, *New York Times*, 28 April 1988.
34. *Ibid.*
35. *Ibid.*
36. Takahashi Yasunari, "Introduction: Suzuki's Work in the Context of Japanese Theatre," in *The Theatre of Suzuki Tadashi*, by Ian Carruthers and Takahashi Yasunari (Cambridge: Cambridge University Press, 2004), p. 3.
37. Ian Carruthers, "Suzuki's Chekhov: *The Chekhov* and *Ivanov*," in Carruthers and Yasunari, *The Theatre of Suzuki Tadashi*, p. 190.
38. *Ibid.*, p. 195.
39. *Ibid.*, p. 196.
40. Senelick, *The Chekhov Theatre*, p. 354.

41. *Ibid.*
42. Lev Dodin, Maly Drama Theatre website, http://www.mdt-dodin.ru/english/spect/index.htm.
43. Freedman, *Moscow Performances*, p. 166.
44. Michael Billington, *Guardian*, 16 April 1994.
45. Quoted by Alastair Macaulay, *Financial Times*, 15 April 1994.
46. Quoted by Mel Gussow, *New York Times*, 7 November 1997.
47. Peter Marks, *New York Times*, 31 October 1997.
48. Senelick, *The Chekhov Theatre*, p. 354.
49. John Freedman, *Moscow Times*, 9 January 2004.
50. Arkady Petrov, "The Shadow of Horrors," *New Times (Novoe Vremya)*, May 2005.
51. John Freedman, *Moscow Times*, 9 January 2004.
52. Petrov, "Shadow of Horrors."
53. Anton Chekhov, *The Cherry Orchard*, trans. Michael Frayn (London: Methuen, 1995), p. 13.

WORKS CITED

Note: For reasons of space, newspaper reviews are cited only in the notes.

Allen, David. *Performing Chekhov*. London: Routledge, 2000.

Baldwin, Jane. "Chekhov, the Rediscovery of Realism: Michel Saint-Denis' Productions of *Three Sisters* and *The Cherry Orchard*." *Theatre Notebook* 53.2 (1999), pp. 96–115.

Barrault, Jean-Louis. *The Theatre of Jean-Louis Barrault*, trans. Joseph Chiari. London: Barrie and Rockliff, 1959, reprinted 1961.

Bely, Andrey. "*The Cherry Orchard*." 1904. *Russian Dramatic Theory from Pushkin to the Symbolists*. Ed. and trans. Laurence Senelick, pp. 89–92. Austin: University of Texas Press, 1981.

Benedetti, Jean, trans. and ed. *The Moscow Art Theatre Letters*. London: Methuen, 1991.

Stanislavski. London: Methuen, 1988.

Borovsky, Victor. *A Triptych from the Russian Theatre: An Artistic Biography of the Komissarzhevskys*. London: Hurst and Co., 2001.

Braun, Edward. *The Theatre of Meyerhold*. New York: Drama Book Specialists, 1979.

Brook, Peter. *The Empty Space*. New York: Avon, 1968.

Threads of Time: A Memoir. London: Methuen, 1998.

Brown, John Mason. *Dramatis Personae*. New York: Viking, 1963.

Two on the Aisle. New York: Norton, 1938.

Calderon, George, trans. and ed. *Two Plays by Tchekhof*. New York: M. Kennerley, 1912.

Carnicke, Sharon. "Stanislavsky's Production of *The Cherry Orchard* in the US." In *Chekhov Then and Now: The Reception of Chekhov in World Culture*, ed. J. Douglas Clayton, pp. 19–30. New York: Peter Lang, 1997.

Carruthers, Ian, and Takahashi Yasunari. *The Theatre of Suzuki Tadashi*. Cambridge: Cambridge University Press, 2004.

"*The Cherry Orchard*: a New English Version by Trevor Griffiths," *Chekhov on the British Stage*, ed. and trans. Patrick Miles, pp. 156–68. Cambridge: Cambridge University Press, 1993.

Crawford, Cheryl. *One Naked Individual: My Fifty Years in the Theatre*. New York: Bobbs-Merrill, 1977.

Croall, Jonathan. *Gielgud, A Theatrical Life*. London: Methuen, 2000.

Demidova, Alla. "Repetitsii *Vishnyovovo Sada*." In *Teatr Anatolia Efrosa*, ed. M. G. Zaionts, pp. 94–112. Moscow: "Artist. Rezhisser. Teatr," 2000.

Dunbar, Janet. *Flora Robson*. London: Harrap, 1960.

Emeljanow, Victor, ed. *Chekhov: The Critical Heritage*. London: Routledge, 1981.

Eyre, Richard. *National Service: Diary of a Decade*. London: Bloomsbury, 2003.

Fergusson, Francis. *The Idea of a Theatre*. Princeton: Princeton University Press, 1949.

Frayn, Michael, trans. *The Cherry Orchard*. By Anton Chekhov. London: Methuen, 1995.

Freedman, John. *Moscow Performances: The New Russian Theatre 1991–1996*. London: Routledge, 1997.

Le Gallienne, Eva. Preface. *The Plays of Anton Tchekov*. Trans. Constance Garnett. New York: Carlton House, 1930.

Gielgud, John. *Gielgud on Gielgud*. London: Hodder and Stoughton, 2000.

Stage Directions. London: Heinemann, 1963.

Golub, Spencer. "Acting on the Run: Efros and the Contemporary Soviet Theatre." *Theatre Quarterly* 7.26 (Summer 1977), pp. 18–28.

Gottlieb, Vera. "Chekhov in Limbo: British Productions of the Plays of Chekhov." In *The Play Out of Context: Transferring Plays from Culture to Culture*, ed. Hanna Scolnicov and Peter Holland, pp. 163–72. Cambridge: Cambridge University Press, 1989.

Chekhov in Performance in Russia and Soviet Russia. London: Chadwyck Healey, 1984.

Gottlieb, Vera, and Paul Allain, eds. *The Cambridge Companion to Chekhov*. Cambridge: Cambridge University Press, 2000.

Griffiths, Trevor. *The Cherry Orchard, by Anton Chekhov, a New English Version by Trevor Griffiths*. From a translation by Helen Rappaport. London: Pluto Press, 1978.

Hackett, Jean. *The Actor's Chekhov*. Newbury, VT: Smith and Kraus, 1992.

Hingley, Ronald, trans. and ed. *The Oxford Chekhov*. Vol. III. Oxford: Oxford University Press, 1964.

Hirst, David L. *Giorgio Strehler*. Cambridge: Cambridge University Press, 1993.

Hunt, Albert, and Geoffrey Reeves. *Peter Brook*. Cambridge: Cambridge University Press, 1995.

Innes, Christopher, ed. *A Sourcebook on Naturalistic Theatre*. London: Routledge, 2000.

Kataev, Vladimir. *If Only We Could Know!: An Interpretation of Chekhov*. Trans. and ed. Harvey Pitcher. Chicago: Ivan R. Dee, 2002.

Kerr, Walter. *Thirty Plays Hath November*. New York: Simon and Schuster, 1969.

Komisarjevsky, Theodore. *Myself and the Theatre*. London: Heinemann, 1929.

Koteliansky, S. S. *Anton Tchekhov: Literary and Theatrical Reminiscences*. London: Routledge, 1927. New York: Benjamin Blom, 1965.

Lambert, Gavin. *Navimova*. New York: Alfred A. Knopf, 1997.

LeBlanc, Ronald. L. "Liberating Chekhov or Destroying Him? Joel Gersmann's Farcical Production of *The Cherry Orchard*." In *Chekhov Then and Now: The Reception of Chekhov in World Culture*, ed. J. Douglas Clayton, pp. 53–62. New York: Peter Lang, 1997.

McVay, Gordon. "Peggy Ashcroft and Chekhov." In *Chekhov on the British Stage*, ed. Patrick Miles, pp. 78–100. Cambridge: Cambridge University Press, 1993.

Magarshack, David. *Chekhov the Dramatist*. Dramabooks edn. New York: Hill and Wang, 1960.

Chekhov the Dramatist. London: J. Lehmann, 1952.

Stanislavsky, A Life. London: Faber, 1986.

Mamet, David. "Notes on *The Cherry Orchard*." *The Cherry Orchard*, by Anton Chekhov, adapted by David Mamet, pp. vii–xv. New York: Grove Press, 1985.

Meister, Charles W. *Chekhov Criticism: 1880 Through 1986.* Jefferson, NC: MacFarland, 1988.

Meyerhold, Vsevolod. "The Naturalistic Theatre and the Theatre of Mood." 1906. Trans. Nora Beeson. In *Anton Chekhov's Plays,* ed. Eugene Bristow, 313–21. New York: Norton, 1977.

Miles, Patrick, ed. *Chekhov on the British Stage.* Cambridge: Cambridge University Press, 1993.

Chekhov on the British Stage, 1909–1987. Cambridge: SAM and SAM, 1987.

Mitchell, John D. *Staging Chekhov: Cherry Orchard.* New York: Institute for Advanced Studies in the Theater Arts, 1991.

Ostrovsky, Sergei. "Germanova and the MAT Prague Group." In *Wandering Stars, Russian Émigré Theatre:1905–1940,* ed. Laurence Senelick, pp. 84–101. Iowa City: Iowa University Press, 1992.

Pitcher, Harvey. *Chekhov's Leading Lady.* New York: Franklin Watts, 1980.

The Chekhov Play: A New Interpretation. London: Chatto and Windus, 1973.

Polotskaya, *Vishnyovy Sad: Zhizin vo Vremeni.* Moscow: Nauka, 2003.

Rayfield, Donald. *The Cherry Orchard: Catastrophe and Comedy.* New York: Twayne, 1994.

Understanding Chekhov: A Critical Study of Chekhov's Prose and Fiction. Madison: University of Wisconsin Press, 1999.

Rudnitsky, Konstantin. *Russian and Soviet Theatre: Tradition and the Avant-Garde.* Trans. Roxanne Permar. London: Thames and Hudson, 1988.

Saint-Denis, Michel. "Chekhov and the Modern Stage." *Drama Survey* 3 (1963), p. 80.

Theatre: The Rediscovery of Style. London: Heinemann, 1960.

Sayler, Oliver M., ed. *The Moscow Art Theatre Series of Russian Plays.* Trans. Jennie Covan. New York: Brentano's, 1923.

The Russian Theatre. New York: Brentano's, 1922.

Schanke, Robert A. "The Legend of Alla Nazimova." *Central States Speech Journal* 29 (Spring 1978), pp. 36–43.

Shattered Applause: The Lives of Eva Le Gallienne. Carbondale: Southern Illinois University Press, 1992.

Senelick, Laurence. *Anton Chekhov.* London: Macmillan, 1985.

Anton Chekhov's Selected Plays, trans. and ed. Laurence Senelick. New York: Norton, 2005.

The Chekhov Theatre. Cambridge: Cambridge University Press, 1997.

ed. *Wandering Stars, Russian Emigré Theatre: 1905–1940*. Iowa City: Iowa University Press, 1992.

Shakh-Azizova, Tatiana. "Chekhov on the Russian Stage." In *The Cambridge Companion to Chekhov*, ed. Vera Gottlieb and Paul Allain, pp. 162–75. Cambridge: Cambridge University Press, 2000.

"Chekhovskaya Trilogia." In *Teatr Anatolia Efrosa*, ed. M. G. Zaionts, pp. 366–85. Moscow: "Artist. Rezhisser. Teatr," 2000.

Sheehy, Helen. *Eva Le Gallienne*. New York: Alfred A. Knopf, 1996.

Smeliansky, Anatoly. "In Search of El Dorado: America in the Fate of the Moscow Art Theatre." In *Wandering Stars, Russian Emigré Theatre: 1905–1940*, ed. Laurence Senelick, Iowa City, Iowa University Press, 1992.

"Chekhov at the Moscow Art Theatre." In *The Cambridge Companion to Chekhov*, ed. Vera Gottlieb and Paul Allain, pp. 44–68. Cambridge: Cambridge University Press, 2000.

The Russian Theatre After Stalin, trans. Patrick Miles. Cambridge: Cambridge University Press, 1999.

Soloviova, I. N. ed. *Rezhissërskiye èkzemplyary K. S. Stanislavskogo*. Vol. III. 1901–1904. Moscow: Iskusstvo, 1983.

Stanislavsky, Constantin. *My Life in Art*. Trans. J. J. Robbins. London: Geoffrey Bles Ltd., 1924. London: Methuen, 1985.

Styan, J. L. *Chekhov in Performance*. Cambridge: Cambridge University Press, 1971.

Suzman, Janet. *The Free State: A South African Response to Chekhov's The Cherry Orchard*. London: Methuen, 2000.

Szewcow, Maria. "Anatolij Efros Directs Chekhov's The Cherry Orchard and Gogol's The Marriage." *Theatre Quarterly* 7.26 (Summer 1977), pp. 34–40.

Todd, Andrew, and Jean-Guy LeCat. *The Open Circle: Peter Brook's Theatre Environments*. London: Faber, 2003.

Tulloch, John. "'Going to Chekhov': Cultural Studies and Theatre Studies." *Journal of Dramatic Theory and Criticism* 13.2 (Spring 1999), pp. 23–55.

Valency, Maurice. *The Breaking String: The Plays of Anton Chekhov*. Oxford: Oxford University Press, 1966.

Van Gyseghem, André. *Theatre in Soviet Russia*. London: Faber, 1940.

Walpole, Hugh. "Epikhodov, Notes on a Russian Character." In *The Soul of Russia*, ed. Winifred Stephens, pp. 34–9. London: Macmillan, 1916.

Webster, Margaret. *The Same Only Different: Five Generations of a Great Theatre Family*. New York: Alfred A. Knopf, 1969.

Whitton, David. *Stage Directors in Modern France*. Manchester: Manchester University Press, 1987.

Worrall, Nick. "Commentary." In *The Cherry Orchard*, by Anton Chekhov. Trans. Michael Frayn. London: Methuen, 1995.

The Moscow Art Theatre. Routledge: London, 1996.

"Stanislavsky's Production Score for Chekhov's *The Cherry Orchard* (1904): A Synoptic Overview." *Modern Drama* 42.4 (Winter 1999), pp. 519–40.

INDEX

Agate, James 79, 97, 99, 106, 107–8
Aleksandrov, Nikolai 45, 53, 81
Alexander, Jane 199
Alfreds, Mike 191–2
Allam, Roger 194
Allen, David 46, 56
Amfiteatrov, Aleksandr 70
Anderson, Lindsay 163
Andreyevna, Marya Federovna 43
Angelou, Maya 198
Antoine, André 3, 4, 80, 123
Arestrup, Niels 173, 177
Art Theatre, London 94–6
Artem, Aleksandr 45
Ashcroft, Peggy 131, 132, 134
Association of Performing Artists
   119–20
Atkinson, Brooks 111, 113

Baranovsky, V. N. 74
Barnes Theatre 100–5
Barrault, Jean-Louis 7, 123–8
Barrymore, John 80
Beckett, Samuel 7, 145, 157, 204,
   205
Bely, Andrey 26
Benedetti, Jean 64
Bennett, Arnold 92, 93
Bernstein, Aline 114, 115
Boleslavsky, Richard 82
Borovsky, David 212–13
Bouffes du Nord, Paris 172
Braun, Edward 73
Brecht, Bertolt 7, 139, 142, 204, 205

Brezhnev, Leonid 148
Brook, Peter 7, 157, 171–81, 183
Brooklyn Academy of Music 179
Brooks, Avery 199–202
Broome Street Theatre, Madison,
   Wisconsin 198
Bunston, Herbert 90

Calderon, George 91
Carnicke, Sharon 69, 82
Carrière, Jean-Claude 172
Carruthers, Ian 204, 205
Chekhov, Mikhail 72
The Chekhov (Suzuki) 204–6
ChekhovNOW Festival, New York 200
Chereshova Gradina (Bulgarian film)
   207
Civic Repertory Company 112–16
Classical Theatre of Harlem 200
Claudel, Paul 123, 128
Clurman, Harold 83
Cocoyannis, Michael 207
Corbin, John 81, 82
Cortese, Valentina 141–2
Crawford, Cheryl 66

Damiani, Luciano 140
Davis, Ossie 197
Demidova, Alla 152–4
Dench, Judi 132, 169, 192
Dennehy, Brian 173, 177
Dix, Dorothy 103
Dodin, Lev 181, 208–9
Dolinov, Anatoly 74

Donnet, Vera 94
Doronina, Tatiana 211
Dotrice, Roy 135
Dreiden, Sergei 213
Dyall, Franklin 91

Efros, Anatoly 7, 147
Efros, Nikolai 59
Evans, Edith 94
Evreinov, Nikolai 72
Eyre, Richard 7, 163, 186

Fagan, J. B. 96–100, 111
Farrah, Abd'elkader 136
Fergusson, Francis 24
Finney, Albert 169
Ford, Mick 167
Foss, Kenelm 90
Foster, Gloria 197
Frayn, Michael 15, 169, 216, 217
The Free State (Suzman) 201

Gaideburov, Pavel 75, 85, 86, 123
Germanova, Maria 79, 123
Gersmann, Joel 198–9
Gielgud, John 17, 96–7, 101, 133,
    134–5
Gill, Peter 169
Golub, Spencer 151, 152
Gorky, Maxim 6, 71, 75
Gottlieb, Vera 169, 190
Greene, Graham 110
Grein, J. T. 90–1, 92
Grey, Mary 96, 99, 111
Gribunin, Vladimir 59, 81
Griffiths, Trevor 7, 162
Gromov, Mikhail Apollinarevich 58–9
Guthrie, Tyrone 105–11

Hagen, Uta 119–20
Hall, Peter 169
Hammond, Percy 81
Hayes, Helen 196–7

Hermann, Karl-Ernst 182, 186
Holm, Ian 135
Hutchinson, Jo 113
Hyman, Earle 197, 201

Ibsen, Henrik 3, 4, 11
Il Giardino dei Ciliegi (Italian film)
    206
Incorporated Stage Society 89–93

Jones, James Earl 197
Josephson, Erland 173, 178
Julia, Raul 161

Kachalov, Vassily 45, 52, 57–8, 59,
    78–9
Kataev, Vladimir 14, 21
Kayoto, Shiraishi 204, 205
Kerzhentsev, Petr 77
Khalyutina, Sofia 45
Kholkov, Konstantin 86
Kleber, Pia 141, 143
Knebel, Maria 149–50
Knipper (-Chekhova), Olga 6, 40, 51,
    53, 56, 63–4, 66, 68, 72, 78–9, 81,
    114, 117, 121
Komisarjevsky, Theodore 96, 100–4
Krejca, Otomar 7, 154–5
Krushchev, Nikita 148
Kugel, A. 70

Lampe, Jutte 186–7
Lanchester, Elsa 109
Larin, Igor 210
Laughton, Charles 104, 105
Le Gallienne, Eva 82, 112–20
Lenin, Vladimir Ilyich 78
Leonidov, Leonid Mironovich 43,
    48–9, 57, 65, 81
Levitan, Isaak 55
Lilina, Marya Petrovna 43, 49–51
Litvinova, Renata 212
Lobanov, Andrey 86–7

Logan, Joshua 196–7
Loquasto, Santo 157
Lunacharsky, Anatoly 78
Lyric Theatre, Hammersmith 96
Lyubimov, Yuri 148, 150, 212

MacArthur Theatre, Princeton, New
    Jersey 199
Magarshack, David 14, 24, 30
Majestic Theatre, New York 179
Maly Drama Theatre, St. Petersburg
    208–9
Mamet, David 28
Mann, Emily 8, 199
Mayakovsky, Vladimir 72, 76
McCowen, Alec 193, 194
McKellen, Ian 191
Mendes, Sam 192
Meyerhold, V. S. 5, 26, 27, 61–2, 70,
    72, 73–4, 75, 78, 86, 88, 171, 178,
    187
The Morning People/The Winter People
    (Yew) 202–3
Moscow Art Theatre 1, 2–6, 40–71,
    73, 75–84, 87–8, 101, 111, 114,
    115, 121, 130, 149, 171, 211–13
Moskvin, Ivan 45, 49, 56, 67, 81
Muratova, Elena Pavlovna 45, 59–60,
    61
Murcell, George 135

National Theatre of Great Britain 169,
    191–2, 194
Nazimova, Alla 114
Nekrosius, Eimuntas 210–11
Nemirovich-Danchenko, Vladimir 2,
    40, 41–2, 47, 57, 64, 65, 67, 73, 75,
    84, 139
New York Shakespeare Festival 147,
    157
Nikolaev, N. I. 63, 70
Noble, Adrian 193–4
Nunn, Trevor 194

Obolensky, Chloe 174
Old Vic Theatre 105–10
Oxford Playhouse 96–7

Paley, Petronia 200
Papp, Joseph 147, 157, 197
Parry, Natasha 173, 175–7
Piccoli, Michel 173, 178
Piccolo Theatre, Milan 137
Pierce, Wendell 201
Pintilie, Lucian 157
Pirandello, Luigi 7, 137
Pitcher, Harvey 22, 24, 32, 37, 42,
    51
Pitoëff, Georges 122–3
Playfair, Nigel 90, 96
Pole, Katherine 90
Polotskaya, Emma 150
Popova, Lyubov 72
Prague Group of the MAT 79, 122
Psacharopoulos, Nikos 156
Public Theatre, New York 197

Rayfield, Donald 15, 24, 27, 28, 34
Redgrave, Corin 194
Redgrave, Vanessa 194
Renaud, Madeleine 126
Richardson, Ralph 169
Robson, Flora 106, 108–9, 110
Royal Shakespeare Company 128, 147,
    162, 191, 193
Russian Revolution (1917) 5, 72, 76

Saint-Denis, Michel 7, 64, 128–37
Sakura no Sono (Japanese film) 207
Savina, Mariya 74
Saxe-Meiningen, Duke of 3, 4, 101
Sayler, Oliver 67, 80
Schaubühne, Berlin 182
Schildkraut, Joseph 118–19
The Seagull (Chekhov) 9, 41
Senelick, Laurence 25, 27, 43, 71, 125,
    147, 154, 162, 199

Serban, Andrei 7, 86, 155–62
Seyler, Athene 106, 107–9, 110
Shakh-Azizova, Tatiana 149, 150,
    154–5
Shapiro, Adolph 8, 203, 212–13
Shaw, G. B. 90
Simov, Victor 4, 47–8, 55, 59–60, 61,
    67, 81
Smeliansky, Anatoly 148, 152–4
Smolyakov, Andrei 212
Socialist Realism 87, 148
Sovremennik Theatre, Moscow
    209–10
Stalin, Joseph 72, 87–8, 148
Stanislavsky, Constantin 1, 2, 3, 4–5,
    6, 19, 26, 27, 30, 36, 40–71, 73, 75,
    76, 80, 81, 82, 83, 84, 86, 88, 101,
    178, 182, 187, 217
Stanitsyn, Victor 130
Stein, Peter 8, 171, 181
Strasberg, Lee 82
Streep, Meryl 159
Strehler, Giorgio 7, 137–46
Strindberg, August 13
Styan, J. L. 9, 20, 27, 30, 34
Suzman, Janet 8, 201–2
Suzuki, Tadashi 8, 204–6
Szewcow, Maria 152

Taganka Theatre, Moscow 147, 148,
    150, 181, 212
Tairov, Aleksandr 72, 78
Tarasova, Alla 132, 149, 230
Tatlin, Vladimir 72

Three Sisters (Chekhov) 9, 37, 41, 72,
    129, 149
Tipton, Jennifer 159
Torporov, Vasily 70
Troughton, David 191
Tulloch, John 169
Turshkin, Leonard 208
Tutin, Dorothy 135
Tynan, Kenneth 127, 131, 132

Uncle Vanya (Chekhov) 9, 41

Vakhtangov, Evgeny 72, 75, 155
Valency, Maurice 24
Van Gyseghem, André 76
Volchek, Galina 209–10
Vysotsky, Vladimir 148, 152–4, 212

Walker, Nancy 120
Walpole, Hugh 49
Weaver, John 83
Webster, Margaret 114, 117
Williamstown Theatre Festival 156
Wilton, Penelope 193
The Wisteria Trees (Logan) 196–7
Woolf, Virginia 94, 95–6
Woollcott, Alexander 111
Worrall, Nick 14, 46, 54, 67
Worth, Irene 159, 160–1

Yew, Chay 202–3

Zavadsky, Yuri 49
Zola, Emile 4

I have no wife.